With thanks and all best in
Clive and Jennifer

Praise for Timeless Treks

*This is a stunning book, written with the discerning eye of
a born communicator with over 50 years of professional
experience in education. I had the good fortune to be taught
by Clive Darley and to accompany him of one of the many
trans-Alpine trekking expeditions he organised. This was a
life-changing experience. Even now, aged nearly 80, he retains
a passion and enthusiasm for the outdoors that floods through
these pages and does so with consuming interest, humour and
deep reflective insights. Read it, enjoy it, and be inspired!*

John Ashcroft, Lt. Colonel (retired)

*Clive Darley introduced me to the hills in the 1960s and this
led directly to a lifetime involved in mountaineering via the
RAF, Gordonstoun School and Mountaineering Scotland. It is
wonderful to see that 50 years later, he and Jennifer continue
to inspire others with their tales of adventure and exploration.
Their exploits, then as now, have become legendary.*

David Monteith (MIC)

*This is an enthralling and eloquent account of treks undertaken
around the world by a couple who demonstrate that the quest
for physical challenge and adventure does not diminish with
age. Its descriptions of differing cultures and geography are
written with real insight, empathy and panache that gives
encouragement to young and old alike.*

Doug Scott CBE

Timeless Treks
tales of an excellent vintage

CLIVE DARLEY

COMMUNITY ACTION NEPAL

Registered charity No. 1067772

www.canepal.org.uk

The mountains of Nepal are one of the world's most inspiring landscapes but life for remote mountain populations has many challenges and difficulties. Mountaineer Doug Scott CBE, the first Englishman to climb Mount Everest in 1975, has seen these daily challenges at first hand when relying on the support of local mountain porters and Sherpas to help him achieve climbing success.

Doug's explanation is: 'In 1989 whilst walking up to Kangchenjunga, I made a decision that would eventually associate me more intimately with the local hill people of High Asia. Sitting around the kitchen fire, our Sherpas and porters were bemoaning the fact that the trekking industry offered little security or return for all their hard work. We therefore launched a trekking cooperative with guaranteed incomes and a chance for porters to determine their own future.'

In 1994 profits from this trekking company were first put into community work. This was at Ghunsa where a school and health post were established at the request of the local community and Tej Tamang, a trek Sirdar. CAN still continues to work with this community today.

Now the charity supports over fifty projects in the middle hill regions, where government welfare provision is limited. These range from running village health posts with trained nurses, where previously patients were faced with many days walk to obtain treatment, to building and staffing schools, which soon become the hub of village life. Nor have the porters been forgotten and, in partnership with the International Porter Protection Group (IPPG), CAN has built three Porter Rescue Shelters in the Khumbu at Machhermo, Gokyo and Gorak Shep. The shelters offer porters overnight accommodation, kitchen and sanitation facilities at very little cost, since they are subsidized by fees charged to trekkers for treatment by the volunteer Western doctors who staff them.

CAN works very closely with local village communities and operates from a UK-based office and an office in Kathmandu. In 2015 all CAN's projects were either destroyed or severely damaged by the two earthquakes which struck Nepal. Now three years later, and following a successful earthquake appeal in which three million pounds was raised, 95% of the rebuilding work has been completed on a 'build back better' principle using earthquake resilient construction design and techniques. More requests have been received and communities in the remote North Gorkha region have requested seven more health facilities so fund-raising remains an imperative.

These projects not only help improve the quality of daily life amongst the Nepalese people, but also help stop the drift from the countryside to the cities thus preserving the Nepalese way of life – so admired by all who visit.

Community Action Nepal are very grateful to Clive and Jennifer for proposing this initiative as all proceeds from the sale of this book will be donated to the charity. For more information please go to CAN's website www.canepal.org.uk or ring the office on 01768 484842.

'I would rather be ashes than dust,
a spark burnt out in a brilliant blaze
than stifled in dry rot,
For man's chief purpose is to live, not to exist.
I shall not waste my days trying to prolong them.
I shall use my time'.

Jack London

'Tho' much is taken, much abides; and though
We are not now that strength which in old days
Moved earth and heaven: That which we are,
We are:
One equal temper of heroic hearts,
Made weak by time and fate, but strong in will
To strive, to seek, to find, and not to yield.'

Alfred Tennyson *Ulysses*

Copyright © Clive Darley, 2018
Published by Burblethwaite Books

British Library Cataloguing-in-Publication data
A catalogue record for this book is available from the British Library

ISBN 978-1-5272-2895-5

Typeset by Scotforth Books
Printed and bound by Cambrian Printers

Contents

Foreword

CARPE DIEM – SEIZE THE DAY – is one of the oldest philosophical mottos in history. It is ascribed to the Roman poet Horace and has come to mean all things to all men. Many interpret it as making the most of a particular opportunity, but rarely does it come to encompass life itself. In practice, our hope is that we shall not reach the end of our lives with regret at not squeezing from our time the last vestiges of opportunity. The saddest litany of our age is the 'cri de coeur' of the newly retired – 'if only' or 'I wish', as the realisation hits home that life is finite and that the freedom to do the things we always promise ourselves when we are battling through the pressures of working life is dashed by loss of health or inadequate finance or domestic responsibilities. Fortunately for the many, life in one's later years still offers prospects of relative freedom and adventure and the possibility of rattling the cage of conformity. Increasing life expectancy is a wonderful boon, but, more importantly, we have the prospect of living more vigorous and fulfilling lives for longer than our parents. There has never been a better time to cast aside the shackles of routine and to reclaim the simplicity and yet profundity of the meaning of 'carpe diem'.

It does not take much to achieve. To learn new things or to re-discover or re-awaken those interests subjugated to the demands of working life requires only an act of will and resolve. We spend most of our lives pre-occupied with the present with little view of the future. When the future arrives it often brings with it a loss of purpose and momentum. This is the opportunity and challenge of the Third Age. As younger individuals, our lives were full of excitement and adventure. Each day seemed full of promise. Why should that be the prerogative of the young? With age, comes choice. That is a priceless gift not to be squandered.

What follows on these pages is intended to encourage and hopefully inspire. For those with dreams to dream do not let age become a barrier. Life is often portrayed as a voyage of self-discovery during which our experiences shape and fashion our understanding of the world but also, more importantly, our understanding of ourselves. Challenge is the catalyst, mental or physical, and our response to that often promotes increased self-knowledge. What better objectives to fill our later precious years! It is one of the paradoxes of our age that although we have never before been so 'connected', we are in other ways more detached from the natural world around us and experience it mainly through digital access rather than intimate personal knowledge. The world, despite its shrinkage, is still a wonderful place beckoning the adventurous to discover its many opportunities. Mass tourism perhaps anaesthetises us from deeper revelations of landscapes and cultures. Sometimes it is more revealing to strip away the layers of familiarity, take a deep breath and cast care and convention aside.

Each of us as we grow older will aim to make the most of our 'golden years' in different ways. My wife and I have always been active sportspeople and keen walkers. It seemed appropriate that whilst health and strength remained, we would try to achieve as many trekking ambitions as possible. This book is an account of some of these travels and the many insights they provided. It may be relevant to disclose that the journeys covered in this book were all made in the writer's seventh and eighth decades not with the advantages of perfect health or bottomless finance but conversely with various joint prostheses and a cardiac pacemaker and on a limited professional and State pension. The rewards have been life-enhancing. It is not possible to quantify such benefits. Physical and mental well-being are comparatively easy to recognise but in their wake come the more profound spiritual and cultural dimensions to a life well-lived. May you dream dreams and seize your days. They will not come around again!

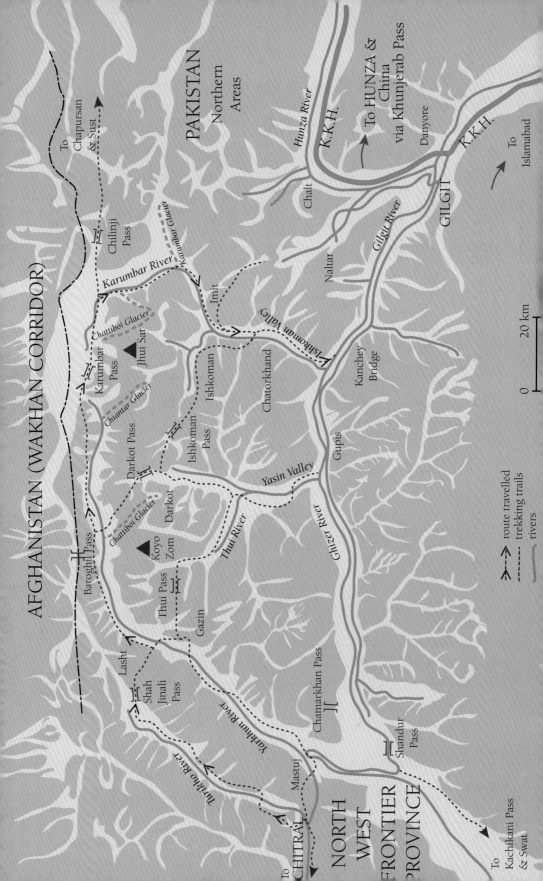

AFGHANISTAN (WAKHAN CORRIDOR)

PAKISTAN
Northern
Areas

To
Chapursan
& Sust

Chilinji
Pass

Karumbar River

Karumbar Glacier

Chattiboi Glacier

Karumbar
Pass

Jhui Sar

Chiantar Glacier

Darkot Pass

Chattiboi Glacier

Koyo
Zom

Darkot

Darkot
Glacier

Thui Pass

Gazin

Thui River

Baroghil Pass

Lasht

Shah
Jimali
Pass

Yarkhun River

Turikho River

Mastuj

CHITRAL

NORTH
WEST
FRONTIER
PROVINCE

To Chitral

To Kachikani Pass
& Swat

Chamarkhan Pass

Ghizer River

Shandur
Pass

Yasin Valley

Gupis

Ishkoman
Pass

Ishkoman

Chatorkhand

Ishkoman Valley

Imit

Kanchey
Bridge

Naltar

Gilgit River

GILGIT

K.K.H.

Danyore

To
Islamabad

To HUNZA &
China
via Khunjerab Pass

Hunza River

K.K.H.

Chalt

0   20 km

→→→ route travelled
------ trekking trails
~~~~ rivers

Hindu Kush

WHEN WE ARE YOUNG, life seems endless. We have energy to burn. There is no thought of mortality. As we grow older we begin to heed more the recommendations given to maintain such youthful vigour and optimism. We listen more to medical advice, however confusing and contradictory this often seems to be. Our diets and lifestyles are more scrupulously moderated. Despite the difficulties we strive to achieve a healthy work and leisure balance and to exercise more. Here the medical advice suggests that the benefits of regular exercise are unequivocal. The cardio-vascular specialists recommend such a regime; their orthopaedic colleagues wait expectantly in the wings as joints begin to fail. Keep a good relationship with your physiotherapist and your orthopaedic consultant is one of the key recommendations of an active maturity!

After a lifetime of competitive sport ranging from rugby, athletics, hockey, squash, fell running, mountaineering and trekking, my body had been put through the mill. By 1994 it was clear that the pain from my left hip could no longer be ignored. At 55, having played good level League squash for over 20 years, it was perhaps not surprising that aches and pains should manifest themselves. When a younger opponent displayed his lean and highly muscled frame in the changing room, an involuntary resigned sigh accompanied the recognition that whilst speed and strength was failing a little, some resort to guile (and gamesmanship!) would probably be necessary to prevail. The diagnosis of osteoarthritis came as no surprise and the exhortation to 'take it easier' was not consistent with the highly competitive nature of the sport. Retirement from League squash did not end my playing days and there was still enjoyment to be found in playing 'social squash', although even this more relaxed form often required the administration of pain-killers after the game. Fell walking, trekking and climbing continued and armed with two trekking poles, formerly dismissed as a Continental affectation, I signed up for a major trek across the Karakorum via Snow Lake. It was to be the last serious expedition for some time. It was evident that some form of surgical intervention would be required if full physicality and vigour were to be restored. Retirement from squash was the first step but to withdraw from fell walking and climbing was unthinkable.

For five long years, therefore, regular work-outs in the gym replaced wanderings over the fells, although occasional shorter excursions such as the round of Wetherlam from Tilberthwaite remained manageable with the aid of pain-killers. By 1999, the die was cast, and my left hip was resurfaced at the Royal Orthopaedic Hospital in Birmingham. This was a new procedure, not endorsed by NICE, but it had inherent advantages over the straightforward hip replacement, which sometimes could dislocate when the leg and hip was contorted through climbing manoeuvres. It proved to be a very worthwhile investment.

Six weeks later and several thousand pounds poorer, a slow but steady ascent was made of Bowfell to profound relief and with much deep satisfaction. The winter beckoned and in the interests of prudence normal convalescence continued until the weather started to improve in the spring. Thoughts now turned to the resumption of guided and supported expeditions. It was the year of the millennium which called for some statement of intent. Having entered the seventh decade, the more challenging options such as the high-level traverse of the Karakorum or the Himalayas were clearly not possible, but inspired by the works of Eric Newby and Wilfred Thesiger, a 'short walk across the Hindu Kush' seemed viable. Both had travelled in this area in a more hospitable political climate. Afghanistan then was included in the 'hippy route' to Kathmandu, but following the Russian invasion of Afghanistan and the rise of the mujahedin, the country was racked by war and civil unrest. It was only when the Russian forces withdrew that an uneasy calm descended on this tormented but beautiful country and the areas of Northern Pakistan adjacent to the border became relatively safe and secure. This amorphous frontier area enjoyed a brief notoriety during the days of the great imperial struggle between the British Raj and Russia that became known as the 'Great Game'. The arbitrary nature of nineteenth-century border delineation produced anomalies that cut across pre-existing trading routes along which caravans of people from the heart of Asia had migrated to and from India. The new borders theoretically provided a buffer zone between the two great nineteenth-century imperial powers that included a long finger of land known as the Wakhan Corridor. This remote area, that subsequently became part of Pakistan sank into obscurity, its isolation aggravated by issues of personal safety and the need to negotiate for permission to travel to small semi-independent kingdoms governed by an assortment of regional chieftains.

The Russian invasion in 1979 condemned this sensitive area to a further period of enforced and protracted isolation. Pakistan had supported the mujahedin, developing supply routes that placed Chitral at the hub of its secretive networks and restricting access for all but authorised military personnel. Only when relationships between Afghanistan, Russia, China and Pakistan began to thaw in the 1990s did it become possible to re-establish routes in this difficult terrain. The attractions were magnetic. A short walk in the Hindu Kush was an objective worth pursuing, travelling on foot in this area where European trekkers were still a rare sight and where the spectacular mountains of the Hindu Kush, Hindu Raj and Karakorum brush against the Pamir-like steppes of Central Asia. Turbulent river valleys represent the main routes of access, and passes linking one valley to the next such as the Shah Jinali and the Karumbar are high (+4000 metres). Glaciers block some of the valleys, presenting further obstacles. Fast-flowing and potentially dangerous tributary rivers and streams must be crossed, either using simple baskets on wire pulleys, called jolas, or simply by wading through turbulent fast-flowing water. Huge silt plains, vertical river cliffs and powerful melt water channels add to the challenges.

The sense of isolation in this remote area is daunting. In the event of accident or emergency, communication can be a real problem even by satellite phone. Helicopter rescue, even if it can be organised by the Pakistani military, takes time and a great deal of money. Tribal sensitivities need to be accommodated in the recruitment of porters along the route. To reach the road head where the trekking begins in earnest is a logistical exercise in itself. Chitral does have an airstrip but planes from Islamabad are few and far between even when the weather conditions allow. Chitral itself is synonymous with 'The Great Game' and is the main centre, along with Gilgit, in this frontier province. From Chitral a 12-hour tortuous jeep trip along vertiginous tracks can be a nightmare for anyone with a nervous disposition. In such a situation, it is necessary to put one's trust entirely in the competence, experience and judgment of the local drivers and guides.

Air travel cocoons and insulates. Within hours of leaving Manchester and landing at Islamabad, the scents and sounds of Pakistan were made all the more striking by the suddenness of the transition to a different culture. An afternoon stroll around the bazaars of Rawalpindi heightened the sense of contrast. The sickly smell of raw sewage was largely masked by the more endearing scents of spices and the beguiling aromas of cooking by street vendors. Browsing the stalls did not have the same air of excitable compulsion or dystopian claustrophobia that would have accompanied a similar visit in India and vendors plied their wares with generosity and good-natured banter. The absence of women was the first indication that we were now in a Muslim state and due deference would be required to avoid offence. Rawalpindi is, of course, a major garrison town and does not share the air of modernity and even sophistication of its neighbour Islamabad, but seems more genuine for that. The hotel was an outpost of westernised habits but even here care was exercised in avoiding water straight from the tap, ice creams, salads etc., that the injudicious might ignore at their peril. Brushing teeth using bottled water became a chore but was preferable to the prospective alternative of an upset stomach or diarrhoea. The food was distinctively sub-Continental and the air hung heavily with the seductive aroma of curry, cardamom, coriander, turmeric, cumin, chillies, ginger and garlic.

A leisurely breakfast preceded a 5.30 a.m. start in the Toyota across the plains towards Peshawar, crossing the Indus at Attock where an impressive fortification commanded the valley. The giant river just east of its major tributary, the River Kabul, was stained a rusty red brown, testimony to the degree of deforestation and erosion taking place upstream. The Kabul was bridged near Nowshera where lines of gaudily painted and ornately decorated trucks, complete with ornamental chains and trinkets, queued up for customs inspection having travelled down from Afghanistan. A brief stop at a roadside cafe for a Coke settled the nerves before the major climb up the Malakand Pass into Swat province. With increasing height, the air should have been clear, but the stench of diesel testified to the antiquity of vehicles struggling to surmount the meandering steep inclines. The descent from Malakund was across a pleasantly rural landscape of lush pastures and forested hillsides dotted with small villages and punctuated by occasional forts. It was here that Winston Churchill nearly came to grief in the late-nineteenth century whilst engaged in quelling an uprising in this remote part of NWFP. Even today the local populace is well armed and almost instinctively rebellious. Swat has now become a place where the Pakistan Taliban exert a presence. It is here that the young Malala was shot for promoting the rights of girls to be educated. It is a long way from here to the Nobel Peace Prize but security here was (and remains) illusory. We were made acutely aware of local sensitivities at a short stop at a tea shop in Dir, where the presence of Western women excited intrusive interest, even though they were appropriately and modestly dressed. It was not a comfortable sensation, a feeling confirmed when the vehicles appeared to be fired on as they climbed sharply out of Dir. Nor was it entirely reassuring to be informed that we were not the target but that the exchanges were between warring factions on either side of the valley!

The trail now steepened significantly and with height gained it became noticeably colder with flecks of snow gathering on the roadside verge. Occasional small settlements appeared to be engaged in cutting down the mature forests for timber, further exacerbating the problems of run-off and erosion. Only the Lowari Pass remained, one of two 'road' links between the Chitral valley and the rest of Pakistan to the south. It is closed by snow from November to May and distinguished by its 45-hairpin bends required to gain the gentler gradient of the Chitral River valley floor. The total descent was in the order of 2000 metres (6500 feet) and meeting other vehicles coming in the opposite direction was an interesting experience. The general tenor of the landscape and the people of this area was perhaps best summarised by a painted inscription on a large rock outcrop declaring 'The Chitrali Scouts love death more than you love life', a somewhat chilling introduction to this decidedly frontier province. This is rough country, subject to earthquakes and populated by hardy, resilient people, including the 'kaffirs' or Kailash, who are non-Muslim and whose distinctive culture is confined to the impossibly steep valleys, such as the Brumboret, that plunge down to the west of the Chitral river.

Eventually after a 14-hour journey, the jeeps drove across a causeway linking the main Chitral road to the Nagar Fort Hotel owned by a relation of the Ul-Mulk family, the traditional rulers, or Mehtas, of Chitral province. Sirajuddin was the cousin of Siraj Ul-Mulk (anglicised to 'Sugar and Milk'), whom we were to meet later at the Hindu Kush Heights Hotel in Chitral. The bluff on which the fort was built overlooked the boiling waters of the river, but it had a garden which lent an air of relative tranquillity. This was disturbed during the evening by the most spectacular thunderstorm. Flashes of forked lightning illuminated the rugged scene and we settled down to sleep trusting that this ferment would not be a portent of things to come.

It was only a couple of hours or so from Nagar to Chitral. Small stone oblongs were all that was left of an Afghan refugee encampment. As we talked to people it became clear that there was a certain ambivalence about the presence of so many Afghans in this part of the frontier province. Most refugees seemed to flow over the more direct passes such as the Khyber into Peshawar and their presence in the Chitral valley was tolerated rather than welcomed wholeheartedly. As fellow Muslims, they sympathised with their plight, but on the other hand there seemed to be limits to their tolerance, the hope being that their presence here was necessarily expedient but should be temporary. By the time we passed the ruins of their encampment, the Russians had long departed Afghanistan and an uneasy stability had settled on the region. The fact that the inhabitants had abandoned the ad hoc settlement seemed to suggest that they had migrated back into Afghanistan or joined other émigré communities further south near Peshawar.

Gradually, the first roadside stalls began to appear as the valley widened into the broad basin in which the town of Chitral is situated. After the journey from Dir this degree of comparative civilisation was quite a contrast. We were taken initially to the Mountain Inn, where lunch was served followed by a leisurely, early-afternoon green tea in the sumptuous courtyard garden. Sitting here talking to a very urbane and articulate lawyer, it was hard to believe that the noise and bustle of the bazaar was just beyond its sheltering walls. The bazaar itself was hardly a frenzy, but all trades plied for custom in its elongated street, representing in its sights and scents a microcosm of India and Central Asia. Outside the corridor of the main street, the snow-capped peaks of the Hindu Kush, dominated by Tirich Mir, served to emphasise the frontier ambience. All types of fresh fruit and vegetables were available. Butchers hung less than appetising strips and chunks of meat and offal on which the flies clustered. Cobblers sold and repaired shoes; tailors made and mended shalwar kameez; metal workers and silversmiths hammered and soldered; sacks of highly coloured spices wafted evocative aromas and workshops maintained and repaired the ubiquitous motor bikes/scooters. We did not spot any arms being sold as we had in Gilgit a few years previously, but it would have been uncharacteristic if they were not available. Semi-precious stones such as lapis lazuli originating in Afghanistan suggested that trade across the frontier still exists. Our presence there attracted no animosity or even undue interest; there were no hordes of children begging for sweets or other gifts. We saw no local women. Only later did we learn that there is an alternative purdah bazaar and that even female foreign aid workers tend not to frequent the main bazaar. Foreign female visitors are tolerated but only if they are accompanied by a man and are appropriately dressed. It was an engrossing and illuminating experience.

Later that afternoon we were ferried to the Hindu Kush Heights Hotel on the northern edge of town overlooking the airstrip. This was a very modern and luxurious place owned by Siraj Ul-Mulk, who had entertained international celebrities here, (including the Duke of Edinburgh), in less troubled times. There was little time to settle in before the jeeps arrived to take us back down into town to visit the fort and mosque and to watch a local cricket game. The fort had an interesting history. During the late-nineteenth century, the British, alarmed at the Russian advances towards the ill-defined border with India, engaged in typical diplomatic manoeuvres involving the Maharajah of Kashmir as well as the local rulers of Chitral. In 1879, a treaty was drawn up giving the incumbent Ul-Mulk an annual stipend and a guarantee against Afghan incursion. However, in 1892 a fractious succession and bloody dispute, in which brother murdered brother, followed the death of Ul-Mulk, who was finally replaced by Amir Ul-Mulk, who allied with the strongly anti-British Afghan ruler of Dir state (some things do not seem to change!) It was resolved to throw the British out of Chitral, where a small garrison occupied the fort. This was now besieged. The British troops held out for 46 days until they were relieved by an expeditionary force from Gilgit that managed to haul men and munitions, including cannon, over the Shandur Pass at 3734 metres. This must have been an epic exploit, much celebrated at the time in the Victorian press. A new pro-British dynasty was installed as rulers and the previous boundaries divided up would be administered by British appointed Governors. When the succession was stabilised to British approval, the province was re-integrated under subsequent generations of Ul-Mulks, who incorporated Chitral into the new state of Pakistan in 1947 and merged the province administratively with the rest of the country in 1969, some 20 years after the state of Pakistan was created.

Today the Ul-Mulks and their myriad family connections still exert a significant influence over political and economic affairs, the relative isolation from Islamabad giving them a degree of local autonomy. The fort still bears the scars of its history. The red walls overlooking the river are chipped and gouged with shrapnel and a line of ancient cannons has been preserved to lend further credence to the imagination. The mosque lies adjacent to the fort. It is not one of the more elegant structures of its kind but is unmistakeably Muslim in its architectural form. Between the fort and the mosque, a cricket game was in progress, excitedly followed by partisan supporters. Hopefully, such activities have supplanted the more serious armed conflicts, although there are still perceptible undercurrents. The valley slopes were decorated with whitewashed stones spelling out the indefatigability of the Chitrali Scouts who make it clear that the regiment brooks no opposition.

It was with a mix of impressions that we were finally escorted back to the Hotel built to a traditional style on a bluff overlooking the river and opulently furnished. We appeared to be the only guests, ate well, but felt some sympathy for the immaculately uniformed young male waiters who were clearly under-employed. Soft drinks cost 25 rupees, about 15 pence, and as this was the last outpost of comfort likely to be

Jeeps ready for departure from Chitral

encountered for a while, a fair number was consumed. A last shower for weeks was the final indulgence.

On a bright and cheerful morning, a small convoy of jeeps waited outside the hotel as kit bags and rucsacs were loaded. It was to be a seven hour journey to the first camp site at Zang Lasht. Initially the route followed a good tarmac road that ran along the valley of the River Mastuj which was boiling with primeval energy. In this wild and dusty country, it seemed somehow incongruous to draw up at a filling station to top up with diesel before the jeeps swung away from the main track onto a dirt road at Buni, heading towards the deeply incised ravine cut by the Turikho. Precipitous side valleys led the eye to glacier tongues and ice fields. This is a complex area both geographically and culturally. We would get to know the river Turikho in its upper course where it also becomes known as the Rich Gol. Downstream it becomes the river Tirich, which drains the highest mountains of the Hindu Kush. This is a sparsely populated area except in the tight-knit valleys and is inhabited by the Kho people whose language, Khowar, is the language of Chitral.

There was now a sense of entering much more forbidding country. Snow-capped peaks loomed on all sides and the jeep track itself was designed to bring idle conversation to a halt. There was no option but to hold on and place complete trust in the drivers who had nerves of steel. Occasionally where the track widened and levelled they would stop to allow passengers to stretch their legs and gaze in awe at this intimidating landscape.

A stop was made for a lunch of peanut butter on crackers and some green tea before the jeeps continued their hair-raising journey. Occasionally, as the valley floor was approached, small mud brick settlements would appear with laughing children draped over the outer walls. Within the walls there were glimpses of vegetables being cultivated. Red onions are now being grown as an income generating crop, but in the midst of their spiky leaves the red poppy flowers could not be disguised. Opium/heroin is still a clandestine earner and the serrated leaves of cannabis plants could often be recognised by the track. It was a long journey but never failed to hold the attention. Slowly the constricted valley broadened slightly and the village of *Zang Lasht* appeared, hemmed in by rocky buttresses above the foaming river, but a real Shangri La in this arid, severe country.

Camp was pitched in an apple and apricot orchard witnessed by scores of captivated youngsters. Very quickly the experienced campers had their tents up; others less versed in the art struggled and had to be assisted. Already two of the party were suffering, one with diarrhoea and one who was simply unaccustomed to such privations. After all was settled we walked through the village accompanied by excitable boys and curious male adults. Of girls and women there was no sign. A conversation held with the local schoolmaster highlighted the desperate shortage of resources and one imagined that medical provision was equally restricted. It only served to confirm that we were now travelling into a remote area where a degree of resourcefulness and self-sufficiency would be required.

The next day we loaded up under the gaze of chattering boys and inquisitive men and the jeeps stuttered into life. Beyond Zang Lasht, the road became even more primitive and crossing the streams using cantilever style wooden bridges proved to be quite a daunting exercise. These are accustomed to carrying the weight of pack donkeys, not a fully laden supply jeep, and it was normal practice to discharge all passengers and baggage, inspect and undertake running repairs to the bridge before driving slowly across it. Despite the snow-capped mountains, the impression was of a very arid landscape apart from the occasional oasis down by the river. The track became increasingly bumpy as it crossed plains of boulders swept down by both glaciers and rivers and it was with some relief that after five hours or so we reached the tiny settlement of *Rua*, at the end of what passed for civilisation. Beyond Rua we would be on our own.

The camp site was by a patch of willows close to the river where it was possible to do some washing and relax, trying to ignore the rumbling guts that are the normal precursor to diarrhoea. Late in the afternoon we went for a walk across the boulder plain above the village to be met by a crowd of children bringing back the herds of goats and small sheep. They chattered away and became very amused when we said 'bye-bye' which translates phonetically in their language to 'goat-goat'! Back at the camp a heated discussion was going on about the recruitment of porters. It became clear that every section of this trek would require a different group of porters with donkeys or horses to be engaged and differential rates to be bargained. It became quite a political issue as to where one area gave way to the next and what rates were to be offered. Eventually the commotion quietened down and our first porter team was recruited.

The guides were under the direction and loose leadership of Ayub, who was an influential figure in his home village of Chattorkand in the Ishkoman valley and carried that natural swagger and authority of the Pashtun. His second-in-command and the one who seemed to do most of the organising was Mahboob, who was endeavouring to develop a private school in his village south of Gilgit in the Indus valley. Both spoke excellent English. The third character was Jahanzeb who was a native of Chitral and very laid back. They were accompanied by a couple of younger boys who did most of the fetching and carrying. By now we had got to know each of the core team quite well and formed some initial impressions. We would be dependent on their local knowledge and on the experience of our two very experienced English guides, Steve and Hazel Bines. Steve was a professional guide, Hazel had formerly worked at Oxford Brookes University and her educational expertise was now being channelled through DFID in Northern Pakistan. Both were reassuringly personable and competent.

Camp was struck the following morning very early amidst a scene of pristine splendour. Across the boulder plain the mountains that formed part of the Wakhan Corridor border with Afghanistan reared up, their snow-capped peaks set against a sky of the deepest blue. On this first day of trekking the route would cross this interminable sea of boulders before climbing sharply against the flank of the enclosing mountains to reach the valley of the Shah Jinali Gol. It was to be a long and eventful day. The first couple of hours were spent threading a path through the mainly level boulder field to the head of the valley where an old shepherd's hut at *Moghlang* lay deserted and disconsolate at the confluence of three thundering streams. A path of sorts clung to the sides of the gorge until it reached a giant chock-stone perched across the narrow defile. This was quite an obstacle, but the pack animals and porters demonstrated the way round it and we continued to climb sharply until the path began to level out at the top of a precipitous gorge overlooking the valley hundreds of feet below. This vertiginous slope was not made of rock but of crumbling clay. The path across it was pencil thin, so much so that the supply barrels were detached from the donkeys and carried across on the backs of porters in case a brush with the vertical wall of baked clay precipitated donkey and load into the river far below. With considerable trepidation we followed nervously, mindful of the consequences of any injury in this situation. The concentration was total and with a palpable sigh of relief we emerged onto safer ground after 200 metres.

Beyond the gorge the river valley opened out into a pleasant landscape of rolling semi-arid pasture dotted with groves of willow that our guides referred to as 'the jungle'. Patches of artemisia, tamarisk and juniper colonised this dry upland steppe. In the background, the higher mountains exerted a powerful presence and a reminder that even more rigorous days lay ahead. With the stomach upset draining energy, it was good to reach the campsite nestling amongst a clump of willows between two small streams and awake the next day feeling more refreshed. This was just as well, because now the altitude of 3500 metres required a more measured pace to be adopted. Thankfully it was a relatively short day of four hours or so across open pastures full of goats and sheep which seemed to wander at will. Small streams came bubbling down the hillsides nourishing areas of dwarf woodland containing willow, birch, dwarf pine and juniper, most of which seemed to have been hacked about for firewood. The camp site at *Shah Gari* was by one of these streams where it was possible to languish in the warm afternoon sun looking out across the open ground to the *Ochhili Pass*, which marked the frontier with Afghanistan. It appeared deceptively close (in reality less than five miles), and a broad glacier col would afford a comparatively easy route, but we were informed that the whole area had been sown with mines to deter its use. It seemed almost sacrilegious. The rhythms of camp life were rapidly becoming established and our guides and porters gradually became more communicative in the mess tent or on trek. They are redoubtable people.

The first main pass of the trek, the *Shah Jinali*, which means 'king's polo-ground' in Khowar, was the next day's first objective, approached by a steep ascent in the cool of early-morning along a series of river bluffs up the left bank of the Shah Jinali Gol almost to the springs that define its source. A gentler gradient then opened out onto an extensive pastoral area grazed by herds of cattle and goats. This almost level area at almost 14,000 feet was a tremendous vantage point looking across to the majestic peaks of the Hindu Raj, such as Koyozo and Thui II, their spectacular profiles glistening with snow. It would have been an ideal place to linger longer but the camp site at *Ishperu Dok* lay another two hours down a steep, rocky ravine lined with colourful wild roses and scented artemisia. Faded Buddhist rock carvings were a legacy of Tibetan incursions in the distant past. The camp site occupied a broad heavily overgrazed mountain valley where herders from the Yarkhun valley below brought their herds in summer. As we pitched the tents, children scurried up the hillsides to bring the goats down for the night and above the encampment a small group of primitive, dour stone houses were occupied by the women. Inevitably our women

Nearing the Shah Jinali Pass

Hindu Raj from the Shah Jinali Pass

were surrounded by grubby children chattering excitedly and gesticulating in ways that we could not understand. What does the future hold for them other than a continuation of this austere and exceptionally tough existence? Before retiring we wandered over to a small stone hut overlooking the Yarkhun valley below and looked out over ranges of mountains turning deep purple in the evening light. Given recent encounters it was impossible not to muse on the transience of life and the human condition.

Despite the fact that the donkeys made a break for freedom in the middle of the night, we awoke ready for the now traditional breakfast of porridge, chapattis, jam, eggs and hot chocolate or green tea. All the recalcitrant donkeys were loaded up ready to go by 7.30 a.m. A steep rocky path followed the Ishperu stream down to its confluence with the much larger and infinitely more boisterous Siru River crossed by a traditional bridge and then lower down by a more modern suspension bridge. At this point the wide valley of the *Yarkhun* came into view flanked by terraced fields and flowery meadows. We stopped by an ingeniously constructed old water mill for grinding grain before ascending sharply up a bluff on a dusty track where we came to a halt to watch a hoopoe that seemed oblivious to our presence. Before entering *Shosht* on the main route to Mastuj and Chitral by jeep, we were fascinated by the village store and post office at *Yashkist*. This was simply a small stone, mud-faced hut and the kindly shop keeper, beset by clamouring kids, shooed them away and offered us sweets to nourish us on our journey. This was such a generous gesture and we thanked him profusely. To refuse gifts so sincerely offered would have been to invite discourtesy. Hot and tired after 4–5 hours of trekking in the dust and relentless sun, we had an extended lunch by the very modern bridge over the Yarkhun linking Shost to Chitral and the rest of Pakistan that seemed a million miles away. Although the Yarkhun valley is an attractive linear oasis, irrigated by the abundance of small streams, it would have been a very long day to walk from Shosht to the camp site beyond Lasht. Following the right bank of the Yarkhun, we piled into heavily over-laden jeeps carrying five passengers and baggage plus drivers and hangers-on (literally) as far as the rough track would go. It was another helter-skelter ride where injury was never far away. After a couple of hair raising miles the jeeps stopped. The tributary stream flowing turbulently down to join the Yarkhun had washed the track away so we all disembarked, waded with packs through the cold, vigorous current and plodded on up the valley. A few hours later and we would not have been able to cross at all.

Lasht was tiny but it did have a 'shop' whose door and windows had received a lick of green paint many years ago. We stopped here to buy scarves to keep out the dust whilst travelling in the jeeps or off the back of our necks whilst trekking. The camp was set on a sandy terrace overlooking the Yarkhun River with a shapely glacier as a frontispiece. Dust was everywhere, seeping into tents and clothes as occasional flurries of wind whipped down from the glacier. The evening meal was graced with fresh mangoes purchased by the guides. They made a tasty addition to the usual fare of dhal bat or corned beef hash.

Leaving the irrigated green pastures, orchards and fields of the Lasht-Shost section behind, the following day was one of indelible contrasts. The Yarkhun valley now opened out into a series of gravel flats and silver-grey silt plains through which braided streams produced a complex dendritic network of glittering channels. The silt in places was quite treacherous and became soft quicksand. It was necessary to try to float across it and not to linger long in one spot. It was at such a point that a Tadjik or Kirghiz horseman came into view on a sturdy horse decorated with coloured woollen blankets. His swarthy complexion and distinctly Mongolian features combined with his palpable ease as a horseman to create a modern-day image of one of Genghis Khan's warriors. He gave us a wordless greeting

Tadjik horseman

before vanishing into the maze of bushes and stunted willows by the bank of the river.

A decent bridge enabled the party to make more solid ground on the right bank of the river and for several hours the route traversed rocky spurs. Across the valley a lineated settlement appeared high above the river where people waved at this alien band of travellers. The first dhzos were sighted, shaggy black beasts that are a cross between a yak

Yarkhun Valley crossing

Koyozum and Thui II

and a cow. These flourish at altitude, a sure sign that we were gaining height towards the Karumbar. Lunch was taken by the river which at this point became very turbulent, its relentless noise stifling conversation. Further small river crossings beneath cliffs of conglomerate and banks of scree led us to *Kishmanja,* where camp was made on the silt amongst a small clump of willow trees. Near the camp site a broad river terrace below frowning crags was being cultivated using two pairs of oxen yoked to a simple plough. It was an evocative sight and a graphic reminder of the harsh everyday struggle to eke an existence in this forbidding landscape. The clear night sky hosted a myriad of stars brighter and more luminous than even on the darkest Cumbrian night. Suitably replete after the evening meal in the mess tent, the porters then provided an impromptu concert, singing and dancing to a drum and a flute complemented by storage drums and fuel cans that beat out a sinuous and haunting rhythm. The young male dancers swayed elegantly to the music, their sensuous gyrations slowly increasing in speed and fervour to the applause of their peers and trekking guests. It was quite a performance and one that would be impossible for a staid Westerner to emulate.

Another early start at 7 a.m. began with a continued stroll by the roaring river across beds of shingle and white silica sand. Occasionally these were interrupted by banks of loose scree that demanded full

Koyozum

attention. The eyes were now drawn to the south where the icy ramparts of the major peaks of the Hindu Raj rose majestically. Of these Koyo Zum and Thui II exerted a powerful and dominating presence. As the valley narrowed beyond a group of huts at Vidinkot, a new suspension bridge took the trail to the opposite left bank where a steeper climb to an upland meadow opened up the stunning vista towards the Darkot An and the snout of the *Chittiboi Glacier*. A challenging route follows this line over the glacier pass at 4650 metres to the Yasin valley and Darkot village, where a jeep track leads eventually down to Gilgit. We were content to sit on a grassy knoll having lunch gazing across at this beguiling landscape before carrying on round the tumbling snout of the Chittiboi Glacier towards the next night's camp site at *Ishkawarz*. As the gradient eased the landscape opened out to a broad open valley. Clusters of huts could be seen, as well as the more substantial whitewashed Chitrali Scout fort that controls the *Boroghil Pass* over into Afghanistan.

It was a gorgeous camp site, located on a grassy terrace below the fort but well above the incised stream, with retrospective views of the Hindu Raj peaks glowing gold and pink in the late afternoon sunlight. We wandered up to the fort before the evening meal to have a word with the group of Chitrali Scouts whose task is to guard the frontier between Pakistan and Afghanistan, which at this point is barely a mile away. They were very coy about the number of troops stationed there and their precise military role, but did point out that the Boroghil Pass is closed to foreigners. It was clearly a major trade route in earlier times carrying trade from Central Asia, much of which was in hashish. When this trade was shut down by events in Afghanistan and China to the north, the Yarkhun Valley made up the shortfall and although the Pakistan Government made hashish illegal in the 1970s, it was clear that a cottage industry still exists. With very little medical provision, cannabis is used as a panacea and particularly to relieve pain. On a cold and windy night, the mess tent was abandoned quite early for the comfort of sleeping bags.

We awoke the next morning to a humbling sight. Sitting quietly outside the mess tent was a line of people all seeking some medical expertise and assistance. Some had travelled quite a distance in the knowledge that a Western party was expected in the area. We did what we could but felt massively out of our depth. An 'old' man in a grubby salwar kameez pointed to his foot and began to unravel a rag covering a red and angry inflamed ankle. His feet were filthy. In all probability, the foot was infected but all that could be done was to wash the foot, smear on some antiseptic cream, bandage it gently and give him some amoxicillin tablets and a small bar of soap. It made us feel incredibly humble. Another more educated young man had trekked a couple of days to see if we could do anything for his mother, who from his description was developing cataracts. One herder, coughing badly and probably suffering from bronchitis or TB asked through our sirdar whether we had anything to help him. By this stage all we had left was a few Strepsils. The sense of impotence was complete. Apparently, the Pakistan Govt. does fund a travelling medical orderly, but he only comes once or twice a year.

At the same time, this was the point where the new porters had to be recruited, as before, a noisy and quarrelsome business, but the haggling soon died down as loads were apportioned and rates agreed. The new team also used donkeys as the main beasts of burden, but a few horses were added to the mix. There was some trepidation at crossing the rickety pole and brushwood cantilever bridge over the foaming torrent, but all crossed with a semblance of dignity even if hands had to held and encouragement given. From here we were able to look back on the snow-capped outlines of the Hindu Raj which now formed the backcloth to a rolling area of Pamir-like steppes dotted with simple herders' huts. The patchy grassland was interspersed with clumps of artemisia and tamarisk amongst which flocks of goats grazed desultorily. At *Gharil*, a broad valley to the north wound its way through thickets of willow to the Boroghil Pass, one of the main route-ways into Afghanistan. It seemed very close and eminently approachable. It is off limits to foreigners, but a permit can be negotiated at the Chitrali Scout fort at Ishkawarz for a day trip for the more intrepid, although a basic requirement would be an approved armed escort. In the foreground of this grassy enclave stood several huts and a new larger building which was still under construction. This was to be the school although it appears that the recruitment of qualified teachers is a real issue even when they receive payment for their services from the central Govt. Nothing summarised more starkly the difficulties of living in such a remote area and once again one could not fail to be impressed with the resilience of these people.

The next couple of hours were spent trekking across a rolling landscape with occasional settlements occupied by Wakhi herders who waved cheerfully at us as we walked by. The overall impression was one of the immensity of this central Asian landscape. Snippets of melodies from Borodin's 'In the steppes of Central Asia' came drifting through at the back of the mind. Slowly the landscape began to change and the open Pamir country with its luxuriant grassland studded

Hindu Raj retrospect

En route to Shower Shah

with turquoise lakes became more constricted. The trail now climbed above the river and afforded a view of the sweeping silty plain of the upper Yarkhun, whose glittering waters broke into a myriad of braided channels. Having surmounted a couple of spurs, lunch was taken on a broad terrace above the river where the shriek of a marmot could be heard. Here the new group of porters gathered in a group to play their own music, the flutes and drums combining to produce haunting, insistent melodies to which some impromptu dancing took place in the heat of the day.

It was only a couple of hours from here to the next camp site at *Showar Shar*. The route now became dustier and the grassland more arid. Breasting one of the many knolls en route, there was a stunning view, one of those occasions that promote an involuntary intake of breath and which leaves an indelible sensation. In the foreground a small circular lake of vivid blue and turquoise led the eye to the ragged tongue of the *Chiantar Glacier* backed by serrated peaks capped by glistening snow. In the far distance, a lone horseman padded noiselessly across the silver-grey silt, the horse kicking up a small spume of dust like a trail of smoke. Set in the immensity of this landscape the sight of one human being was a highly emotional moment. The sense of perspective emphasised the insignificance of man against the scale of this primeval landscape. Showar Shah was a broad sloping embayment of green, well-watered pasture looking across to an alternative route

View South towards the Darkot Pass

over the Zindikharam Glacier to Darkot. It is an important summer grazing area for local Wakhi or Tadjik herdsmen and the area was well populated with flocks of goats and herds of yak and cattle, to which were added our own donkeys and horses. Showar Shah lies at an altitude of nearly 3700 metres and yet there were a few villages perched on ledges above the verdant plain, simple mud-bricked structures which are presumably only occupied in summer. Where this congregation of livestock is wintered remained uncertain.

There was a degree of anticipation as we gathered after breakfast to begin the gentle climb up to the climax of the walk along the Yarkhun

Caravan emerges from Shower Shah

Elemental Pamir landscape

valley to the pass at *Karumbar An* at 4230 metres. This was reputed to be one of the most beautiful places in Central Asia. For the first time on this trek we were accompanied for some of the way by the Wakhi herders and their flocks and a crocodile of donkeys, horses, goats and yak began to climb gently towards the tawny coloured mountainsides seamed by clear crystal streams. In places the colours of the rolling hills to the north became kaleidoscopic, varying from slate-grey to purple, ochre to yellow. Cloud shadows drifted across the clear blue sky and the glaciers and snow-capped peaks to the south glinted in the cold mountain air. The over-riding impression was one of space and

Lunch halt

cleanliness as the expanse of the desert and the presence of the high mountains came together.

At one point a trail of dust marked the approach of a highly decorated yak on which was seated an equally ornate and well-jewelled woman and her baby, the two being led along with palpable pride by the young husband. As we stopped for a picnic lunch by a crystal-clear stream to take in the view, a group of local herders came down from the village above to join us. Generously they offered us some of the local yoghurt, but mindful of the possible consequences, we declined with as much politeness we could muster. One was clearly the elder of the village, a minor ruler with pronounced Tadjik or Uzbek features. He was regarded as venerable and exuded a natural authority. Unlike his two guards who wore the traditional Chitrali cap, he sported a turban. They wore rather garish pullovers; he wore a well-used tweed jacket. None was able to speak English but through our sirdar, Ayub, we were able to establish that he was allegedly in his mid-50s, which in this part of the world classifies him as 'old'. After the refreshment halt, we continued the climb up to the pass, the flocks of goats and their herders having left us to spread out across the lush grazing, where pools of very blue water were interspersed with golden-yellow sedges and bog. The sandy slopes and scree were covered with alpine flowers; sedum, aster, sempervivum and saxifrage. As the pass was approached, the gradient became easier and we looked across to the embryonic river winding its way through channels of silver-grey silt. Above, deep-blue mountain slopes reared sharply, their summits gleaming with the whiteness and purity of the snow.

As we breasted the pass, marked by a prominent cairn, the view down the valley exceeded all expectations. For several miles the vivid blue waters of Karumbar Lake stretched out between sandy coloured arid slopes to the north and the spectacular mountain rim to the south. The camp site, which was clearly well used by herders and traders as well as trekkers, was positioned in a shallow grassy basin where some simple stone huts had been built and where our porters took up residence. This magnificent site was to be home for two nights. We wandered around the broad plateau for a couple of hours before the evening meal assimilating the solitude and serenity of the surrounds. To lighten the mood, a herd of mainly black yaks brought up by a herder gave a highly amusing and uncharacteristic display of frivolity, gambolling around like frisky sheep much to the consternation of their herder. Flocks of ubiquitous choughs wheeled around the site, their guttural cries breaking the silence. At 4300 metres, the evening became cold and we retired to our tents early complete with flasks filled with hot water. The altitude and rigour of the trek at this point had claimed a few victims. Tim, from Cambridge was obliged to pay for the services of a young porter to carry his day sac without realising that the lad himself was unaccustomed to such height and was suffering altitude sickness; Brenda had been suffering with diarrhoea almost from the start and her problems were now exacerbated by altitude; Stuart had also had a bad day. A good night's rest was needed by all.

The morning was clear, cold and frosty. This was scheduled to be a day of rest, but the option was given of some local walks, one of which was to trek round Karumbar Lake. On such a morning, this enticement was too much to resist. The two of us set off, hotly pursued by a porter who apologetically handed us fresh water bottles which had been dosed with iodine to sterilise. The colour of the lake was mesmerising. Perhaps it was the clarity of the air that gave the blueness an additional vibrancy; perhaps it was the proximity of the dominant peak of Jhui Sar whose snowfields and glaciers spilled down towards the lake. It was rough going but after a couple of hours we had emerged at the outflow stream which had to be forded.

Karambar camp site

We sat on a large boulder to dry our feet and put boots back on and as we turned to head back along the northern shore we were suddenly confronted by four horsemen, all resplendent in their costumes and all heavily armed. It was difficult not to feel uneasy. The Afghan border was less than an hour away on horseback and the camp site was only barely visible in the distance. They were as surprised as we were and when we greeted them with clasped hands and proffered 'salaam aleikum', they acknowledged the courtesy and wheeled their horses down the valley. It was a reminder that this could be a hostile and dangerous place for unarmed, unaccompanied Westerners to be. The trail on the northern side was much more worn and frequented and we were back at the camp site by early-afternoon. It was time to wash some of the grime of the previous week away, but the water of the lake was so cold that cupping water over the scalp froze the brain quite painfully. As we walked back to the tent, the night sky was incredibly clear, mountains and glaciers lit by soft moonlight and the Milky Way close enough to touch. It was a memorable awe-inspiring scene.

The following day was relatively short and began with the walk along the northern shore of the lake before following the stream down to the camp site at *Shuinj*. The Karumbar An is an important watershed and our route was now to follow the course of the Karumbar River to its confluence with the Ishkoman, which finally drains into the Gilgit River on its way to join the Indus. This eastern side was similarly lush grassland bordered by a chain of steep mountains to the south. Herds

Impromptu polo match

of goats and yak increased in numbers as we headed down the valley. Intriguingly as we descended we were overtaken by a few horsemen, all with roughly hewn polo sticks over their shoulders. The horses looked lean and muscular, their riders in grubby shalwar kameez looked the same. It was only when we arrived at the camp site at Shuinj, perched on a grassy terrace overlooking the incised river, that the penny dropped. This was the local polo 'field' and that evening we were to be treated to an impromptu polo match. This was exhilarating in its pace, ferocity and skill. There seemed to be no rules. Riders and horses careered across the stony pitch with utter abandon, the polo horses often accompanied by their younger foals. It was exotic, powerful and highly competitive. This was no choreographed display for tourists but a genuine full-blooded match. The clouds of dust generated slowly settled as the riders called a halt after about an hour of frenzied riding. To be able to witness a genuine exhibition of the indigenous sport of this frontier region was a rare and unforgettable privilege.

Significant challenges now lay ahead. The Karumbar River enters a turbulent section as its valley narrows and we were introduced to some distinctly scary bridges made of rickety planks bound loosely together that enabled us to traverse the steep rocky bluffs. Even these paled into insignificance when compared to the supports that led the path across crumbling rock faces. These consisted of poles wedged between convenient lines of weakness in the rock or jammed by large boulders. The base poles were then topped by further poles to leave a creaking causeway barely wide enough to support one walker and their traverse was made with considerable trepidation, given the probability of serious injury or worse should footings or balance fail. Somehow, the donkeys found their way across although at a later stage the porters were obliged to unload the store barrels and despatch the donkeys into the boiling rapids for them to make their own way downstream. This was trekking at its most elemental. The hair-raising section gradually eased, and the valley floor was again reached. This was now a chaos of boulders, pebbles and gravel brought down by the river. As we made our way carefully across this rocky plain, the next challenge soon presented itself. The valley was blocked by a major glacial tongue that reared above the foam-flecked river, which now disappeared under the glacial snout. This was the *Chashboi (or Chatteboi) Glacier* and the challenge was to cross the river and climb up onto the main body of the glacier.

High jinks in the jola

Fortunately, the answer soon became apparent. A cable was strung across the river which supported a wire cage or jola. It was the unenviable job of two of the porters to hang onto this lifeline and make their way to the opposite side of the river to release the jola. This was achieved with cheerful abandon. Loads were transferred from the horses and donkeys and ferried across. The pack animals somehow made their way via a considerable detour to find an alternative route across the river. It was then our turn to be squeezed into the basket and winched across. This mode of transport was not designed for arthritic limbs, but it was curiously exhilarating nonetheless. All that now needed to be done was to cross the glacier, or, as it transpired, two glaciers, as another major glacial tongue cascaded into the Chashboi from the south. Traversing a glacier with an evident abundance of crevasses normally requires ropes and crampons but fortunately the icy surface was blanketed in rubble released by frost-thaw from the vertical rock faces above. This mantle of gravel gave the necessary purchase for both humans and horses. Sometimes this built up into a ribbon of morainic debris; sometimes the finer particles locked into the ice were sufficient to prevent slipping. This was a major glacial crossing where the human scale was dwarfed by the immensity of the ice-flow and the severity of the active rock faces above the glacier. These were mainly granitic, polished and near vertical. It was a sombre place. Fortunately, our guides were knowledgeable and the weather held so that visibility was never an issue. In less clement conditions this could have been a very hazardous crossing. The constant crack of rocks falling from the crags above hastened the traverse until at last a broader outwash plain was visible to the south-east. It was possible to move off the bare ice onto a pronounced medial moraine which finally led to a steep but safe descent onto the outwash plain. Ahead a small clump of willows could be seen by the re-emerged Karumbar River and one or two dwellings. This was the camp site at *Sokhter Rabot*.

It had been a mentally draining as well as a physically tiring day and we camped on the river silts amongst the trees, thankful that this section had been safely negotiated. A strong wind whipped up the dust into devils that whirled around the camp like demons. It was time for an early night after the evening meal. There was now a palpable feeling that the most demanding section of the trek was over. Fatigue was slowly building but it is a wonderful sensation to confront any sort of challenge and to sense that it had been overcome. Hubris would be the right expression to describe such naivete in the light of what was to follow the next day, but we fell asleep oblivious of the future.

The following morning gave us a little time to wander round the now becalmed camp. One of the buildings was a mosque under construction, a simple one-storey building. It was hard to imagine where the worshippers would come from. We were now entering a section where major passes crossed the mountains such as the *Chilinji* into Hunza and the *Khora Bort (Khoderg Werth)* into Afghanistan. The latter is high and steep, but it appears that the Pakistani Govt. intends to build a road into Tadjikistan over this pass. This would be a major undertaking as would be the approach from Gilgit. We were now in the province of mainly Gujar herders. The linguistic diversity of this area reflects its physical isolation. Most of our porters and sirdars were now Gujar but Ayub and Mehboob spoke to them in the common language of Urdu, which most understand. With Wakhi, Khowar and Burushashki, (the mysterious language of Hunza) all spoken, it is linguistically complex and diverse.

This was to become a traumatic day. Within minutes of setting off, John, our Yorkshire colleague, slipped on one of the many rounded and smoothed boulders and twisted his ankle so badly he was unable to walk. A broken ankle in this situation was serious. He was strapped up, loaded on to a donkey with his feet almost touching the floor in evident pain. At a later stage the conclusion was reached that although the ankle was probably not broken, the ankle ligaments were shot. His lack of mobility was now to condition the future route taken, which included glacier crossings, turbulent melt-water fording and the possibility of a high glacier pass, the Chilinji, at the height of Mont Blanc. Clearly something would have to give, but the immediate problem was that an angry glacial melt-water stream, tantamount to a small river had to be crossed. The horses came in useful here and the porters took the opportunity to guide the lady members across. The first objective was the small summer grazing area at Chilinji, where another jola crossing was available to ferry people and supplies across the now very turbulent Karumbar to the opposite bank, where the ascent to the Chilinji Pass would begin. At this point the Chilinji Glacier comes down almost to the river whose boisterous passage made conversation difficult. However, conversation there had to be! John was not in any condition to attempt the scheduled high route over the Chilinji Pass to the Chapursan valley and Hunza. To some extent, neither were we! We were by far the oldest members of the party and the prospect of a major high level glacial crossing and a very steep descent on snow and ice was perhaps less attractive than it might have been even a week ago. In all honesty, we were probably beginning to tire. There were some dissenting voices but clearly the whole party had to stay together, and the decision was made to take the alternative lower level route, following the Karumbar River down to Imit, Gilgit and Hunza.

This was to prove a very interesting diversion. It is an old mountaineering adage – 'never follow a river valley down-slope', but the die was cast and when river cliffs barred the way, the pack animals were unloaded again and made to find their own salvation in the turbulent rapids downstream. Loads were now portaged across another series of ingenious but hair-raising pole-supported 'paths', which presumably must be renewed annually. None of the sections were much wider than a boot. It called for maximum concentration. Finally, we emerged onto a more placid alluvial fan through which the river braided into more gentle channels with silt and grass in equal abundance. This calmer section was transient. A final glacier crossing loomed where a tongue of ice and compacted snow came right down to the river. Fortunately, this was of minor inconvenience and the trail kept high following a lateral moraine, before curving south to the sheltered camp site at *Maturamdas*. This was shielded by trees, contained a few stone huts used by herders and looked out on the impressive snow-capped outliers of the Karakorum Range. There was not much flat land, but we spread our tents out over the undulating rocky ground and began to relax.

From here it was mainly downhill with only one more major glacial crossing to undertake. John had survived the day which almost certainly contained more of interest than a stiff glacial climb under the searing sun. It was still a dusty place and subject to squalls of wind which whipped the dust into tents, eyes and lungs. A persistent cough was beginning to develop which was put down to the inhalation of dust, rather than the effects of altitude. By now camp life had settled into a rhythm, but the prospect of a bed and shower after nearly two weeks on the trail was beginning to cause unwelcome hallucinations.

The *Karambar Glacier* was not quite as daunting as some we had already traversed but it proved a challenging couple of hours. Unlike the Chashboi with its rolling folds of ice this was a steeper tongue broken into unstable sections of morainic debris by melt-water streams. The path soon disintegrated underfoot after the pack animals had made their way across and we approached some of the sections gingerly giving thanks for the stability and security afforded by the trekking poles. The written guides had declared this to be a 'serious obstacle' but once again our sirdars had found an uneventful way through. The river valley beyond the glacier slowly began to open out and clumps of trees, including both willow and cultivated poplar began to appear. The first sign of civilisation was a fence protecting a stand of trees where we slumped down for a lengthy picnic lunch and enjoyed another impromptu concert. John's ankle was holding out and he was able to hobble around with the aid of a stick.

From here to *Bort* was relatively easy going after the glacial traverse in the morning, a strip of silt easing the way between the chaotic sea of glacial and alluvial debris. Bort itself was a small collection of huts sited on the edge of a sloping fan of debris but with a few cultivated areas irrigated from the abundant tributary streams. It was not the most comfortable of camp sites. Local boys came to see their strange visitors taking in the rare sight of someone shaving with rapt interest and responding to our ad hoc lessons in English. The porters were now much more relaxed, realising the end was nigh and although we were not able to converse with them other than by gesture, they were quite happy to allow photographs to be taken. They had been a resolute and reliable team but their (and our) trials were not quite over.

Porter struggles through meltwater stream

It was a short day to the road-head at *Bilhanz* but this contained a sting in the tail. The trail between Bort and Bilhanz involved quite a few innocuous river crossings but then came one that made even the most experienced members of the party blanch. A raging torrent of obvious power flowed sharply down to join the main river. It was not very wide but incredibly ferocious. Trekking packs were taken from the donkeys and hoisted onto the backs of the porters in case one of the donkeys should slip (indeed we were to learn later that only a few days before this had happened, carrying donkey and load into the Karambar River). In our case, one of the porters did slip and was briefly washed down the torrent complete with pack, but fortunately managed to regain his footing. We were helped across by pairs of porters who did a magnificent job. It was some way to complete an epic trek. It was not far from here to the road-head, but our recent experience had demonstrated why even jeeps could not progress as far as Bort. The camp at Bilhanz was in a potato field, not the most prepossessing or dramatic of sites. At least it was largely free of boulders and beyond it we could see the dusty track and the tyre tracks that denoted the passage of vehicles.

Sure enough, the next morning over breakfast we heard the unmistakeable burble of diesel engines as two cargo jeeps came bouncing and jolting into view. Trekking bags, provisions and people were piled high and squeezed into the jeeps and we set off bouncing and swaying on this very rough 'road' to join the much better track south of Imit where the Karumbar River, which had been our constant companion since the Karambar Pass, flowed into the broad *Ishkoman valley*. We were now following a well-defined trail heading towards the sizeable settlement of *Chatorkand*, the home of Ayub, our Chief Sirdar. Just when it seemed that our trials and tribulations were at an end, the jeeps slowed and then stopped at a point where the track had been undermined by a landslide. The damage seemed irreparable, but soon a team armed with the simplest of tools, mainly two-man shovels, had reinstated the track sufficiently for a large jeep to cross. Passengers disembarked and watched courageous drivers inch their way cautiously across the still unconsolidated section, below which was a steep drop down to the stony river valley. To rounds of applause, they managed the crossing with aplomb and we continued our journey to Chatorkand. The trekking party was invited to join Ayub at his home for lavish refreshments. The complex of buildings was surrounded by a delightful orchard containing a wide variety of fruit trees – apple, pear, walnut, almond, figs, mulberry and grapes. It was something of an oasis after our journey across the harsher terrain of the Yarkhun and Karumbar valleys.

There was still some way to go to Gilgit, so with some reluctance, we piled into the cramped quarters of the jeeps to continue the long, dusty ride accompanied by the tinny sounds of Pakistani music coming from the driver's transistor radio. It was about 5 p.m. when we pulled into the grounds of the Chinnar Inn and slumped onto the beds waiting for the hot water to arrive after 6 p.m. Eventually we settled for cold showers to wash away the grime and dust. It seemed strange to feel clean again. Breakfast was taken at 8 a.m. It was a day to explore this interesting place that figured so prominently in 'The Great Game'. *Gilgit* is one of the main markets of the northern frontier region and a tour of its main street was an education. Exotic cloths and spices, meat and vegetables, shoes and pottery, household goods, motor repair shops, all jostled for space in adjacent stalls. There was, however, no sign of the stall which only five years ago had been selling Russian armaments including AK47s and rocket launchers. After a fascinating wander round, we all joined up for lunch at the Serena Hotel, the 'poshest' place in town. Lunch here cost the princely sum of 250 rupees or about £3. After so long in the cramped quarters of the mess tent, such luxury was a welcome change. We continued to explore Gilgit including its famous polo ground where the highly competitive rivalry

Morning light on Rakaposhi, Hunza

between Gilgit and Chitral is enacted, before making our way back to the Chinnar Inn to relax in the garden. It was here that we said our farewells to all our Pakistani guides and cook, an emotional moment. They had accompanied us through thick and thin and we would always be grateful for their loyalty and commitment. Our porters had been paid off and thanked at the last camp and it seemed strange to be without their company after so long. It dawned on us that these farewells marked the beginning of the end of this adventure but there was still the jeep journey to be made to *Karimabad* in *Hunza* via the Karakorum Highway.

Hunza was allegedly the basis of the concept of 'Shangri La', its linear oasis of green fields and productive orchards contrasting with the harsh, austere Karakorum landscape that encloses the valley. It is dominated by the peak of Rakaposhi, one of the most photogenic mountains in the whole of the Karakorum. At its foot we stopped for freshly baked chapattis to see us on our way and trundled into our lodgings at the Park Hotel by mid-day. Having settled in, we joined the rest of the party for a tour of *Baltit Fort*, the home of the Mir of Hunza, an impressive and formidable fortress perched on a terrace overlooking the valley and backed by the glittering snows of the *Ultar* peaks. The fort has an interesting history, formerly commanding the trade routes over the *Khunjerab Pass* to *Kashgar* and central Asia and some of the wealth of Hunza was accumulated by exacting tolls from trade caravans using this route. During the Great Game the fort was taken by the British in December 1892, after a campaign in which the futility and incongruity of organised warfare in such a setting was compounded by the realisation that no invading force of Russians or Chinese would be likely to make much progress down the Hunza valley given the near impregnability of its natural defences. It had taken outstanding courage by sappers and Ghurkas to overcome a handful of defenders whose ancient matchlock rifles were matched against Gatling machine guns and artillery. In this historical context the tour round Baltit was instructional and fascinating. We wandered down to the bazaar in Karimabad during the afternoon stopping at the chocolate shop for a pancake topped with Hunza honey. Dinner at the hotel included apricot soup, the local speciality, and afterwards on a moonlit night of pristine beauty we spent time on the flat roof looking across 'Shangri La' towards Rakaposhi, its snows gleaming in the subdued light.

Below the main bazaar of Karimabad, a track leads down to *Altit*, a broad basin of irrigated land where vegetables and fruit crops are carefully tended. Most of the flat-roofed mud brick houses had harvested crops of apricots, tomatoes and peppers drying in the sun. It was a colourful and productive place. Overlooking the river Hunza and the course of the present Karakorum Highway (KKH) is Altit Fort, high on a bluff commanding the point where the valley narrows. It is centuries old and to withstand earthquakes has a laminated construction, alternate layers of wood and hardened mud designed to stretch and yield to the forces imposed upon it. It is in this novel way a forerunner of many much larger buildings erected in areas subject to frequent earthquakes. Across the Hunza River lies the Shia settlement of Nagar, which the KKH passes by and the contrasts between it and the more cosmopolitan Ismaili Karimabad are huge. Walking back to the hotel we were accosted in the nicest possible way by groups of inquisitive children, smiling, giggling and often speaking passable English They were a delight. The women in Hunza are clearly more emancipated as Ismaili Muslims. They do not wear veils and are openly more confident and forthcoming.

After a brief rest it was decided to walk up to the 'Eagle's Nest'. With hindsight, we should have taken a taxi which would have cost a pittance but, being purists, we hauled our tired bodies up a dusty track to this famous viewpoint. The subsequent tea and Coke at the teashop on the summit was very well received. Below, the terraced fields of the Hunza valley bounded by lines of elegant poplar trees led to the glittering peak of Rakaposhi. It was here that we met the Headmaster of the local secondary school and received an invitation to visit which was accepted with alacrity.

Had we surmounted the Chilinji Pass we would have entered the *Chapursan* valley that leads down to *Sost* on the KKH. The following day we took the easy option and drove up in jeeps. The surface of the KKH is well maintained. It climbs steadily through the most impressive mountain landscapes to the Khunjerab Pass that leads over into China and Kashgar. The Karakorum mountains are every child's idealised mountain forms; they appear like spiky triangles inset in layer after layer. Below the perpendicular crags, fans of scree spilled out into the valley. To the south a pronounced notch leads through to the *Shimshal* valley to which access is possible by pack animals, but current plans are to blast a jeep track through. As in the Alps dynamite and bulldozers have, and are, changing the nature of the

Karakorum Highway truck, Gilgit

landscape and transforming the lives of local people who were formerly very isolated. To the north, the Batura Glacier flows down almost to the KKH itself, its surface blackened with piles of debris. We stopped here for a while to assimilate the elemental grandeur of the landscape, and also to view the outlines of the buildings that housed the largely Chinese construction workers who were responsible for the building of one of the world's most impressive highways. The cost in human life was staggering. It is estimated that it cost one life per mile to build and even today the Pakistani engineers and army regularly lose personnel in endeavouring to keep the KKH open against the constant problems of massive landslides, exacerbated by severe earthquakes.

We left the KKH on the return journey to drive up to the teashop at Borit Lake set in small gardens and looking out towards an archetypal Karakorum landscape of serrated blue mountains and tumbling ice fields. The final stop was at the Marco Polo Hotel in *Gulmit*, where stooks of grain nestled against informal gardens of sunflowers, phlox and roses. Weeping willow trees and stately poplars framed this splash of colour in one of the most forbidding landscapes on earth. A picnic lunch emptied the last of the blue barrels that had accompanied us for the whole of the expedition and we were able, unusually for a Muslim country, to purchase ice-cold cans of Chinese beer. A visit to the museum at Gulmit followed. Inside its gloomy, dusty interior were displays of stuffed animals including markhor, Marco Polo sheep and probably the world's worst example of a stuffed snow leopard. One wondered how many visitors the place received but it deserved full credit simply for its existence. Around the corner was a weaving workshop where groups of women worked in almost troglodytic conditions. However, they were cheerful at their looms, the clatter of which halted as we crowded in. It was our thirty sixth Wedding Anniversary (15 August), and the women were astonished at this longevity. In an area where life expectancy for women is in the mid-40s, arranged marriages take place in the mid-teens and childbirth begins early, it must have seemed unusual to be confronted by an aged couple who had had only one child. It became a very interesting cultural insight and we bade them farewell to their evident camaraderie. There was time back in Karimabad to have another frothy coffee with walnut cake before the return to the hotel. It was quite an emotional evening because all recognised that the adventure was coming to a close. The next day we would begin the long journey back to Rawalpindi via Gilgit and the KKH. On a warm, still evening we went up to the roof terrace again and watched the sun sink slowly behind the reddening snows of Rakaposhi. It had been a momentous journey.

On the final morning in Karimabad, I went to the local English medium secondary school with Hazel, the trek leader who had many years of educational experience both in the UK and with DFID in Pakistan. Even with my 40 years of working in English secondary schools, I did not know what to expect, but as we assembled in the staff room, the very smartly turned out pupils gathered on the dusty playground for assembly, very much in the English tradition. A brief peroration was followed by a rendition of the national anthem and the raising of the Pakistani flag. Already the relatively liberal Ismaili influence was detectable. There were as many girls as boys, a situation not commonly found in Sunni or Shia Pakistan. In the classrooms boys and girls were taught together, although as is the way the whole world over, boys did not sit with girls. Introduced by the 'Humanities' teacher, the lesson plan was to provide some insights on England. It was a very wide-ranging brief and one which provided some challenges. English was not one of them nor was discipline. All the pupils spoke good English and were impeccably behaved. When asked to describe the geography of England there were immediate issues. How does one translate the concept of an island bounded by the sea when the Indian Ocean is over a thousand miles away and only a few large lakes are accessible from Hunza? How does one describe the flat industrial plains and rolling green countryside of most of England when at the back of the school the Ultar Peaks rose almost vertically to over 20,000 feet and most of the surrounding landscape is semi-arid and severely mountainous? Factories, cities, railways, traffic lights, multi-storey buildings, noise, pollution – it must have seemed a strange and alien world to them. They were also politically very astute. What was the feeling on the Partition of India in 1947? That called for a diplomatic response. The 'lesson' itself lasted for more than an hour and at the end the learning process had been mutual. They were delightful students but one went away both reassured and mightily encouraged, whilst recognising that in most parts of Pakistan this situation is far from the norm. What talent there must be waiting to be unlocked? One's mind shifted back to the schoolhouse at Boroghil where any children enrolled would never be able to aspire to the opportunities presented to the youngsters in Hunza.

Back at the hotel, group photos were taken, and we piled into the jeeps for the ride down the KKH to Gilgit. This took us to *Alliabad* with its queue of gaudily decorated trucks whose drivers were having refreshments before the long climb over the Khunjerab Pass into China. Inevitably, the final impression of the Hunza valley was the view across the valley to the imposing and beautiful outline of *Rakaposhi* framed by spires of poplars. Entrancing, daunting and utterly unforgettable! We were back at the Chinar Inn in Gilgit by late-afternoon and after another last wander round the bazaar turned in early for what we knew would be a tiring last day. Breakfast was taken at 4.30 a.m. and the Toyota coaster set off at 5 a.m. It was somewhat cramped, and a 14-hour journey lay in front of us. The KKH, however, never fails to concentrate attention. In the first couple of hours the road descends into a mighty gorge with crumbling towering cliffs above. Resident bulldozers were already at work clearing fallen debris, like miniature insects against the immensity of the towering crags above them.

We halted at the information stone near *Bunji* that marks the point where tectonic plates collide. This is the point where the leading edge of the Himalayas, identified by the sheer icy cliffs of Nanga Parbat visible in the distance, is forced inexorably against the continental plate, producing the Karakorum and the Hindu Kush. Mighty rivers have exploited these elemental fractures, the Indus, Hunza and Gilgit. This was geography/geology at its rawest and most dramatic. We continued down the KKH across a high semi-arid plateau above the right bank of the Indus towards Nanga Parbat, a mesmeric peak revered and respected in mountain lore as 'The Killer Mountain', a reference to the number of climbing fatalities it has caused over many years. Its north face falls almost sheer some 7000 metres to the Indus valley. Its name in Kashmiri means the 'naked mountain' because its rock faces are so steep that snow rarely sticks to them. It is approached via Fairy Meadows where an approach track deviates from the main KKH as it crosses to the left bank of the Indus over the spectacular Raikhot Bridge, whose abutments are decorated with Chinese dragons identifying its provenance. The highway clings to the foot of the mountain wall below Nanga Parbat until finally it escapes the confines of the gorge and reaches *Chilas*. This place is renowned as 'bandit country', where even in the halcyon past Western trekkers went missing. Western women, in particular, do not receive a cordial welcome although it seemed quiet today as we strolled past the pomegranates into the PTDC Motel for refreshments.

Chilas is the northernmost outpost of Kohistan, an area of unruly factions that hide away in the steep valleys that branch off the Indus. Tribal warfare and blood feuds are apparently quite common. The Sikhs, the British and even the Pakistanis accepted the inevitable, and administration of this lawless area translates into police garrisons based in Chilas to prevent blood feuds from boiling over. Schisms between Sunni and Shia add fuel to the flames. After the construction of the KKH a stronger military presence was provided; road blocks are common and occasional garrison barracks have been built. However, even today this is not a place to linger and away from the KKH authority diminishes quickly.

The transit of Kohistan is also marked by the spectacular defile of the Indus Gorge where the KKH clings to almost vertical rock walls and where the construction of the road cost many lives. It is a dizzying section, and not one for the squeamish. The drop down to the Indus is vertiginous and a number of rusting vehicles at its foot testify to the dangers of getting the line wrong. After winter weathering or intense

summer rains the crumbling rock walls have a habit of sliding down
into the Indus creating a constant problem of maintenance. The rule of
the road seems to be very basic; the largest vehicle takes precedence.
At times, vehicles almost touch as they inch past each other. Lorries
pass with jangling decorative chains, their drivers seemingly prey to a
nihilistic abandon. Trust is surrendered to the driver and fortunately
ours was alert and competent. Suddenly the constriction of the gorge
fades and a broad embayment appears where a tributary valley has
spilled a large delta into the Indus valley. A huddle of house bazaars,
motels and shops marks the provincial centre of *Pattan*. This fertile
bowl was the epicentre of a catastrophic earthquake in 1974, when
entire sections of the valley wall collapsed burying villages, killing
thousands and disrupting communications for some time. Today, it
seemed a more placid place than Chilas although an interest was taken
in our vehicle. We did not halt here but carried on for lunch at *Besham*,
the half-way point on the journey back to Rawalpindi. It was a good
place to restore sanity and shattered nerves. Besham is technically in
the administrative district of Swat, so in that sense we had come almost
full circle. It was a noisy place full of choking diesel fumes and honking
traffic so that the relative quiet of the motel tea shop was a boon.

The rest of the journey was relatively uneventful. The KKH
followed the broadening valley of the Indus as far as Thakot where the
road crosses the river and ascends steeply through pine plantations to
a high plateau and gently rolling countryside. This is the province of
Hazara and it seemed that we were re-entering civilisation after the
various nerve-tingling episodes on the upper part of the KKH. By the
time we reached the provincial centre at *Mansehra*, where we stopped
for an evening meal, dusk was beginning to fall. We drove on through
Abbotabad, the garrison town where Osama bin Laden was finally
apprehended, accompanied by increasingly dense traffic to arrive back
at the Shalimar Hotel in Rawalpindi at about 10.30 p.m. All credit must
be given to the driver whose concentration never seemed to waver and
who had driven over 400 miles through some of the most hostile and
intimidating country in the world apparently without breaking sweat.

Sleep came easily that night and we went down for breakfast at
well past 8 a.m. It was our last full day in Pakistan. First port of call
was the King Faisal mosque in Islamabad, a highly futuristic and
commanding structure whose minarets appear like space rockets.
As a building, it was hugely impressive. Women were separated and,

King Faisal mosque, Islamabad

although there were one or two frowns, we were received cordially into the main body of the mosque having been punctilious in observing the correct protocols. 'Islamabad is not Pakistan' is the adage that confronts any visitor to the capital. It is built on a rectilinear pattern and is much more westernised than Rawalpindi. It has shops rather than bazaars and the inevitable searching for pashminas and other souvenirs began. In the afternoon, we were driven to a restaurant in the Marghalla Hills overlooking the city. Here we sampled lassi, a cold and highly tasty drink comprising a yoghurt or buttermilk base mixed with fresh mango juice. This gourmet theme continued into the evening when we assembled in the Pearl Continental Hotel to partake of excellent ice-cream and a splendid Chinese meal. The mind buzzing with reminiscences and flooded with cultural contrasts, we returned to the Shalimar for the briefest of rests interrupted by the pipes and drums of a wedding feast. By 1.30 a.m. we were on our way to the airport to be whisked back to an entirely different world.

We arrived in Manchester at 10 a.m and immediately headed for a kiosk selling bacon butties before catching the train back to Cumbria. When we drew up the lane to home, Pip, our tolerant and characterful tabby cat was sitting on the garden steps, a mixture of nonchalance and obliviousness, but clearly pleased to see the humans return. The garden was lush, the lilies highly scented. And yet even as we soaked up the familiar atmosphere, the mind was disorientated, with flashes of recall – the gardens at Gulmit and the splendour of the Hunza valley; the ruggedness and majesty of the valleys of the Hindu Kush and the Karakorum; the dignity of local people in conditions of extreme adversity.

All expeditions take time to assimilate. For days if not weeks a degree of disorientation exists as the return to familiar routines and domestic life impose themselves. Even more than previous trips to the Himalayas and the northern territories of Pakistan (Snow Lake), the expedition along the Yarkhun and Karambar and down to Gilgit was hugely fulfilling and unforgettable. Such experiences shape lives. One learns a great deal not only about the country and the people of the area but also, as importantly, about oneself. An inescapable truth is that often the people who have the least material possessions and tangible wealth are in many ways richer than more affluent Westerners. To be made welcome in such rudimentary social contexts is humbling. The worlds of Islam mean more; Sunni, Shia and Ismaili. Understanding of the wider political and social issues improves. In the years since our return the growth of extreme religious divides in Swat and Kohistan where fundamental Sunni practices have spawned the emergence of the Pakistani Taliban have contributed to making the area hazardous for travel. We may have been one of the few trekking groups to make this trip; today Hunza is often approached via Kashgar to the north to avoid the incipient dangers of travel from the south. This is saddening. Not only is the North-West Frontier Province one of the most ravishingly beautiful places on earth but the loss of hard currency as the number of tourists dwindle must have hit the local economy hard. One has only to think of Mehboob, our estimable sirdar, who was guiding us to raise funds for the school he was founding in the upper part of the Indus valley. What hope for him and his seven sisters?

It is chastening to think that we are unlikely to visit northern Pakistan again, but its attractions are etched deep in the memory. Very few areas in the world combine such grandeur and spectacle, present such a challenge, provide such a startling cultural insight or leave such an impact. We shall miss the high places of the Hindu Kush and the Karakorum!

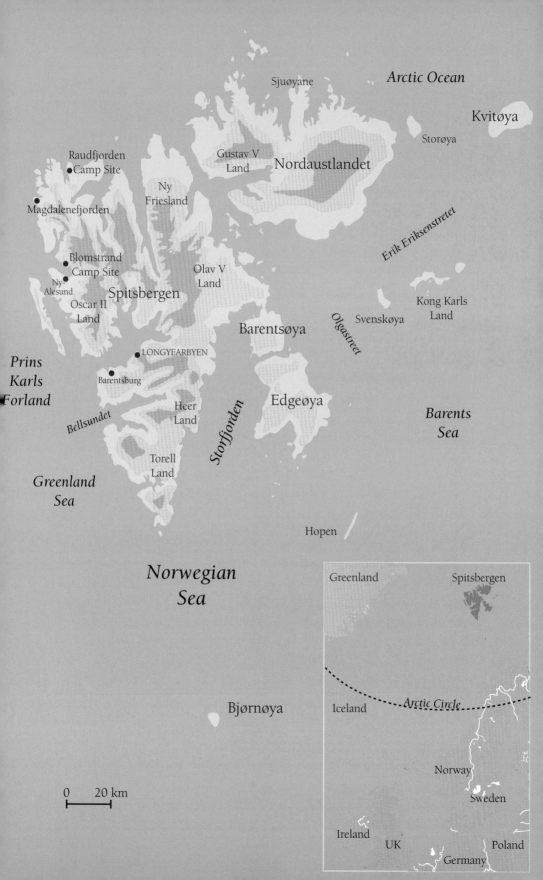

Spitzbergen Expedition

SPITZBERGEN: THE VERY NAME conjures up notions of Ultima Thule, the end of the world, bearing with it a romance, mystery and allure. In a sense, Spitzbergen is the end of the world, being the most northerly inhabited land on the planet. The bare statistics do not do it justice. About the size of Scotland, 60 per cent of its land area is covered by ice, although there is no other place so close to the pole (about 900 miles) that can be reached by ordinary ships that are not specialist ice-breakers, at least in summer. For a place on the same latitude as northern Greenland (80 degrees north) this is entirely due to the last ghost whispers of the Gulf Stream. The broader archipelago of Svalbard does not, however, enjoy the benefits of the latter. Away from the western and northern coasts, the second largest island of Nordaustlandet is almost entirely covered in permanent ice and in winter the entire archipelago is often locked in the pack ice drift from the polar sea. It has always exerted an attraction, excited by its forbidding terrain and daunting location. Today, the possibility of visiting it has been enhanced considerably by the development of the airport at Longyearbyen with regular flights from Oslo or Tromso. After recent visits to Norway, it seemed a natural corollary to include a trekking holiday to Svalbard in celebration of an impending seventieth birthday. The days when such an arduous prospect can be met with appropriate physical energy may not last forever and whilst confidence remains, the time seemed ripe.

It was with these thoughts in mind that we embarked on the first leg to Oslo with some degree of trepidation not knowing quite what to expect. A night at the Radisson re-introduced us to silly Norwegian prices but the buffet breakfast set us up nicely for the early-morning flight of nearly four hours to Longyearbyen. This in itself was an indication of how far north we were travelling. After touching down at Tromso, the flight continued and looking around the packed plane, there was some attempt to pick out prospective trekking colleagues. Prominent amongst our fellow passengers was a group of very excitable Chinese whom we were to become acquainted with later on the voyage north from Longyearbyen. The clouds below obscured the approaches and it was only as we burst through the cloud layers some 200 feet above the runway that the first views of the stark and seemingly barren Spitzbergen landscape were revealed. From above, Longyearbyen gave all the first impressions of being a frontier town at the very limits of human existence in the character of its buildings and wholesale evidence of industrial detritus. There was not long to ponder this sobering view before we were led through the terminal building resembling a hangar to meet with our tour guide, Ole. Inside, the stuffed polar bear hinted at a savage polar world; outside, the temperatures were quite mild although a chilling mist dampened spirits a little after the long journey. From here the minibus took us to the first night's accommodation at the Spitzbergen Guesthouse. This was housed in the collection of barrack style buildings formerly erected to accommodate coal miners and managerial staff and whilst rudimentary by Radisson standards, we have stayed in much worse. The journey from the airport to the Guesthouse passed through the main strand lineated inland up the valley of Adventalen and flanked by clear evidence of mining activity – spoilheaps, pylons, crushing plant etc. It was not the most appealing of vistas on such a bleak and cheerless day, but the rudiments of civilisation appeared to be in place. Many of the buildings nearer the harbour are more modern and whilst obviously fabricated

Chalets at Longyearbyen

for ease of construction, have been painted in the Norwegian style to add some colour to the harshness of the physical surrounds. Outside most of the houses was a collection of snow-scooters or snow-mobiles, which are clearly the main mode of transport for much of the year. There was a shopping centre, post office, school and numerous hotels. For a permanent population of just over 1000, dependent wholly on imported supplies of foodstuffs and construction materials as well as oil, this seemed to mock its frontier position more than 78 degrees north. Buildings were placed on wooden piles above the permafrost and all utilities were raised in pipes and conduits above ground to avoid fracture as the underlying frozen earth moved under the influence of freeze and seasonal thaw. The mists swirled along the valley obscuring the surrounding hills as we booked in and transferred to our simple sleeping quarters.

A briefing at 6.30 p.m. summoned us to the Spitzbergen Hotel, an altogether more sophisticated place, where the cuisine would not have disgraced one of Lakeland's classier restaurants. The evening meal of fillet steak, impeccably cooked with fresh vegetables, was almost surreal in this setting but very welcome nonetheless. To walk off the effects of such a hearty meal, we strolled around the environs back to the lodgings, passing en route yet more evidence of the initial importance of coal mining in the early development of Longyearbyen. Looming through the mist were the ghostly relics of the wooden pylons

Adventalen, the end of the world!

used to support the cableways carrying the coal in iron skips down to the harbour. These could have been dismantled as they are no longer in use but have been preserved as part of the industrial heritage of the place. They certainly provide a grim reminder of the conditions endured by the early miners. On the way back, a small graveyard of simple white crosses was passed. This stands out on the journey up the valley on its southern side and marks the resting-place of miners killed in an accident almost 100 years ago as well as those that succumbed to Spanish flu in 1920. Interestingly, some of these latter graves have been exhumed in an endeavour to discover the DNA traces that will give some insight into more recent viral pandemics such as swine flu. Graves are rare in Svalbard as the permafrost has the habit of raising bodies back to the surface as it continues to expand and contract due to freeze-thaw so today bodies are transferred to the mainland for conventional burial or cremation. There was much food for thought as we trudged back to the guesthouse.

It would be futile to pretend that much sleep was had during the 'night'. The problem, of course, is that there is no 'night' and the flimsy curtains could not dim even the misty light. Ironically, too, there was road noise as vehicles made their way down to the airport for the two morning planes at around 2 a.m. linking Longyearbyen with Tromso and Oslo. Somewhat blearily, therefore, we presented ourselves for breakfast, which was again quite a surreal feast. Quite what we were expecting is uncertain, but the profusion of fresh fruit again confirmed that the supply chain with the mainland is very efficient. En route down to the Spitzbergen Hotel to meet Ole for the morning's walk, we called in at the local art gallery, which was impressive. Displays of early maps pointed to the competition between the Dutch and the English during the late-seventeenth and eighteenth centuries to explore and map the archipelago and to the influence of early whalers and hunters from both nations as well as the Russian Pomors in temporarily colonising the more amenable fringes of Spitzbergen in pursuit of their trade. We could have spent longer here. Like all buildings in the town, it is very well heated, incongruously so. There is also the custom of removing footwear on entry to each building, which demonstrates both pragmatism and civility. The school buildings are modern and functional accommodating the surprisingly large number of children for a population of about 1000. This may be due to the short-term employment contracts and the fact that the pioneer nature of the place and its consequent salary inducements attract a younger group of inhabitants. There is also a University devoted mainly to Arctic geology, biology and environmental studies but one can only assume that many of the older students must leave the island to pursue their studies.

The walk with Ole was to the top of the shaly hill above the town, a climb of perhaps 1500 feet. It was our first introduction to the gradients and the rough scree created by the very active weathering in this extreme location. It also gave an opportunity to study the profusion of wild flowers that provide a subtle splash of colour in this harsh terrain during their short growing season. There are no trees on Svalbard. Arctic willow and dwarf birch creep along the ground, a strategy employed by most plants, few of which attain a height of more than a few centimetres to avoid the rigours of the extreme environment. Nevertheless, the tundra and broken scree is alive with plants. With so few insects to pollinate flowers, it is assumed that many will reproduce through scions or runners. They were certainly very hardy and in this setting had the effect of softening the rugged, raw nature of the landscape. Mountain sorrel was prominent along with knotweed and Arctic mouse-ear, a flower not dissimilar to our snow-in-summer or cerastium. Vivid green mounds of moss campion with their dainty pink flowers dotted the tundra. The locals refer to this as the compass plant because the flowers appear in rotation according to aspect and according to the time of year, the abundance of flowers on one side of the mound hints at direction. Perhaps the most ubiquitous species is the saxifrage, both purple and yellow casting carpets of colour across the dull sward of the tundra. The national plant is the Svalbard poppy, instantly recognizable, not only by the colour of its flowers, predominantly white and yellow, but also by the distinctive small poppy leaves. Clumps of mountain aven, white flowers with a yellow centre, form little colonies along with low growing bell heathers of white and rose. Scurvy grass is common, and its name denotes its significance in the early days of settlement in keeping scurvy at bay. It is not as distinctive as some of the above but seems to grow out of almost bare rock and weathered grit. On the marshier areas of the tundra, wispy tassels of Arctic cotton-grass fluttered in the wind. Many of the rocky surfaces are coated with colourful lichens and occasionally fungi of various kinds protrude from the mat of spongy, barely consolidated earth. The morning showed conclusively that even in this stark world of extreme climate and inimical conditions, the tundra is alive with flowers much more subtle than their alpine relations and yet more evidence of nature's capacity to survive in the most hostile environments.

Apart from the flowers, there was little view to be gained from the cairn at the summit. Longyearbyen spreads itself from the concentration of buildings around the coast, which includes the simple church and the Governor's residence, southwards along the main valley inland for about two kilometres, after which even the barrack-like buildings end abruptly. The hazy outlines of snowfields and glacier fronts mark the last tentacles of habitation.

Isfjorden, Longyearbyen

The main store (Svalbardbutikken)

At the hotel we were introduced to our second guide, Gunnhild, who during our stay was to prove an absolute delight. Her flaxen, plaited hair, blue eyes, vivacity and enthusiasm could not have been more archetypically Norwegian. We had time to explore the town centre with its two shopping precincts, before moving down to the main museum. Life on Spitzbergen may be hard but whilst choice may be more limited, the inhabitants of Longyearbyen did not seem to lack any of the essentials and also some of the luxuries. The main store (Svalbardbutikken) next door to the Post Office, has an attractive array of foodstuffs, hardware, clothing and other goods. Not exactly a Tesco, but in this setting revelatory. Opposite is the other main shopping precinct, the Lomponsenter, with its pharmacy, clothing and outdoor equipment shops. There is, inevitably, a pizza parlour and even a kebab/hamburger van!

The Svalbard Museum was also a revelation. Housed in a modern building constructed with familiar prefabricated wooden or aluminium sections but imaginatively designed and assembled, it provided a graphic insight into the early days of hunting, whaling and coal mining. Until 1920, when Svalbard came under the jurisdiction of Norway, this land must have resembled the Klondyke where claims to land could be made by the most rudimentary and basic of methods. Claims were marked, staked and lodged, although the legal process attached to the latter seemed fairly perfunctory and unclear. An international agreement at Versailles in 1925 gave all signatory nations rights of access to Svalbard providing that Norwegian sovereignty and law was respected. Even today, however, there is a distinct Russian presence, mainly at Barentsburg, which must have made for an interesting relationship during the Cold War. Displays of native fauna and flora also whetted the appetite for what was to come.

During the walk down to the harbour to embark on the MS Expedition, the sun finally broke through, casting away some of the gloom that seemed to have engulfed us since arrival. At the quayside, the MS Expedition lay at her mooring, dressed in her former Hurtigruten colours, but now Liberian registered and crewed largely by Philippinos. There was a courteous and friendly welcome as we were escorted to our cabin but little time to explore before the ship cast off and Longyearbyen drifted slowly from view. This was quite a dramatic moment, laced with both excitement at the adventure ahead but also some trepidation now that the 'civilisation' was being left behind. The boat itself was well equipped and very comfortable and this feeling of cutting loose would, of course, be of nought compared to the moment when we would leave the vessel for our first camp. Dinner followed quickly as we sailed down Isfjorden towards the open Arctic waters. Again, it was of very high quality much like that enjoyed on the main Hurtigruten ferry service on the mainland.

After a brief sojourn in the lounge we met our final guide, Ingrid who was born and raised on Svalbard. She was to prove a fount of knowledge, dispensed with great charm and impeccable English. She was the ideal partner to Gunnhild – same age (29), with stunning auburn locks again tidied into plaits. What a team this was turning out to be. Ole was the counterpoint. In his late-40s, he was more laconic but with a dry sense of humour and fathomless patience. In a crisis, this is the sort of man anybody would want around. By now we were also becoming familiar with our fellow trekkers after both formal and informal introductions.

There were four Americans. Victor and Barbara were from Chicago, both in their late-40s, both clearly bright and very personable. Corey was from Virginia, an extremely clever neuroscientist with a Yale, Stanford background. He was with his daughter, Anya, a mature, communicative 12-year old, who was a very impressive young lady. The Dutch contingent consisted of Peter and Eesje from Utrecht and Vera and Willard from Amsterdam. All were probably in their late-30s or early-40s, all spoke shamefully perfect English and were to prove exceptionally good company. Willard was perhaps the most impressive, a doctor by trade but a real polymath able to discuss almost any topic with intelligent insight. That left our fellow Brits, Andrew, an IT consultant working at the Hadley Climatic Centre at the University of Reading, and Alex, a former Bedford School pupil and geography graduate from Durham, now working for the BBC. The party was completed by a Norwegian, Bard, from Stavanger, who worked for BP, and Marida a very pleasant professional lady from Milan whose English was again perfect. The final member, Stefano, clearly had some language problems, but he managed to communicate via talking English in the same way as we use 'franglais'. This was unquestionably, the most congenial group of people one would have wished to spend the two weeks living with in difficult circumstances – lively, communicative, experienced, sensitive and enthusiastic.

After the safety drills and a final briefing, we had just time for a group gathering before the boat pulled in to Barentsburg at about 10 p.m. This is a Russian mining town of about 500 people that seems to operate as an autonomous enclave within the framework of the Svalbard Treaty accords. The first impressions do not compare favourably with Longyearbyen. It has the look and feel of 1950s Stalinist Eastern Europe in its ranks of ugly apartment buildings, most of which seem in a state of actual or incipient dilapidation. Its initial raison d'etre may have been the mining of coal and there is plentiful evidence of its former significance, but mining problems and marketing costs suggest very strongly that the Russian presence

Barentsburg

here is symbolic. In its modern way, Russia is staking a claim as a major player in Arctic politics to the possible resources to be found offshore in Arctic waters both adjacent to its own landmass and beyond here in Svalbard. The access to the settlement is by daunting wooden steps leading from the quayside to the main street. The Ukrainian guide, Oleg, was punctilious, polite and enthusiastic but around him the gulls cried mournfully and the buildings told a less optimistic story. Today, Soviet style hoardings exhorting the workers to fulfil their collective purpose decorate some of the larger buildings and this place must be one of the few remaining to boast a statue to Lenin. If this is what East Berlin looked like in comparison to the West, the only surprise is that it took so long for the Berlin Wall to come crashing down. There are only a handful of children in the local school, the buildings look forlorn and dejected and the only spiritual uplift provided was in the local Russian Orthodox shrine built to commemorate the tragic air crash at Longyearbyen in 1996 that claimed the lives of 130 miners and their relatives returning from the Ukraine. It was an interesting port of call, essential to understand the economic history and politics of Spitzbergen, but on a gloomy, misty night it left a dispirited feeling.

The boat beckoned, and we settled down in the cabin to a good night's sleep. Unfortunately, the cabin must have been directly above the drive shaft of the propellers and whilst the throbbing pulse

Polar 'dip', Magdalenefjord

resembled panting huskies as it drove us north, it proved difficult to settle to uninterrupted rest.

We rose to a grey, misty morning with occasional revelations of brooding mountains peering through the cloudy screen. By mid-morning there was a sight of a building on a gravel strand at the entrance to Magdalenefjord. Glaciers streamed down to the water and seabirds clamoured around the floes, taking their turn to feast on the body of a dead whale floating in the icy waters. Our first landing by Zodiacs was quite adventurous. We were escorted by Gunnhild, armed with a high velocity rifle as always, to the protected graveyard of over 150 whalers where we were given some insight into the rigours of their lives, often cut short by the nature of their work, disease or scurvy. The simple wooden building was the summer residence of the Governor of Svalbard, (Syssalmannen) but no trace remains of the whalers' shelters. Only rendering buckets remain to tell the story of this formerly lucrative trade that drove the Greenland whale to near extinction. Two yachts lay in the sheltered cove with blue ice floes floating around them, amongst which Alex launched himself briefly for the first of numerous swims in the polar waters.

On the way back to the boat a diversion in the direction the dead whale was made quietly as a polar bear slowly hauled itself onto the carcass and began to feed. The fjord went very quiet, only the sound of camera shutters disturbing the peace. It was the first contact with

Polar bear at Magdalenefjord

the iconic symbol of Svalbard. These are not zoo animals or semi-tame scavengers that populate Churchill on Hudson Bay. Svalbard has the highest concentration of polar bears in the Arctic, some 3000 in total and there are sufficient anecdotal references to their lethality. A hungry male bear weighing 700 kilos and as fast as an Olympic sprinter is not something to approach lightly! Its appearance here certainly excited the Chinese contingent with their telephoto lenses and shots of this sighting were to wend their way around the globe via news agencies to which the images were electronically transferred.

After all this excitement, it was time for a splendid lunch before the boat made its way cautiously into Smeerenburgfjorden at the head of which the vivid blue glacier wall was busily calving icebergs into the mist-draped waters. There was an ethereal light and atmosphere as we drifted slowly amongst the sculptured blue floes towards the glacier snout. Another Zodiac trip took us to the ice-wall itself, gently surveying the iridescent seracs which would crash into the water as they became unstable. Glaucous gulls, kittiwakes, guillemots and auks bobbed on the water or rose in flocks as they wheeled and then dived into the water. The remoteness and elemental character of this scene was mightily impressive.

Calving blue ice

Back on the boat, dinner was interrupted by the sighting of a Finn whale and then there was a general invitation to the party that celebrated the crossing of 80 degrees latitude. After this jollity, thoughts now turned to severing this umbilical link to the mother ship that had proved so accommodating and comfortable as we boarded the Zodiacs to be taken ashore. Raudenfjord is a north-south inlet at the very north of Spitzbergen and derives its name from the red coloration of the Devonian sandstones and conglomerates laid down when Spitzbergen was a desert at 30 degrees north. The geology is remarkably similar to that of Torridon in the North West Highlands of Scotland in that these rocks lie on top of the base gneisses. MS Expedition gently introduced us to a view of glaciers and snow-streaked mountains bathed in Arctic light but swathed in mist. There was an indefinable and distinctive atmosphere. Only the quiet hum of the ship's engines could be heard as we slowly edged into the calmer waters of the fjord. From the decks, eyes scanned for a possible landing site and then a cluster of tents and people came into view at the head of a gravel embayment. It was time to leave the comfort of the ship, its soft bunks, its warmth and excellent cuisine and cast off into the wilderness. Normally this would sound melodramatic or metaphoric but as the Zodiacs weaved between the floes to the shingle strand at Alicehamna, the term castaway seemed appropriate. Reassuringly, the mess tent had a wisp of smoke coming from it that hinted at a stove, but the eagerness of the previous party to leave for the comfort of the ship was less encouraging.

As the last Zodiac roared back to the 'Expedition', we cast a final glance at the ship anchored in the fjord and concentrated on the practical business of carrying materials up the beach to the camp site and sorting out the tent that would be our home for the next four days. The site was stony but with camping mats this presented few problems. The immediate agenda was to explore the bounds of the site beyond which it would not be safe to move without protection. Instructions were given as to the priming and firing of the flares to be used in an emergency to dissuade approaching bears and the procedures for the bear watch fully explained. The polar 'night' would be divided into two-hour watches which delegated pairs would staff in rotation. If a polar bear was sighted we were exhorted to make a hell of a din, shout 'BEAR' at the top of our voices whilst one of us would rouse our Norwegian guides who would bring rifles with them to deter the ursine intruder. The flares could also be employed. These were about the size

Polar bear invades Raudenfjord camp

of a fat biro and were primed by springing back a lever, which could then be used to trigger the charge. Normally these were located by the primitive toilets and the instruction given was to aim in front of the advancing bear if caught inconveniently performing one's needs on the bucket with its detachable seat. Misdirection of the flare behind the bear would only serve to accelerate its advance, not a happy thought with one's pants literally down!

As we sauntered back to the tents, a shout of 'BEAR' elicited initial scepticism, but the call was repeated more urgently by Alex. Sure enough, a polar bear came padding into view about 100 metres above the camp. It stopped, sniffed, stopped again, turned its head in our direction but then dismissed us as being of little immediate interest and carried on towards a snow slope. There it stopped, deliberated briefly and then spread out its front paws and slid gracefully and amusingly downhill. It looked back at us again, probably expecting applause, but then headed for the fjord, swimming strongly through the placid waters. The timing was perfect and added an immediate urgency and relevance to the bear-watch rota. Ours was the 5–7 a.m. watch, quite a convenient start, in that it did allow for some fitful sleep.

The stillness and solitude was total. Near the camp, a pair of Arctic terns was trying to raise two incredibly cute, fluffy and vulnerable chicks. Incoming parents were mobbed by other terns in an attempt to dislodge their cargo of sand eels to much general shrieking and crying. The delicate Arctic silence was punctuated by their insistent calls. The aerobatics of these birds was a joy to behold, hovering above the fjord with wings fluttering like a humming bird before kissing the surface of the water to emerge with shrimp or sand eel. They moved too quickly to establish how they managed to extricate themselves from the water and resume flight. A threat to the chicks was the Arctic fox, one of which loped through the boulders during the watch, and great skuas which would sometimes fly by with evil intent. On the fjord, large rafts of eider ducks cruised along cooing gently as they went. With these occasional interruptions, the watch passed quickly and gave time for us to assimilate this awesome and formidable setting.

Breakfast was made by Ole and consisted of porridge, laced liberally with cinnamon or blueberry jam, followed by excellent bread, cheese and various spreads. Of these the pate and 'caviar' went down well. Breakfast became a social occasion as the bleariness of waking was slowly replaced by convivial chatter and laughter. Sandwiches made, we now prepared for the first day's excursion to the summit of the neighbouring peak to the north of the camp, setting off in rapidly improving weather. Rents of

Polar bear heads off into Raudenfjord

Polar summit

blue sky allowed the sun to burn off the shreds of mist that remained. It was to become a day to remember. As we climbed higher across jumbled rocks and patches of flower-dotted tundra the whole of northern Spitzbergen was laid out to view in brilliant sunshine. The glaciers of Trollhattenhalvoya plunged down to the fjord and snow-streaked, serrated peaks studded the horizon. Their spikiness gave Spitzbergen its name and how appropriate it seemed today in such clear visibility. To the south-west, ice-shattered pinnacles protruded from the larger ice caps. North lay the open water of the polar sea. Banks of persistent mist hinted at the confluence of the relatively mild, Gulf Stream warmed waters with the permanent drift ice of the polar ice pack. It was indescribably beautiful in a raw, elemental way. The climb had generated warmth but at the exposed summit rocks, the wind became more biting, so we found a more sheltered spot for lunch. The group separated at this point, some to climb up to the neighbouring whale-backed mound, others, including us, to descend back to the shoreline to make our way back to the camp. In the intense sunshine and blinding light, it was almost impossible to believe that we were at nearly 80 degrees north but this was an exceptional day in every respect. To celebrate, as we returned to the campsite, Victor swam and we paddled in true British fashion. Dinner was fish cakes in mushroom sauce with potatoes, vacuum-packed by the Spitzbergen Hotel for our delectation and delight. The quality of our evening meals was to become almost legendary and certainly lifted the spirits on the darker days.

By now we had lost all track of time but deduced that the next day was Sunday. Overnight the weather had resumed its docile character, shrouding the views of yesterday in a pall of clammy, cold mist. At the confluence of warm and cold air, this was to become a familiar pattern. More ambitious plans were rejected in favour of a stroll south along the eastern shore of the fjord. Stroll has connotations of a leisurely ramble, but this was altogether more rigorous. The bouldery nature of the ground became a trial; numerous melt water streams had to be negotiated with improvised bridges or by leaping or paddling through the braided channels. Occasional interventions by Arctic terns nudged us away from nesting sites. Beachcombing here was certainly interesting. The skulls and vertebrae of two beluga whales were examined by Willard in forensic fashion and piles of timber on the shingle had floated here on the currents from Northern Russia. We took advantage of the latter to take lunch by a camp fire before turning back to camp. Ingrid continued her inimitable

Camp site, Raudenfjord

accounts of early settlement and the lives of hunters and whalers, complemented by contributions from Ole and Gunnhild. Between them they provided a constant stream of interesting and amusing information. It was never intrusive or boring and certainly enhanced our appreciation of this sublime wilderness.

One group opted for the high trail back through the impenetrable mist. We again opted for the more sensible route along the strand and tundra at a lower level. It was tough work and jarring on the joints but interrupted by speculation on the origins of the periglacial stone polygons and garlands of stone necklaces that pattern the tundra landscape. Conventional explanations suggest that repetitive freezing and thawing causes expansion and contraction in the saturated tundra, separating out the coarse and fine particles. Stone rings or polygons consisting of an outer coarser ring of stones and gravel up to three metres in diameter develop, with an inner core of silt and clay. They were certainly striking in breaking up the sea of boulders. This was another interesting day not for the distance covered or the views obtained but for its absorbing atmosphere and developing understanding of the interplay between landscape and man.

Bear watch during the 'night' was from 3–5 a.m., not the most congenial time to have to rise from a warm sleeping bag, but again the

Trapper's memorial

Trapper's hut

hours passed quickly. The bonfire became a comfort as we huddled against the freezing mist, but the tern chicks kept us amused and enthralled and the Arctic fox resumed its trail through the outer margins of the camp. Two hours sleep remained before breakfast after which plans were again amended as the mist persisted. Visibility was now less than 100 metres as we set off in the opposite direction northwards along the beach to the remains of a trapper's hut. This was in a good state of repair, simply constructed and our visit was again embellished by relevant background information from Ingrid. The remains of fox traps could be seen and more recent litter of rusting cans with Russian labels hinted at its more recent occupation. The hut was cobbled together from the driftwood lining the strand and, whilst small, it did have a stove and separate sleeping and living space. It seems, unsurprisingly, that many trappers and hunters became 'hut-crazy' possibly due to the loneliness and isolation of their existence and possibly due to inadequacies of diet before the need to combat scurvy was recognised. Many just gave up the ghost and died in the long winter night; others more resolute took to the rigours of this indescribably lonely existence with tenacity and resilience. Some, incredibly, lived like this for decades and became the stuff of folklore. The grave of the last known occupant lies beneath a pile of stones at the crest of the nearby hill. It was a hauntingly melancholic place to spend eternity. It became remotely possible in this setting to imagine the problems that such men would face, divorced from human communication and utterly reliant on the vagaries of the pack ice to enable re-supply or return to 'civilisation'. As illustration, we were treated to the saga of Nansen and Johansen who lived in such circumstances, locked in each other's confined company for years.

We had lunch back at camp and with the day slowly deteriorating into obscurity, we hatched a plan to combat the inevitable listlessness that can develop when the mists thicken by suggesting to our Norwegian guides that we should organise an international tournament. There were, after all, four obvious teams of four; four British, four Dutch, four Americans and four Norwegian/Italians. Four events would be staged. The first involved accuracy in knocking down numbered tins using selected tundra pebbles at a range of twenty metres; the second pitching pebbles into a defined target area; the third

Obstacle course takes shape

Gunnhild starts polar sports

casting a home-made ring over a reindeer's antlers and the final event consisted of an apple and spoon relay over a brutish course. All would be refereed by Gunnhild, who was firm and impartial. The Americans fluked a win in the first event, the Dutch won the second, the British team were handsome winners of the third. That left the deciding relay where the British brought up on egg and spoon events had no trouble in quelling the opposition, coming up on the rails to beat the Dutch. It was a bizarre and surreal occasion, but it did have the effect of keeping everyone warm and engaged on a dismal afternoon and of further generating a strong sense of camaraderie.

All that remained before dinner after this excitement was a ramble around the immediate environs of the camp to see the remains of an Arctic fox in its winter coat, surprisingly left un-scavenged, and to get our first view of Richard Lake. This separated the site from the shore of the polar sea on the north coast and it remained largely frozen

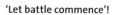

'Let battle commence'!

'Near miss'!

Unbridled laughter

except for the occasional fractured leads of water where a small flock of barnacle geese hooted their disapproval at being disturbed. Two months later a skein of barnacle geese was to pass overhead as we stood on the summit of Great Dodd in the Northern Lakes, heading for their winter feeding grounds in Morecambe Bay or the Solway Firth. It was an emotional moment. Were these our Spitzbergen geese? The wonders of seasonal bird migration never cease to astonish.

The last day in camp at Raudfjorden saw the mists and water merging into a grey/blue blanket with visibility down to 100 metres. The higher-level option was once again abandoned in favour of the long low-level trek to the north coast. The boulder field by the side of the lake was something of a trial, straining sinews and jarring joints. The lake was deeply frozen, but the edges had thawed sufficiently for bands of blue/green ice to denote fracture lines and occasional leads of open water in which eider ducks and barnacle geese paddled. The lake was only discovered a century ago and was given the name of Richard Lake after the British surveyor of the Prince of Monaco's mapping expedition. It is apparently renowned for its population of Arctic char, which, like their distant cousins in Windermere, grow slowly but can survive in such cold-water conditions.

In the mist, the northern shoreline seemed distant and progress tended to be circuitous as we meandered from one flat stone polygon to the next across the acres of shattered detritus and more gentle tundra. The latter was preferable but became increasingly boggy as

Paddle in Polar Sea

the permafrost beneath held the melt-water at the surface. Eventually a ridge-line of banked shingle, spread liberally with stranded logs and driftwood, came hazily into view, marking the end of land as we approached the tide line of the Polar Sea. Headlands brooded in the mist, waves lapped lazily against the pebbles and in one of the trapped lagoons a pair of red-throated divers swam gracefully away. Beyond lay nothing but a narrow strip of open water and then the floes and solid ice of the Arctic ice sheet, which would shortly be advancing again as the brief summer waned. It was quite a poignant moment to stand and stare. The mood was broken as Alex stripped off again and launched himself into the freezing water. Not to be outdone, the 'oldies' went for a paddle, to much general amusement. It was cold enough to make the toes numb but surprisingly refreshing!

We were not looking forward to the return journey across the shattered boulder fields, but a different line was taken along the very edge of the lake. It did not seem long until the welcome sight of the mess tent with its billowing stovepipe came into view. Events now moved quickly as we struck camp and began to assemble equipment prior to shifting the entire load down to the shore of the fjord across the newly mended 'bridge'. The timing was impeccable. Eyes scanned, and ears strained for the burble of diesel engines signalling the arrival of MS Expedition around the obstructing headland. At 2050, its familiar outlines appeared, and it dropped anchor in the fjord. There was both relief and sadness and one can only imagine what it must have been like for the early trappers for whom such a moment would have meant so much more.

The Zodiacs whisked us back to the ship to renew briefly our acquaintance with a world of warmth, relative comfort and hot showers. It had been an eventful four days and there was a great deal of nostalgia as we watched the gravel strand, now denuded of any evidence of our occupation, slowly subside back into the embrace of the cold Arctic mists.

Wednesday, 5 August began with breakfast as the boat nudged its way into the long finger of Krossfjorden, heading for the six kilometres wide blue glacial end wall of the Lilliehookbreen glacier. The upper fiord was dotted with recently calved floes of all shapes and sizes and the lichen-covered, almost vertical rock slopes rose sharply along the margins of the water. We passed on another Zodiac trip to the snout, preferring instead to languish in the warmth and gather strength for the next stage of our journey. The 'Expedition' continued on its passage south after lunch, passing by the guano-stained cliffs of Cadiopynten, where flocks of kittiwakes and black guillemots nested in their thousands. Ahead of the boat occasional pairs of puffins with their stubby wings and distinctive beaks took off against all the laws of aerodynamics, beating furiously to escape the clutch of the water. The white banks of guano created a fan of brighter green moss beneath the nest sites and extensive red lichen stains on the rock gave this austere setting a splash of colour.

By mid-afternoon we were anchored opposite the 14 July glacier where we did take advantage of the Zodiacs to land on the platform of tundra above the shingle beach. Above lay another raft of nests and the constant flood of guano supported a wealth of Arctic flowers beneath the cliffs. A couple of Svalbard reindeer padded quickly from view in one of the deeply dissected gullies and the air was alive with auks, kittiwakes and guillemots. On the shingle beach an Arctic skua, perfectly camouflaged, sat motionless on her nest and a bearded seal patrolled the waters offshore. After our more intimate walks, the size of the landing party seemed intrusive and certainly inhibited more unfettered exploration.

The rest of the afternoon was spent just relaxing in the lounge. Being back on the boat conferred obvious advantages, but strangely the lack of momentum and clear purpose felt more tiring. It is curious that in many ways we already missed the rigours and discomforts of camp life. This lassitude is a familiar theme. All expeditions generate a momentum. If this is interrupted by bad weather enforced rest is sometimes paradoxically debilitating.

It was a late call at Ny Alesund, the world's most northerly permanently occupied non-military settlement at 78 degrees 50' N. However, there are no families or children in year-round residence. Like Longyearbyen, it owed its existence originally to the extraction of coal and high on the bleak hillside above the cluster of buildings, the old slagheaps could still be seen. It stands on the southern shore of the large W-E inlet of Kongsfjorden, which has in its past seen other entrepreneurial ventures come and go. One was the development of 'marble' extraction at New London by a persuasive businessman at the beginning of the twentieth century but this venture collapsed when the marble disintegrated as the frost binding the fractured rock melted on transit. The old locomotive and trucks that carried the stone now have pride of place near the quayside at Ny Alesund. Coalmining effectively ended in the 1960s due to geological difficulties and the catalyst of a serious methane explosion in which 21 miners died. The land itself is still owned by the mining company, Kings Bay AS, but the place has transformed itself into an international research base. In summer, up to 150 scientists live here, but in winter that reduces to about 30. The Norwegian Polar Research station is based here and many other nationalities have colonised the

Ny Alesund harbour

Relic of coal mining days, Ny Alesund

former mine buildings as well as erecting new buildings. The British, French, Italian and German scientific communities are represented but there are also research facilities for the Chinese, Japanese, Indians and South Koreans. Because of its cosmopolitan scientific community and evident recent investment in infrastructure and energy, the place has none of the down-at-heel forlorn look of Barentsburg, but nevertheless, there is a distinct awareness that this is the end of the line in terms of human settlement.

We wandered through the settlement examining a former miner's cottage, viewing the most northerly post-office in the world, (which does a roaring trade in franking postcards) and inspecting the various research stations. Tourists are shown the old mast that tethered the airship of Nobile and Amundsen that successfully flew over the North Pole, although to a British mindset that seemed like cheating and we maintained jingoistically that Wally Herbert was the first person to complete the trans-Arctic land crossing. We took time to linger in the small museum before purchasing some mementos for the three guides at the only shop, Kongsfjordbuttiken. The tour did not take long on a rather dank and drizzly night and we were back on board by 11 p.m.

We cast off and headed across Kongsfjord towards the second camp at Blomstrand in heavy fog that brought a melancholic air with it. It was late, and we had visions of having to set up camp well into the early hours. In the gloom, we passed Blomstrandhalvoya, named after a Swedish chemist. 'Halvoya' means peninsula but it transpires that this

Camp site at Balestrand

is now an island, the connection with the glacier having been severed as the latter retreated. It was here that Ernest Mansfield set up the Northern Exploration Company to exploit the low-grade marble in 1913.

The ship now nosed into a sheltered bay littered with floes of all sizes and shapes that had calved from the Blomstrandbreen glacier and gently laid anchor amongst the floating ice. On the south side of the bay lay the Blomstrand campsite, its tents strung out along the sandy, gravelly shore and what appeared to be a yurt, its stovepipe billowing a plume of smoke. It was a very welcoming sight. The Zodiacs weaved amongst the ice and we stepped ashore onto the sand. Sleeping on sand made a pleasant change to the unyielding boulders but throughout the night we were constantly awakened by the heaving and groaning of the glacier. Occasional thunderous crashes occurred as huge blocks fell away into the water, creating a mini-tsunami that washed against the outer limits of the camp. We were on watch from 3–5 a.m. on a bleak night but again the time passed swiftly. The site was visited by long-tailed or mountain skuas and the Arctic terns continued their aerobatics over the icy waters. Although the horizon between land and sea was imperceptibly blurred, the bands of light reflecting off the vast ice sheets of the interior made the prospects for the following day more optimistic. The warmer waters off west Spitzbergen mingling with the colder air above the Arctic seas produce persistent mist that had plagued us for too long and the memory of that first splendid day at Raudfjorden was beginning to recede.

The mess tent/yurt was a real godsend. It was a pre-fabricated structure with tables and benches to make life less primitive. We gathered there for our first breakfast, in our case a little blearily after our late watch. With there being no distinction between night and day, the passage of time became difficult to track, a situation exacerbated by the continuing mists. The day did have some promise and we set off to climb Olsentoppen at 915 metres. The first section of the climb was across tundra awash with delicate flowers – moss campion and yellow saxifrage as well as mountain avens, bell heathers and mountain sorrel. Dwarf birch and willow sprawled in carpets across the barely consolidated silts and gravel.

The climb began across recently glacially scoured rocks before we encountered the jumble of frost-crumbled scree that led up to the first sugar-loaf peak. From here a testing shattered ridge created some excitement for a few hundred metres before we came to less challenging ground. Puffins appeared, peering cheekily from behind the precipitous rock faces on the northern side of the ridge, inquisitive at this human invasion but not at all apprehensive. We had barely noticed during this period of rapt concentration that the mist was thinning and by the time we spread ourselves out for lunch just beneath the summit slope, the clouds parted and a spectacular temperature inversion lay beneath us. Above it, the view to the east was far ranging. Pyramidal nunataks rose above the vast swathes of glittering white in the ice-locked interior of King Haakons Land. The flat-topped summits of the Three Kings (Tre Kroner) were more immediately identifiable. These are composed of Permo-Carboniferous sediments and have been named Dana, Nora and Svea, symbolising the ancient Norse kingdoms of Scandinavia.

We could have stayed here for quite a long time soaking up this

Arctic mouse-ear	Mountain avens

vista, but the mist was becoming twitchy and we occupied a sandwich of clear sky between the descending cloud and the inversion layers above the glacier beneath us. The option of trudging the hundred metres or so to the top did not appeal, so with Peter, Eesje, Marida and Ingrid we opted instead for the steep descent via the snow couloir by the glacier. This was almost too steep to descend other than by bum-skiing, which created great amusement. This small group made for a highly congenial walk back to camp where the evening meal of reindeer meat and mushroom sauce was again of the highest quality.

Friday began promisingly after a night listening to the haunting cries of the sea birds and the thunderous crashes of ice cascading from the glacier wall into the floe-studded waters. At breakfast, the bay was full of drifting icebergs, many of which had been washed against the shore by wind and currents. The sun glinted on their sculptured surfaces and the plaintive call of a red throated diver echoed across the icy expanses. Its colloquial term of 'loon' suits it well, the call resembling a sad wail, constantly repeated.

The destination for today was the glacier itself, the blue ice presenting a formidable wall of crumbling seracs but behind this façade, the smoother slopes of crevassed white ice sloped into the far distance. We donned all protective gear at the glacier's edge – helmets, crampons, ice axes and harnesses and roped up into two long

Ice sculptures, Balestrand

Balestrand glacier and fjord

lines headed by Gunnhild and Ole. The route across the glacier was circuitous to avoid the many deep crevasses that scarred the surface, many falling deeply into the bowels of the ice sheet. Blomstrandbreen is a classic Spitzbergen glacier, penetrating many miles inland and bounded by frost shattered pyramidal nunataks. On the seaward side, many other glaciers came into view all ending similarly by the water's edge, but the grandest view of all was beyond the head of Kongsfjord to the vast expanses of inland ice above which rose the Tre Kroner peaks. It was a scene of complete isolation where very few people must have trod. The atmosphere and the translucence of the light enhanced this unforgettable image.

By now the cold air funnelling down the glacier was beginning to chill the bones and we rested for lunch in a convenient declivity above which rose several spectacular (and probably unstable) seracs. It was here that most had a stab at ice climbing and abseiling. Technique was a trifle rusty, but it was mightily enjoyable nonetheless. It only remained for us to trudge back across the glacier to the beginnings of the rock moraine and unharness. Down by the shore, it was comfortably warm as we began to thaw out. We had watched the clouds gathering menacingly over Prins Karls Forland for several hours and by early-evening a malignant pall of heavy cloud and drizzle had

Glacier abseil

engulfed the camp. The rains began at 8 p.m. just as we sat down for another splendid evening meal of reindeer meat. It was not the most conducive bear watch (1–3 a.m.) but donning the guides' polar suits made light of the penetrating cold and wet. From the hillock above the camp the scene in all directions was from the pages of the beginning of time, elemental in its eerie stillness and desolation. The cries of the skuas and the terns littered the silence and the crashing blocks from the glacier continued to resonate across the bay like claps of thunder.

We awoke a little tired for the final day. The spitting drizzle constrained objectives but we decided to take a walk across the glacial debris and the softer, flowered tundra to the north coast of Kongsfjord. A small party of Swedish scientists from Ny Alesund had a small encampment by an old trapper's hut and we stopped to exchange pleasantries and to plead for a 'proper' tea bag, not one of these fruit-flavoured infusions that we had become grudgingly used to as the tea bags ran out. They informed us of recent polar bear activity and within minutes we came across the huge imprints of tracks along the soft sand and shingle. Clearly a polar bear had passed this way recently. Guillemots, auks and terns flew above or bobbed unconcernedly in the water and our progress was tracked by an inquisitive bearded seal. Wildlife here seems to have little intrinsic fear of man.

We stopped for lunch by the bones of a Greenland whale that were at least 200 years old. Their scale and state of preservation was impressive. It is little wonder that these behemoths, slow moving and vulnerable, were almost hunted to extinction in a little over 100 years. Ole continued to regale us with further trappers' tales as we made our way back across the tundra for the last time. Back in camp, we filled the remaining hours before dinner with a general knowledge quiz, which the Dutch team edged by half a point. The last meal of whale, seal and reindeer meat, cooked patiently outside by Ole on a barbecue, was as excellent as ever. It was time then to make our presentations to our guide team, Gunnhild, Ingrid and Ole. How we shall miss them and this hauntingly atmospheric place of Blomstrand!

Although we were not on watch, we got up early at about 5.30 a.m., which with hindsight was probably a mistake. Ole was up by 6.30 a.m. to prepare porridge and the rest of the party stumbled in to breakfast by 7 a.m. It was going to be a busy morning. The 'Expedition' was due to pick us up at 12.30 p.m. and we had the entire camp to pack up for the end of the season. It was easy to understand why the trekking expeditions end even by mid-August. The ice floes were jostling along the shingle and the bay in front of the glacier was packed with floating sheets or lumps of ice. A change in the wind direction or a fall in temperature would have had interesting consequences. We all pulled together for a couple of hours and stored camp timber away behind a shingle dune and piled tents, equipment and gear on the beach, assuming that the Zodiacs would be able to negotiate the ice.

There was again a perceptible feeling of both anticipation and genuine sadness as 12.30 p.m. approached and the soft purring of the diesel engines signalled the arrival of the 'Expedition' around the ice encrusted headland. It nosed its way gently towards the glacier and then dropped anchor. What a glorious but also highly emotional sight this was. It was time for group photographs and a last lingering, poignant look at the site where we had spent the last few days. The first Zodiac was hoisted into the water and with obvious care and circumspection meandered through the ice obstacles to land on the shingle. We were being whisked back to an environment of comfort and modernity and we all probably recognised that the rigours that had honed us as a collective unit were receding with each beat of the outboard engines. Lunch, shower and sleep followed in sequence before the party reassembled informally in the lounge to exchange reminiscences over proper tea and coffee. Outside the blurred misty outlines of the cliffs and headlands of Prins Karls Forland drifted slowly past in the increasing swell of the open waters. A certain unreality pervaded the atmosphere.

After dinner, the group assembled for the final time directed by an inimitable exhortation from Gunnhild to the debriefing session. Dispersal was made reluctantly after the genuine expressions of comradeship and affection. There was not much sleep to be had before the ship docked at Longyearbyen at 1 a.m. and the buses arrived to take us to the airport. A last, fond, lingering look at the MS 'Expedition' and we were in another world of queues, bustle, impatience and cumulative fatigue. Anticlimactic would be an understatement. It was a long wait before the flight to Oslo at 5 a.m. and many of the party left on the earlier flight to Tromso to heartfelt farewells. Will we see any of these people again? We shall certainly not forget them in a hurry. That left Victor and Barbara in Oslo awaiting their flight direct to Chicago, Marida who was accompanying us to Copenhagen and Andy whose flight to Heathrow preceded ours by several hours.

The seven-hour wait at Oslo airport was excruciating. We were exhausted but there was no opportunity to allow this to take its natural course. Eventually, and with huge relief, we boarded the plane to Copenhagen, survived a distinctly hairy landing and spent the last hour with Marida before setting off on the last leg to Manchester. We arrived here nearly 18 hours after disembarking from the boat, a long time but in the annals of early exploration, inconceivable. The pace of transfer from one environment to another made the drive back up the motorway utterly surreal. As dusk fell by 8 p.m., the car lights were switched on – we had to readjust back to the concept and reality of day followed by night, as well as to the obvious pace and frenzy of the modern world. It was distinctly disorientating.

And so, the expedition to Svalbard came to its close. We have been privileged to have visited many of the most spectacular parts of the world, seen many awe-inspiring sights and met many interesting people, but Spitzbergen will linger in the memory as perhaps the finest experience of them all. It has an indefinable atmosphere and allure. Pristine, forbidding, starkly beautiful landscapes, a huge diversity of fauna and flora and fascinating cultural, historical and political dimensions combined to make this endlessly interesting. Above all, however, it was the people. Most trekking groups contain some potential for schism and tension, social tectonics that under strain rupture the social cohesion of the group and diminish the quality of the overall experience. Our

Norwegian guides could not be surpassed. Their vitality, enthusiasm and sensitivity enabled the group to cohere and enhanced the enjoyment of the experiences shared immeasurably. Our fellow trekkers were an interesting and companionable crowd from a range of backgrounds and nationalities. All were united in their desire to learn and contribute and threw themselves into all activities with genuine commitment and resourcefulness. The affinities were evident from the outset and grew perceptibly as the days went by. By the time we boarded the Zodiacs for the last time we had bonded into a group which had found each other's company interesting, entertaining and amusing. There was respect, admiration and sincere affection for our guides who had also become an integral element in this social equation. We were destined to go our separate ways at the end, but those two weeks had grafted us into a real team, whose camaraderie and common purpose had done so much to enhance our collective experience and enjoyment. Emotions at the end ran deep, but there is a lingering hope that we shall meet some of our colleagues again and one day even return to this uniquely beautiful place.

Gunnhild, Ole and Ingrid, guides extraordinaire

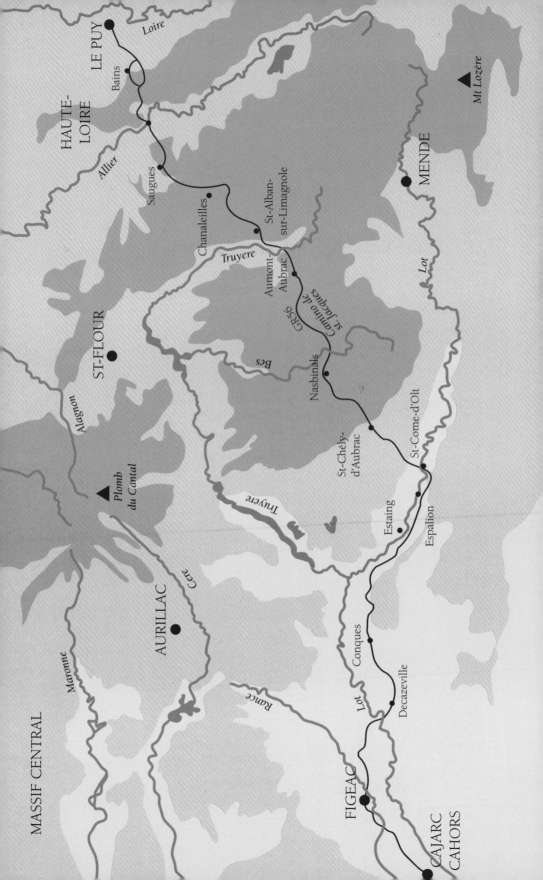

Chemin de St. Jacques –
Le Puy to Cahors

Tempus fugit! Now well into our seventies, we reluctantly accepted increasing aches and pains as the price for maintaining our walking and trekking activities. No longer burdened with heavy rucsacs, it seemed sensible to let others take the strain. So was born the notion of fully assisted treks which enabled full kit to be carried forward to a pre-arranged destination. With this assistance the concept of adventure and exploration could be extended, as long as it was possible to carry a day sac and put one leg in front of the other. Sensibly, too, the rigours of such treks could be reduced in terms of distance and altitude gain per day without compromising the inherent enjoyment of such journeys.

This was the rationale behind the decision to walk the Pilgrim's Way, the Chemin de St. Jacques, that begins at Le Puy in the Central Massif in France and extends in its ultimate form to Santiago de Compostella in Spain. The latter section through northern Spain is infinitely more popular and well-publicised, if scenically less diverse, but the section across the heart of France traversing the Central Massif seemed much more appealing.

There was some trepidation in advance. Would we be able to contend with daily walks of over 20 kilometres over ground that we did not know, would the trail be well marked, would the baggage transfers be logistically sound, and would we be able to withstand the momentum and rigours necessitating a daily commitment whatever the weather? The concept of a journey from A to B has always been an attraction. The foreknowledge that there will be inevitable challenges to face, the new experiences one is bound to have, the people to be encountered and the physical and cultural landscapes to be assimilated are all powerful motivations. There is also the seductive draw of personal fulfilment in rising to the challenge of any such trip and the experiences it brings and of reaching journey's end with the glow of satisfaction in realising one's objectives. In that, such a trek is a microcosm of life itself and a compelling metaphor.

Europe is wonderfully endowed with long-distance footpaths. In France, for example the Sentiers de Grande Randonnee, (GRs) with their distinctive red and white horizontally banded markers, traverse the Alps from St. Gingolph on the southern shores of Lake Geneva to Nice (GR5) or the Pyrenees, from Hendaye on the Atlantic to Banyuls sur Mer on the Mediterranean (GR10). These major walking routes often interlink locally with the Chemins de Petite Randonnee (PRs), marked with yellow signs. In the Lake District, we have frequently had cause to redirect walkers undertaking the Coast-to Coast Walk who have gone astray for although our paths have often become worn into major tracks they are not marked as precisely. Following GRs, it is almost impossible to become disorientated or lost. If the way is in doubt, for example where two routes diverge in close proximity, the red and white markers have a black cross advising the confused not to follow the wrong one. This is a great boon and not only for the elderly!

Using maps and guides, therefore, it is perfectly feasible to design bespoke walking routes using gites, dortoirs, mountain refuges (CAF – Club Alpin Francais) or even, on occasions, country hotels. Even old dogs can learn new tricks via the internet and Google Earth!

The rationale behind choosing the GR65 in France was partly based on previous experience of the French Grandes Randonnees in the Alps and Pyrenees and partly on the attraction of walking across the geographical, cultural and historic heart of France by traversing the Central Massif. In the former we were to be slightly disappointed in that the Chemin de St. Jacques is not a path as such and differs from the alpine GRs by following minor roads and farm tracks for much of its course, thereby creating a somewhat unrelenting pounding for the feet and joints. In the latter we were certainly not to be disappointed. The route began in the volcanic east with its distinctive 'puys' and sombre basaltic landscape, which gave way to the broad, open rolling grasslands of the granitic Aubrac plateau and culminated in a crossing of the distinctive limestone 'causses' of Quercy.

Throughout this traverse the major watersheds of famous French rivers are crossed from the Loire and Allier in the east to the Lot, Tarn and Aveyron to the west. The Lot and its tributary, the Cele, was to be our constant companion during the latter part of this autumnal walk, its course the setting for many mediaeval villages with a distinctive Gallic charm and whose architecture and style was quintessentially French. We met many interesting people, stayed in some strange places, including a convent, savoured some splendid French cuisine as well as foraging like squirrels on walnuts, hazelnuts, chestnuts and figs, reflected on European history and improved the standards of 'franglais' no end as confidence grew. In short, we saw a great deal, learned a great deal, walked a long way without too much difficulty, slept well and ate well. It was a good trip and all to the background of sunshine which was the constant for the first half of the trek, becoming more changeable and autumnal for the second half. We never got seriously wet and the joy of being able to walk for much of the time in shorts in warmth was a huge bonus.

The starting point for the 'camino' is Le Puy-en-Velay in the Haute Loire department of south-central France. Wary of intense summer heat, we flew out to Lyon from Gatwick on Wednesday, 18 September. Despite the ungodly hour of departure, it was an excellent flight courtesy of Easyjet. Lyon airport is a work in progress and some distance from the city centre where the rail connections awaited. Part of the developments is a new high-speed tram track linking the airport to the city. It made for an easy if somewhat expensive connection (15 euros each) and required the first of many trawls through school French to obtain tickets. However, the tram dropped us off opposite the Gare du Part Dieu where, fortuitously, we were able to board an earlier train taking us to Le Puy. By contrast with the tram this was excellent value for money, a two-hour journey costing just 16 euros.

The train rattled through the commercial and industrial suburbs of Lyon before crossing the broad alluvial plain of the Rhone valley and climbing steadily up the eastern slopes of the Central Massif to St. Etienne. The declining industrial base of this area was clear to see; rusting pitheads, derelict rolling mills and forges and scars of rock waste. This part of the Central Massif (St. Etienne; Decazeville; Ales) does have coal measures and being at some distance from the main coalfields of the north-east, which are strategically more vulnerable, they attracted disproportionate industrial development. Clermont Ferrand, the home of Michelin, just north of here is a classic case in point. Like the older coalfields of Britain, the same legacy of industrial decline exists. There is a sad melancholy to the tangible evidence of this decay.

Slowly these scars receded as the train approached the upper reaches of the Loire valley where the wooded slopes were punctuated by pillars of basalt and distinctive lava plugs, on top of many of which statues and churches had been erected. It also began to rain! Burdened by kit bags we stumbled from the station at the terminus at Le Puy and despite some local difficulties, both geographical and linguistic, we soon managed to arrive at the Hotel Bristol. This was fairly basic but reasonably comfortable, a typical commercial hotel of fading glories. There was sufficient time for a quick stroll around the town centre to begin the process of familiarising ourselves with its geography and practising the 'franglais' that would be the mainstay of communication for the next month.

Time had been allowed in the schedule for a full exploration of Le Puy, which proved to be an interesting place in terms of its geology, history, culture and ecclesiastical background. The town is dominated by several volcanic plugs or 'puys' and at its heart overlooking the centre lies its cathedral. Early in the morning we walked from the Place du Plot just behind the main strand to the Place des Tables at the foot of the cathedral steps. Much of this fairly steep ascent was on ancient cobbled streets made of lava blocks. The cathedral itself is impressively austere and architecturally distinctive. It broods. Inside, the interior is massive with a high vaulted ceiling. Memorials to religious martyrs feature prominently. Many of these were local clerics executed in the 1790s by revolutionary zealots. The place is famed for its black Madonna and for the statue of St. Jacques, its patron saint. Our impressions were that this sombre cathedral was not as ostentatious as many, but nevertheless gave a reminder of the rationale behind the Reformation. It is the focal point of a large mediaeval religious centre which proved fascinating to explore.

The atmosphere was certainly enhanced by the fact that we had timed our arrival unconsciously to coincide with a mediaeval festival. The old streets were populated by people dressed in convincing mediaeval costumes. Most endearing were the crocodiles of children being escorted around and imbued with a sense of civic tradition and history. From the cathedral precincts and the heart of the old town, we wandered out towards the Notre Dame de St. Michel, perched spectacularly on top of a perpendicular volcanic plug. This is an incredible example of engineering and human endeavour. The initial vision of St. Michael is alleged to have taken place in Italy and early pilgrims' routes linked Turin with Le Puy with connections to Mont St. Michel in north west France, St. Michael's Mount in Cornwall and ultimately the Skellig Islands off the coast of Kerry in West Ireland. All share the same philosophical and ecclesiastical premise and certain geological and architectural characteristics. Austerity, 'lift up mine eyes', 'nearer my God to thee' all spring to mind in a process of focused reflection on

Notre Dame de St. Michel, Le Puy

the deeper meaning of life and on the development of faith. Whatever the precepts, the structure of Notre Dame is deeply impressive. Access to the church containing its original tiny chapel is via a vertiginous staircase of steps cut into the bare basaltic rock with protection today thankfully afforded by a guardrail. The original (and humble) chapel itself is hewn out of the solid basalt rock and could readily be imagined as a place of quiet contemplation high above the mediaeval bustle of the town below. The view across the volcanic basin from the church was worth the climb.

We settled for a coffee in a nearby cafe as the sun finally made an appearance and, suitably refreshed, continued our exploration of the town from its mediaeval core elevated above the more modern spacious squares and streets. It was fascinating but ultimately exhausting. Le Puy seems to be a conservative place, acutely mindful of its history and traditions and exhibiting a palpable civic pride. It has variety, character and colour and is certainly worthy of a longer visit. In the evening after dinner, we walked down to a local church where a free choral concert had been advertised, fully expecting that this would be full. However, it transpired that we were probably the only members of the audience unconnected to the Church or to the singers. It was superb! Three singers performed a mediaeval choral programme, which in this setting and with highly musical acoustics and harmonies, perfectly set the scene for our own pilgrimage through the history and culture of the French heartlands over the coming month.

The trek began on Friday, 20 September on a morning of glowering cloud and intermittent rain. The climb out of Le Puy was steep and unrelenting and, as we were to discover throughout most of the journey, on roads or farm tracks. The road soon gave way to a track composed of rusty red volcanic rubble bisecting fields bounded by blocks of basalt. The D59 road was crossed at La Roche and the path wove its way from here towards the first tiny village of St. Christophe-sur-Dalaison which lies at the centre of a deeply dissected volcanic plateau. It was a predominantly arable landscape with cereals, lentils and maize much in evidence. The weather began to improve, and the scenery opened up after the tiny hamlets of Liac and Lic, comprising just three or four buildings built of the local stone that gave them a dark, dour but durable appearance. Farm tracks led to the D road, just below the village of Montbonnet, where the Chapelle St. Roch (the patron saint of pilgrims) provided a convenient resting place. This was

Chapelle de St. Roch, Montbonnet

the first of many such chapels devoted to St. Roch that we were to meet on the journey and like the others it had a simple dignity, a place to reflect and shelter if need be.

By now today's route had climbed to well over 1100 metres and as the GR 65 wound its way through the large, prosperous looking village it met the D road again opposite La Grange Bar where the temptation to halt and have a beer was irresistible. This was a long first day of 24 kilometres together with a climb from Le Puy of 2000 feet culminating in a steady descent to St. Privat d'Allier, mostly in warm early autumn sunshine. The auberge was basic and after settling in we made for the local bar for another restorative beer before climbing up to the church for a view over the town and the surrounding countryside that marked the following day's route. The views from this minor elevation were almost nautical in nature, the swells of green-blue, wooded hills stretching like an ocean, wave on wave, to an almost imperceptible horizon, the waves cut by troughs of gorges and deeply dissected valleys. The light was wonderful, the atmosphere soporific. Humming bird moths played around a buddleia in full scented flower and pink autumn crocus decorated the edges of the green fields. It was good to reflect on a successful first day of walking and to settle down

Camino crosses, St. Privat d'Allier

for a filling communal evening meal presided over by a hyperactive, supremely efficient Madame. Main item on the menu was Puy lentils served in a large bowl with some lettuce to alleviate the palate. It was to become a familiar theme over the next week. What it does to the digestive system is not polite to describe.

A pristine morning of sheer perfection greeted us the following day and we were off and away by 8 a.m. Many other walkers had the same idea, but competitive instincts had now matured into a more companionable togetherness. We contoured round the valley above St. Privat, the sun in our faces and a sharpness and clarity to the air. A procession of docile cows padded towards us through the morning mists that became thicker as we gained height. By the time the distinctive church and tower at Rochegude had been reached, the mists cloaked the site, lending it an air of mystery. From this vantage point, it was possible to peer down to the Allier gorge and valley far below and begin to understand the strategic value of such defensive sites that enabled tolls to be exacted and control exerted over medieval travellers.

It was a long descent through the woods and then along lava strewn lanes to finally reach the town of Monistrol-sur-Allier. This seemed a very functional place whose significance lay in the bridging points across the river, one of which was built by Gustav Eiffel who went on to design the famous tower in Paris that bears his name. Crossing the river, a coffee revived before we began the long ascent out of the valley to the basalt plateau at 1200 metres. The R. Allier is hemmed in by granite bluffs and lava crags, which showed evidence of a series of separate lava flows in their structure and coloration. The route took us towards a seemingly impregnable lava cliff but then snaked its way with the aid of railings to the tiny hamlet of Eskluzels perched at the top of the crag. A brief road section then gave way to a tree-shaded and beautifully graded forest path that led to the open fields on top of the plateau at Montaure. From here there were immense views back across the Allier valley and its deeply dissected tributaries. The gently undulating road was dry and dusty linking large farms with huge barns that seemed to have been built recently, probably with the help of EU grants. Certainly, agriculture seemed profitable and productive. The farming hamlets of Roziers and Le Vernet came and went before we finally stopped at the gite in Rognac for bilberry tart and a drink. By bitter experience we have found that as the years advance any excuse for trail side refreshment should be taken! The descent into Sauges was again mainly on roads except for the last section, a steep rocky path that piled on the agony for tired and aching joints. Sauges was a small, compact, historic provincial market town and the Hotel La Terrasse was excellent, a marked improvement on the rather basic first night. We had enough energy left to explore the town, have a beer and then a thoroughly revitalising shower before settling down to a splendid evening meal, dominated by le patron's love affair with his cheese trolley.

After two long days, it had been decided to break the next even longer day, originally scheduled as a 28 kilometres walk, into two. This proved to be wise if only because it introduced us to the Gite des Deux Pellerins at Villaret. The route out of Sauges was again largely on farm tracks and metalled roads through small farming hamlets such as Le Pinet and Fauzet where we stopped for a picnic comprising three biscuits and three dried apricots. No wonder that we appeared to be losing weight already! The hard surfaces were a pain but slowly the rhythms of the journey began to assert themselves. This area, Lozere, must be almost the geometric centre of France. It certainly feels deeply rural but also affluent. Buildings are made of solid granite blocks and there seems to be little elaboration on a general theme of four-square solid and sturdy with red terracotta roofs. There is an abundance of

Villaret

tiny allotments and often the houses abut each other, as if huddling in the swales of the land, which rolls on in a great sweep of forested hills and cultivated valleys with open sections of granite heath dotted with tors and boulders. It seems timeless except for the burble of tractors and the silver drapery of electricity pylons that the French seem to love to festoon across even the most sensitive of landscapes.

We reached the gite early on a gorgeously sunny and warm afternoon and introduced ourselves to the host who welcomed us cordially with refreshments. There was some prior apprehension about staying in a gite run by two former pilgrims, where the atmosphere and connotations of pilgrimage may have cast a piety over the place, but we need not have worried. Our hosts were charm personified. Although their English was non-existent, there were a further four guests, a retired French couple, and two PhD students from Paris, who were able to translate as requested. The evening meal began with aperitifs and Mr. and Mme. Bouffar then orchestrated a rendition of the Chanson des Pellerins, in which we were all encouraged to participate. This could have been an embarrassing disaster but it was cheery and charming. The verses were in French, but the chorus was in an unidentifiable mediaeval language explained as a mixture of Gothic Spanish and Middle Ages Latin, with snippets of Basque and Catalan included for good measure. Ultreia, which means 'further', featured prominently, symbolising the pilgrim's quest not just to complete a physical journey but also an inner journey of self-discovery. The other expression commonly re-iterated was 'E sus eia', which means 'higher', reflecting the fact that with the past below him, the pilgrim lives within the present only and has no thoughts on the future as day after day develops its own rhythms and pre-occupations. The present is viewed as the gate which opens up onto the invisible – eternity. These were ancient but also relevant modern sentiments with which we could fully empathise.

After this choral preamble, the main meal was served, and conversation flowed freely, mainly in French but with us stuttering into 'franglais' from time to time, lubricated by jugs of wine regularly replenished. At the conclusion of the meal copious quantities of very strong Chartreuse liqueur were made available. Neither of us is accustomed to more than a small glass of wine to accompany a meal and with some embarrassment we realised that the Chartreuse had administered the coup de grace to our senses, rendering our franglais even less coherent! During the course of the evening, Mr. Bouffar revealed that his home is in the Isere valley and that in two weeks the gite would close for the winter and he would return to pursue his other musical interests and to conduct the local choir. They were a lovely couple and we bid them farewell the following morning with a genuine regret. They had taught us a great deal in our brief stay including,

Aubrac bull

regrettably, the fact that we should be on our guard against the dreaded 'punaises', or bed bugs, which have reached epidemic proportions in certain refuges along the camino.

We set off on the morning of Monday, 23 September into the most perfect autumn day. Tendrils of mist clung to the wooded valley slopes and filaments of rime converted the cobwebs draped across the broom bushes into spangled jewels. We traversed the valley slopes passing fields full of impressively muscled cattle before climbing steadily into dappled woodland comprising mainly oak and beech. The route through the woods brought us face to face with impressive and impassive bulls guarding their harems of cows but, fortunately, they seemed quite docile. The immediate objective was the Domaine Sauvage, a former mediaeval hospital, which stood at the edge of a broad open heathland, dotted with rounded, crumbling granite boulders. An ancient barn, or buron, stood in the middle of this intensively grazed rough pasture, shielded by its clump of trees. Today the Domaine Sauvage consists of a gite, farm and restaurant where we were glad to avail ourselves of Oranginas to slake a growing thirst in the hot dusty conditions. The climbing was not yet over and a broad forestry plantation track brought us to a road col at 1300 metres that marks the administrative boundary between Haute Loire and Lozere. Emerging from the shaded forest, we blinked into intense sunshine and a cauldron of heat. There was not a cloud in the alpine blue sky and the temperature must have been well over 25 degrees Celsius with little breeze to offer relief.

We stopped to rest and have a snack at the Chappelle St. Roch (another one!), before descending gently on a good path shaded by occasional trees that led to the D987 and via open fields and meadows to the day's final destination, the Hotel l'Oustal de Parent at Les Faux. Sitting in the garden here the heat was redolent of high summer but during the day we had also been aware of the bronzing of the deciduous woodland, testimony to the inexorable advance of autumn.

As the comfort of the hotel receded the following morning, there was a distinct chill in the air. We opted to follow the road down towards Le Fouget and were not surprised to find the broad basin in which the village was situated touched by the first frosts of the season. The main town towards which we were heading was St. Alban-sur-Limagnole, the outskirts of which seemed to go on forever. The place is dominated by a huge hospital complex built around an ancient chateau, but it lacked the character of Sauges and did not detain us. After tramping through streets and busy roads, the open countryside finally beckoned on what was already becoming another very hot day. Workmen were renovating one of the larger crosses that mark the route which led down to the village of Grazieres and which brought us back to the main road.

Thankfully at this juncture, having crossed the tarmac, a real path beckoned, climbing through gnarled conifers and broom. This was not to last and at 1050 metres the path became another dusty gravel track circling round a forested coombe before leading to a rather unpleasant steep, eroded gully, which in wet weather would be positively lethal. Les Estrets was rumoured to have a bar and a gite, both selling drinks, but the former seemed to have closed and the latter was like the 'Marie Celeste'. There was no choice but to carry on up a long drag via another relentless gravelly track for several kilometres. Shade was infrequent and there was no obvious stopping place so with the junction with the D7 in sight, we found a fallen log shielded by a canopy of trees to crunch on the remaining biscuits and empty the water bottle.

In many ways, it was like being adrift on an ocean. There were precious few landmarks and the hills seemed to stretch to infinity. To relieve the tedium, it was amusing to watch the crickets springing around the track, flitting off in a display of red or blue metallic under-wings. Larger cicadas waddled around the gravel, some clearly enjoying a meal of the smaller crickets and grasshoppers. It was stinking hot! God knows what this section must be like in high summer. It would be futile to pretend that this was the most enjoyable day. We had walked well over 20 kilometres and as the outskirts of Aumont Aubrac were reached, the prospect of a bar and a beer loomed like a mirage. The latter was found opposite the Town Hall, where the illuminated information display indicated a temperature of 29 degrees Celsius. We were not inclined to explore but made straight for the Hotel Prunieres, which was something of a disappointment after recent experiences. It was shabby and not particularly welcoming. The capacity of the human body to recover from physical excess meant that after a bath and a brief respite we headed for the Tourist Office to find that the weather forecast for the next few days was for more unseasonably hot but sunny conditions. As the next day was on paper the longest stage, this would mean an early start.

Pre-existing trepidations about the section from Aumont to

Nasbinals centred on the fact that this would be the longest day of 28 kilometres, following yesterday's gruelling section of 26 kilometres. and that cumulative fatigue might make its influence felt. The map showed a lack of escape routes, so it would require complete commitment in continuing debilitating very hot weather. Notwithstanding all the above, we set off in good heart at 7.30 a.m., armed with a baguette from the local boulangerie and relieved to be walking through cool, damp misty conditions. The atmosphere was quite ethereal, but the enveloping mist presaged another scorcher. By the time the pretty Chapelle de Bastide had been reached at Laibros, about five kilometres away, the mist was already beginning to clear and the early-morning colours started to break through. Swales of wooded hills were ablaze with autumn tints as the track undulated upwards through open stands of conifers, oak and beech. It was a very attractive landscape.

The first objective of the day was the Cafe Chez Regine at Les Quatres Chemins, some 11 kilometres from Aumont. After yesterday's enervating experience there was a resolve to incorporate as many convenient refreshment-stops as possible, rather than keep plodding on. Fortunately, today did offer strategically located possibilities to do just this. After the first drinks halt, there was a sense of revival as the longest stage of the day loomed ahead. A brief road section led to a

Resistance Memorial, Fineyrols

clearly marked path through banks of broom which then opened out onto a panorama of classic granite moorland studded with boulders and mini-tors. The views were expansive, the path much more yielding and grassy, even boggy in places, almost English in character, vaguely reminiscent of the limestone plateaus in the Yorkshire Dales.

We followed this drove road or 'draille' across a sea of rough grazing with sedges and tussocky grasses, the lack of any semblance of field boundaries accentuating the openness of the landscape. Stocky Aubrac cattle gathered in great herds, the bulls distinguished by their bison-like chestnut coloured ruff, the cows attractively dun coloured with lighter cream ears and eye patches. Young calves gambolled endearingly. It was a wonderfully bucolic scene. The profusion of hairy knapweed and gentian was visited by hosts of butterflies, including a rare Imperial and numerous swallow-tails. There was always something of interest to distract as we headed towards the Ferme Gentianes, just outside the hamlet of Fineyrols, where we stopped again for refreshment.

By now we had traversed a good six kilometres across the moor and had reached the half-way point. Suitably revived, we set off again towards the highest point of the granite moorland at 1273 m, its summit marked by some giant boulders, the Rocs des Loups, from which a vast panorama opened up of almost endless, featureless open countryside. It was almost akin to being in a boat on a placid sea without form or shape or points of reference. However, in the distance could be discerned a small road and the roofs of buildings at Rieutort d'Aubrac glinting in the dazzling sun. Like so many villages in the deep rural heart of France there were signs of depopulation and decay as well as evidence of more recent refurbishment. Old houses still occupied exuded a durability that perhaps economic circumstances had eroded. The place felt sleepy in the hot sun, quiet and soporific.

The next four kilometres to Montgros were probably the least interesting of the day and the most exhausting. The GR65 followed the line of the D road to the bridge over the Bessiere stream, the heat reflecting mercilessly off the baking tarmac. It was stiflingly hot, but with only another four kilometres to go from the bridge to Nasbinals, we dug deep and found refuge in the extremely welcome Maison de Rosalie where, once again, a cold sirop de citron with Perrier did the trick.

Nothing now could impede progress, not even the last cruel ascent up a roughly gravelled, boulder-fringed track. With a palpable

Les Rocs des Loups 1273m

sigh of relief, the nucleated, pretty village of Nasbinals was now in view over the final rise. It was such a reassurance not only to complete this longest of days in decent condition but to do so in a very respectable time in unremitting heat. The Hotel La Route d'Argent was a real oasis, clean and comfortable, the only downside being that it was adjacent to the attractive church whose sonorous bells chimed the hours, not once but twice for effect! Unlike functional Aumont, Nasbinals was pretty and characterful, buildings of evident antiquity blending well with more recent residential developments. This was probably the day that saw us turn the corner, apprehensions not entirely dismissed but immediate anxieties assuaged. The prevailing mood was that if we could manage two consecutive days of this rigour, we could cope with anything else that the camino could place in our way. To cap it all, the cuisine was first class with the emphasis on the carnivore!

It was hard to believe that today we had been on the road (often literally) for seven days and had travelled some 126 kilometres. The weather continued to hold as we left Nasbinals on a soft, scented morning with diaphanous mists drifting across the fields. For two days we had crossed the Aubrac plateau, a place that would exert a lasting memory with its sweeping vistas, its herds of sturdy Aubrac cattle, its isolated burons and scattered granite outcrops. In spring, it is apparently awash with wild flowers, narcissi, jonquils, wild crocus

Buron, Aubrac plateau

and primrose. It would be fascinating to return here at that time of year.

The next stage began with a gentle climb along an ancient track bounded by granite boulders and fringed with trees and shrubs such as wild roses, whose vivid crimson hips added a splash of colour. Before long, the broad sweep of open moorland came back into view. It is startling country because of its enormity of space and sheer emptiness apart from the ubiquitous herds of cattle. In blinding sunshine and sharp early-morning clarity, it seemed that we could walk for ever across this terrestrial ocean. The path made a broad sweep around a gentle coombe, climbed again and reached its highest point of over 1300 metres by an obvious wooden cross near the Trois Eveques, a cone shaped hill that marks the boundary between the departements of Cantal, Lozere and Aveyron. It was such a relief to walk on gentle forgiving grass and the path continued like this into the settlement of Aubrac, a small village that was founded as a place of refuge for pilgrims. It seemed something of a tourist magnet although at this time of the morning, the first coaches were only just arriving as we left the cafe and headed up the road to begin the long descent down narrow shady lanes to St. Chely d'Aubrac.

This was a descent of nearly 700 metres into a completely different world from the openness of the plateau. It seemed that the route was now much more confined, with occasional glimpses through the trees across a number of deeply dissected wooded valleys. Although the views were more constrained, the benefits of shade were very much appreciated. We were now back on ashes and lavas, epitomised by the small volcanic puy at Beznet. Eventually on an increasingly humid afternoon, we left the rough track with its loose boulders and came to a tarmac road which led directly into the main street of St. Chely and the Hotel les Coudercous.

St. Chely was an attractive place with clusters of tall mediaeval houses, many corbelled over narrow alleyways. It did not exude the understated prosperity of Nasbinals and there was some indication that the modern world has passed it by. Many houses were for sale and there was very little obvious bustle and energy on display. Nevertheless, it had a distinct charm and the hotel was certainly one of the best that we stayed in during the trek, despite its lowly official rating. The tourist office was a mine of information amongst which was the forecast that the fine weather was shortly to be replaced by a more unsettled thundery and cloudy atmosphere. Even sun-starved Cumbrians can tire of unremitting heat!

Friday's destination was St. Come d'Olt, the latter spelling the Occitan version of Lot. It was another interesting and very hot day. We crossed the bridge at St. Chely as dawn was breaking deep in the valley. The bridge is an ancient pellerin (pilgrim) crossing and from it

Autumn sunrise over St. Chely

there were excellent views of the village blinking in the sunshine. Old footpaths led us through beech and chestnut woodland to the top of the bluff line where the views became more open and expansive. We reached the sleepy hamlet of L'Estrade where an enterprising madam had laid out a refreshment stall in an old communal bakery and laverie, or communal washing area, by the road side. It was a welcome halt before the descent began again on cobbled shaded tracks bounded by dense forests of chestnut, whose spiky green cases littered the floor and became distracting objects to kick around. It was a long descent to the bridge over the tiny stream at Cancels where the path began to climb again to re-join the D road. Impelled by a series of notices proselytising the virtues of 'Chez Muriel', we opted to abandon the hard tarmac and took a steep path to La Rozere, where we sat in the shade at Muriel's and enjoyed an excellent salad with l'eau gazeuse. This is one of the joys of such an ad hoc trek and the cuisine at such wayside farms became an attractive feature of the walk.

By mid-day, the heat was bouncing off the track as we resumed the descent towards St. Come. Lizards scuttled on the path and amongst the rocks; old vineyards and orchards provided samples of fruit to taste. When the D987 was finally reached, it was a short climb to the Couvent de Malet, where we were booked to stay the night. The convent was a very impressive building. Clearly the Catholic Church is not short of money! There were again some apprehensions in staying here, but these were again allayed when it became clear that we were not to be assailed by evangelical overtures. The room was spotlessly clean and cool but rudimentary as befits a convent. There were no locks on the doors and no decorative embellishments.

Having settled in and unpacked, we then wandered into the town, distinguished by its church with a crooked spire to rival that of Chesterfield. It was a lovely place with delightful mediaeval streets, corbelled houses and a magnificent church. Place names were both in French and Occitan, an unusual combination that hinted at its antiquity. This was symptomatic of the sense of history and cultural distinctiveness of the town. One of the oldest and architecturally interesting buildings was the Church of the Penitents, tucked away at the edge of the town centre, which must have been at least 800 years old. The whole place had a historic atmosphere about it unburdened by tourist trappings or an overweening pretentiousness. It was a good way to spend a couple of hours as the intensity of the afternoon heat

Central square, St. Come d'Olt

began to subside. At the convent, the evening meal was a communal affair with long tables enabling us to converse with fellow travellers to the best of our improving abilities. We reflected on our English reserve. Had we been ushered to such a communal table in an English pub or restaurant we would probably have bridled at the prospect of sharing our meal and conversation with others, but here it seemed perfectly natural and indeed preferable. Fortunately, our knowledge of French did not include any expletives which might have been less than decorous in this setting!

After a good night's rest, we awoke to a different sort of day. The blue skies and intense sunshine had been replaced by a much cooler, cloudier and more humid atmosphere. Steps were re-traced to the bridge over the River Lot to join the road parallel to the river for the six kilometres walk into Espalion. Even on such a grey morning, the entry into Espalion was spectacular. Mediaeval houses with 'toy-town' roofs lined the river, many with stone slabs overlooking the water where hides were washed and cleaned as part of the old tanning industry.

An impressive chateau and an ancient bridge enhanced the historic ambience of the place. We wandered into town to have a coffee before regaining the path by the river that now led into more modern suburbs where the scent of flowering sarcococca filled the air.

A few more kilometres of road walking eventually led to a side road leading down to the ancient village of Bessejouls where we halted for a while to view one of the oldest churches on the route, St. Pierre-de-Bessejouls, an eleventh century chapel with an even older altar. Beyond here the village of Bessejouls nestled charmingly in its tight, wooded valley, but now the GR65 struck relentlessly upwards through wooded bluffs on a meandering and slippery path before emerging on the open plateau. Tractors were at work in the fields ploughing and harrowing, creating dust devils in their wake. Large slabs of creamy yellow Jurassic limestone littered the fields or had been collected to form the field boundaries. It was a landscape highly reminiscent of the Cotswolds but with a more evident arable emphasis. Farming hamlets such as Griffoul could easily have been a simulacrum of a fifteenth century settlement if it were not for the huge barns on its fringe. The lane was fringed by sweet chestnut and walnut trees. The former were readily identifiable by spiky green spherical pods but the latter took some time to

Estaing Chateau

recognise. Peeling back the soft fibrous outer lining revealed the new season walnuts in their hard casings. Walnuts as fresh as these were a gastronomic treat!

Without a great deal of warning the path suddenly began to descend through a narrow, wooded track that led to the chateau-like farm of Beauregard overlooking another very ancient church and a broad highly fertile basin. The path wound round the edge of the latter before cutting a more direct line to the very pretty hamlet of Verrieres, whose mediaeval houses and church were lineated along the banks of the river Lot, which at this point describes a sharp left-hand meander. Rather than continue on the road, we took a short cut uphill on a rocky path that brought us back out on the road, where we obtained our first view of the fairy-tale chateau at Estaing. This is the birthplace and home of Valery Giscard d'Estaing, the rather haughty and aristocratic former French President. We crossed the elegant bridge over the Lot and made our way to our hotel situated on the banks of the river. Estaing is an ornate and picturesque place dominated by its chateau that stands on a bluff of schist overlooking the bridging point. Its architecture is classically French, its mediaeval vernacular style punctuated by towers, stone pillars, and ornate projections built onto the main structure of the building. It is undoubtedly spectacular, and the craftsmanship is superb, but like the chateaus of the Loire, it sometimes seems over-elaborate and flamboyant and one yearns for the elegant simplistic lines of a Salisbury or Durham Cathedral, which were built at roughly the same time. Only some of the more extreme German castles could rival this exuberance of style so quintessentially French in its capriciousness. Unfortunately, our tour of the densely packed heart of the village coincided with grey skies and spats of rain. The chateau would certainly have looked even more unworldly on a brilliantly sunny day.

There were some reservations as we left Estaing for Espeyrac some 25 kilometres away with a 700-metre climb to negotiate through the wooded slopes overlooking the incised course of the River Lot. The weather forecast was also less than encouraging with intense thundery rainfall predicted. Thankfully that never came to pass, but the heavy downpours during the night had left a legacy of clinging mists as we set out along the road by the left bank of the limpid River Lot. Shading trees dripped with moisture, but soon the road was left behind as the path meandered steeply and sinuously uphill by-passing the broad meanders of the road. Climbing up well-graded ancient tracks was infinitely preferable to pounding out the kilometres on the road and as the trees thinned, the sky brightened and ribbons of mist could be seen filling the wooded valleys that now lay below. Dogs barked, and shots reverberated in the still air. The official opening of the French hunting season is 1 October but clearly some people were having an early practice.

On the high plateau, the mist relented and the sun now broke through as we settled to the inevitable rhythms of walking on tarmac again, relieving the monotony by kicking the sweet chestnut casings down the road. After a good hour of this, the GR65 left the road and followed a delightful forest track towards the upland village of Golinhac, the approximate half-way point of the day. With the climbing mainly behind us we had spurred ourselves on with the prospect of a leisurely lunch and/or drink at the well-publicised bar-restaurant, but to our disappointment the place was closed due to 'exceptional circumstances'. This was a real blow. The whole village seemed devoid of life. Two French women who had waved to us from a bus from Estaing were highly complimentary about our speed of progress. We had walked the 16 kilometres in about four hours but this was also an uphill section so perhaps we do not give ourselves sufficient credit.

Somewhat flattered by this unsolicited congratulation we carried on – onward and upwards (Ushaia!). Again, after a brief section of pleasant path, we spent much of the rest of the day on the all-too familiar tarmac road. The last 8–10 kilometres to Espeyrac continued against the background of an increasingly threatening sky. There was much more evidence here of rural depopulation and decay in the numbers of semi-derelict barns and poorly maintained farmhouses. Ancient terraces were covered with brambles and scrub and the former orchards seemed untended and wild. It was now becoming very hot.

Espeyrac remained screened from view almost to the last minute, when we traversed round a small coombe on an ancient track to see the spire of the church in front of us. It was Sunday, but the whole place seemed devoid of life. We scuttled into the hotel just as the anticipated thunderstorm finally broke, only to find this a somewhat soulless place. The room was more like a cell and there was a dispiriting, uninterested, detached atmosphere that continued through the evening meal to breakfast. The latter seemed to sum up the Hotel de la Vallee – stale bread and tepid coffee. We could not get away soon enough. This was our least favourite accommodation to date.

Monday morning was gloomy with drabs of drizzle in the air, but we were heading for a rest day in Conques at the half-way stage and walked with commensurate vigour. Trees dripping with moisture lined the track leading to the small village of Senergues which, unlike Espeyrac, seemed energised and relatively busy. A small cafe provided a much more satisfying coffee and croissant and even at 8.30 a.m., the small local shop was already busy. Armed with yet more energy bars and dried apricots we wandered steadily uphill, joining a forestry track on the edge of the town until this inevitably led to a small tarmac road that undulated on top of a rolling plateau studded with ancient farmhouses or 'mas'. The fields were grazed by herds of ubiquitous Aveyron cattle but, interestingly, there were also herds of Friesian, suggesting that this is a milk-producing, cheese making area. There was a glut of blackberries and walnuts to keep us happy as we strolled along with one eye on the weather which was beginning to deteriorate gently.

We stopped at the church in the hamlet of St. Marcel to eat our pain au chocolat, but soon after the rain began in earnest and for the first time it became necessary to don full waterproofs. Thankfully, the

Conques

Cottages at Conques

road was soon left behind as we descended sharply down a rutted, slippery path towards the outskirts of Conques. The historic town was obscured by curtains of trees until we were almost upon it when, even in the rain, it revealed its full architectural splendour.

Conques is a beautifully preserved mediaeval town, lineated above a densely wooded valley along a natural terrace. It is dominated by its twin-spired cathedral that features prominently in the history and traditions of the Pilgrimage de St. Jacques. The whole town is a UNESCO World Heritage Site and it is easy to see how it acquired this status. It is very child's picture of a medieval town. Most of its houses were half-timbered buildings and many were corbelled to extend living quarters over narrow cobbled streets. The picturesque historic scene was accentuated by the quaint and often idiosyncratic roofing tiles, made of schist and sculpted into heart shapes (called lauzes), above which rose assorted chimney stacks, some like barley-sticks, some Tolkienesque in character. Defensive gateways punctuated the embracing defensive walls that surrounded the nucleus of the town around the cathedral. As we walked through the town gaining these initial impressions, it was now possible to understand that for many pilgrims or walkers starting at Le Puy, Conques would be a logical climax to their walk.

The Hotel St. Jacques was very close to the cathedral and after some confusion as to our booking, which was for two nights and not just one, we were shown to our room, a full 68 winding steps to the fourth floor. At this point medieval character, however fascinating, could have been exchanged for the modern luxury of a lift! However, as we stumbled out into the town after settling in, the rain stopped, and a watery sun appeared. Opposite the hotel was a very convenient cafe/restaurant where we embraced the notion of rest day indulgence by ordering a late lunch and a beer. It would be easy to get used to this! Postcards were bought and written, the tourist office sought for more information and a tour of the town organised in the couple of hours or so before the evening meal was ready. The last embers of a crimson sunset burnished the distinctive twin towers of the cathedral before we descended the 68 steps for dinner.

It was good to know that tomorrow there would be no necessity for an early start but we could relax and take our time. Unfortunately, we do not do repose very well. The concept of a rest day to dally, amble, wash and indulge ourselves conflicted with the instincts to move on, climb another hill, turn another corner and descend another path. However, the rest did give us time for reflection and Conques was an ideal choice to break the daily rhythms that had consumed us for the last 10 days. We were both sustaining the rigours well and feeling and looking much better. The sun had helped, of course, and daily practicalities, unfettered by domestic trivia, created a simple purpose and generated an inevitable momentum that sometimes daily life lacks. The hotel TV gave us access to the BBC World Service and re-introduced us to a world and a time that seemed strangely alien and irrelevant.

The simple objectives of the journey had taken over and in their wake came a degree of emotional and spiritual clarity and refreshment. So far the challenges of the journey had been met and although journey's end was still not in sight, there was a confidence that we could cope with most things that might lie in front of us. With this reassurance, we approached the rest day in relaxed mood, exploring this lovely town thoroughly and once again availing ourselves of a tasty lunch at the restaurant over the road. We seemed to have developed a penchant for sirop de citron and Perrier as the preferred refreshment and the hot chicken salad set us up for the rest of the day. At one point, we tagged on to an Australian party led by an academic from the University of Melbourne who was explaining the meanings behind the world-famous stone sculpture, or tympanum, that forms the centre piece above the impressive cathedral entrance. It demonstrates graphically in stone the unspeakable torments inflicted on non-believers 'pour decourager les autres'! This was described with characteristic antipodean irreverence and macabre humour. The cathedral does have a majesty and serenity about it and as a point of pilgrimage, it carries authority and status. Even in just one day, we had come to know and appreciate the many delights of Conques. It had been an excellent choice of venue for a rest day.

The next day's destination was Livinhac, some 26 kilometres from Conques and we resumed the routines of packing, taking an early breakfast and setting off within 30 minutes. We were now into October and the mornings seemed darker at 8 a.m. The day started well enough. Mists clung to the valley sides as we descended beneath the rocky outcrop on which stands the tiny Chapelle St. Roch (another one!), and the view back to the narrow streets and cathedral spires of Conques appeared ghostly. An attractive medieval bridge spanned the fast-flowing stream and from here the pilgrims' trail followed a well-graded circuitous line through dense woodland of mainly chestnut trees. It was refreshing to be back on the sort of path we know and love! Height was gained effortlessly and soon the trees thinned and the path crossed a high bluff overlooking the valley with late flowering ling and decaying bracken adding autumn colour to the slopes. From this viewpoint, Conques remained obstinately shrouded in mist and its now familiar valley receded from view as we began the road walk along the plateau towards Noilhac.

We learned to break the rhythms of walking whenever opportunity presented itself and a morning coffee in the pleasant village bar in the sunshine gave some respite from the road. Unfortunately, this was short-lived for after a brief uphill section on a farm track, the next tarmac strip was reached at the Chapelle St. Roch (yes, another one!). This was interesting in that it featured a couple of sculptural renditions of the patron saint of pilgrims. Mythology has it that he suffered from bubonic plague and was dependent on his faithful dog to bring rations from the villages he passed. He is often depicted in his medieval costume baring a thigh to show his affliction. The only problem here was that the offending 'bubo' appeared on his left leg on the outside sculpture above the chapel entrance but on his right leg on the smaller statue inside. Artistic licence, perhaps, or maybe he was more diseased than history recounts!

After this diversion, the next couple of hours involved a

12-kilometre tramp on the D road to Decazeville across fertile farmland where the maize harvest was being garnered by giant machines and their accompanying tractors and trailers, chewing up the entire crop, cobs, stems and all, chipping the residue into cattle feed. At about the half-way point, a very pleasant garden area had been laid out for the benefit of pilgrims. It was welcoming and much appreciated. It was here that we met the charming couple from Bordeaux who would be trekking companions for the next few days. They had halting English, we had halting French, but it did not seem to matter and where our fluency came to a halt a few Gallic gestures seemed to suffice. Shortly after this oasis, the GR65 left the road at last and followed a sandy track descending gradually towards a nexus of open valleys, some of which bore the scars of open-cast mining despite valiant efforts at reinstatement and reclamation.

It was now becoming oppressively hot and humid and the sweat was flowing freely. When the path inevitably re-joined the tarmac road on the upper outskirts of Decazeville, there were views below to a broad, heavily industrialised trench with some urban sprawl spreading up the lower hillsides. Expectations that the road would lead down to the heart of Decazeville were dashed as it continued to wind down for several kilometres in the now baking heat. By the time we finally reached the outskirts of the town we were shattered, but consoled ourselves with the knowledge that the guide indicated that there were only four kilometres more to go. Unfortunately, most of these were uphill on an unforgiving road with no evident source of refreshment. Then came the realisation that Livinhac was far below us in the valley of the Lot and to reach the town would mean another lengthy descent, mercifully through shaded woodland. As we staggered into the village square, the first task was to purchase some iced tea which slaked the raging thirst and paved the way for a beer shortly afterwards. This, without doubt, had been the most punishing day. However, the chambre d'hote was clean, comfortable and welcoming and the evening meal featured the largest duck breast ever consumed with stacks of French fries. We came to the distinct impression that this was not a route for the vegetarian! Once again, it was miraculous to feel the restorative effects of rest, drink and food and, unsurprisingly, sleep came easily.

In planning the trek, some of the longer days had been broken down into two and today, fortuitously, was one of them. The stage from Livinhac to Felzins on Thursday 3 October was only about 14 kilometres, which after the previous day would seem like a stroll. The weather was also cooler and cloudier. This made it easier for walking and infinitely preferable to the desiccating conditions of the previous day, which surprisingly did not carry over any ill-effects. Once again, the day started with a climb on tarmac out of the Lot valley to an undulating plateau. However, with the pressure now off to have to complete another 20 km+ section, it was possible to ramble through a rolling pastoral landscape of large farms, although there was much evidence of crumbling farm buildings and of general rural decay. Although the land was well cultivated, it did seem like the back of beyond.

In the event, it would have been perfectly feasible to have reached Figeac in the day, but we wandered into Felzins at just past noon to find that there was no shop, no bar, no cafe. The only place open was a hairdresser's. The agricultural store, where it might have been possible to buy cheese and bread, had closed for the afternoon two minutes before we arrived. To cap it all, the Chambre d'Hote, Le Pentadou, was also closed until 4 p.m., although there was an annexe in which to sit. Four hours was a long time to hang about, so we spent a good hour foraging around the church for hazelnuts, walnuts, chestnuts and figs like human squirrels. A couple of gentle meanderings around the village, where there was some recent development and a lively primary school, and we settled down to await the arrival of our hosts for the evening. It was worth waiting for. The room was delightful and Anne and Peter Gysbrecht were the most charming of hosts. As at Valloret, all guests sat around a large farm table for the evening meal, a pork pot-roast, and although all our fellow guests were mainly French-speaking, there was sufficient comprehension of English for us to understand what was going on and for them to understand our more basic French. Wine again flowed freely but that was not to blame for the slip on the bottom stone step descending to the room which demolished some garden furniture. Not the best way to end a very pleasant evening!

We said a reluctant farewell to Pentadou in the morning and headed for Figeac, one of the larger towns on the route. The weather now had settled into a pretty sombre pattern and the clouds loomed threateningly as we followed the GR65 mainly on roads above the Cele valley, one of the main tributaries of the Lot. The descent into the town was steep and coincided with the first bursts of rain which would turn out to be heavy and prolonged. Fortunately, we missed most of it and were able to find the hotel without any trouble. Unfortunately, Reception was closed until after 3 p.m., so we took the opportunity to cross the main bridge into town, have a coffee and then a lunch, an unaccustomed treat. Energy bars, dried fruit and nuts do pall after a while and the enticement of steak and chips was far too strong to resist.

The rain persisted all day and it was fortunate that our arrival had preceded the worst of the downpour. By early-evening the heaviest rain had passed and there was an opportunity to explore the nucleated old town overlooking the crossing points of the River Cele before dinner in an Italian restaurant. Figeac had a major role during the War as a base for the French Resistance. The installation of an engineering works to manufacture propellers for Heinkel aircraft was destroyed and communications constantly harassed. The penalty was vicious reprisals and mass deportations to German concentration camps or as forced labour. It was obviously a harrowing part of Figeac's history, commemorated, as we were to find next morning, by a major memorial overlooking the town.

The rain receded into showers during the early part of Saturday 5 October as we accompanied a very pleasant Australian couple on the day's walk to Grealou. This was another day broken in two and one again that with hindsight we could have incorporated into one. As the sunshine reappeared, we strolled into a very neat hillside settlement of Feycelles where a welcome cup of coffee relieved the continued road walking. The countryside was slowly changing into more subdued, rolling wooded hills with distinctive igloo-like stone shelters called caselles dotting the fields. These were made of limestone blocks and caused some puzzlement as to their construction. They were made in dry-stone fashion with no apparent wooden supports for the toadstool cap roof. It seemed an ingenious but also very durable form of construction. Many had been around for a long time, although some were slowly starting to crack and crumble. It was assumed that these must have been shepherds' shelters or simple stores. They certainly looked weather-proof and we were to meet scores of these over the next few days.

The limestone paths made a change from the tarmac but their 'knuckly' surface brought little respite for the feet. The causses landscape of Quercy was highly distinctive. The GR 65 seemed at

Casselle

times to be buried in a canopy of oak and walnut trees that encroached almost impenetrably on the track. Beyond the bounding limestone walls the untended forest could have engulfed thousands of people without trace. For this reason, as it became clearer when we reached the Museum in Cahors, the French Resistance simply melted into this arboreal maze. Occasionally, the forest had been tamed and regularised into orchards of walnut and chestnut and even oak. This is one of the main areas in France for the harvesting of wild mushrooms and, even more importantly, of the 'black diamonds' – truffles. We did come across quite a few people with baskets delving into the edge of the forest, but many areas were fenced off with 'Chaussee Prive' signs that did not invite trespass for hunting or foraging.

The weather had become sultry and menacing by early-afternoon and just as we met up with the Australian couple again, a heavy thunderstorm broke, the first and only occasion in the three weeks that we were seriously troubled by rain. They were going on to Cajarc and as the man was suffering with a bad case of plantar fasciitis that was giving his heel a great deal of pain, we wondered subsequently how he must have fared. He was in his 50s and mildly astonished that the intrepid 'poms' could give him a couple of decades.

The Accueil Ecoasis at Grealou, where we were staying the night,

Ancient dolmen, Quercy

was closed when we arrived at 2 p.m. and the next two hours were spent rather aimlessly relaxing in the sun. This place was not quite what we expected. The atmosphere was like a youth-hostel and there was a discernibly worthy, sanctimonious and slightly condescending air to it. As its name suggested it endeavoured to espouse environmental sensibilities which extended to 'dry' toilets and a communal washing area. There was a lengthy lecture on 'punaises' to greet us and despite our solitary German companion and a group of Austrian cave-divers, we felt rather isolated in a way that had not happened at Pentadou. The evening meal was fine, but in truth we were glad to get away the following morning.

It was a short three and a half hour walk to Cajarc. Initially the mist cast a ghostly silence over the embracing oak woodland but slowly the sun began to burn through. The limestone causses relented in places to give open scrubland, in which there were

Pilgrim cross, Quercy

ancient dolmens and some of the oldest of the stone crosses that had accompanied the camino all the way from Le Puy. This openness did not last long and the forest closed in again. In its favour, the GR65 was impeccably marked. Indications of the track were clear as were, just as importantly, indications of where not to proceed. In country riddled with tracks this was a blessing. To be lost in this country would have been a serious proposition.

The green lanes were rough, but eventually led to a broad basin rimmed by limestone cliffs and bluffs, in the middle of which, curled round a meander of the River Lot, sat the neat and pretty town of Cajarc. This became one of our favourite places. Its broad market square with its shops and cafes, most of which were open when we arrived just after mid-day, and the old centre of the town huddled around its church were picturesque. On a sunny afternoon on a Sunday it had the relaxed feel of a southern French town. It was the birthplace of both George Pompidou and Francoise Sagan and had also played a key role in the French Resistance. The Hotel La Peyrade on the outskirts of town was clean and pleasant and had the refinements that we had missed the previous day such as flushing toilets and a shower. It was an agreeable change.

It was understood that the last couple of days to Cahors would

Cajarc

involve consecutive 24 kilometres + walks after today's slightly shorter amble of about 18 kilometres. By now, however, limbs, joints and muscles had become attuned to the rigours of the trek and confidence had grown. We were also tangibly fitter, and the weather had taken a turn for the better. In thick mist, we left Cajarc heading for the Mas d'Ambeyrac near Limogne, a farm chambre d'hote. The way out was through the suburbs and industrial estates on roads to cross the Lot near Gaillac, some four kilometres away. It was testimony to increasing fitness that this was covered in only 45 minutes.

Thankfully, the road walking ended here for a while as a steady climb began on a forest track fringed with untended box and oak woodland. The emerging sun created dappled effects through the canopy of leaves and occasional clearances in the forest allowed extensive views over the rolling hills of Quercy. Eventually the shaded track emerged onto a minor road with open fields and large farms such as the Mas Couderc. The land shimmered in the developing heat and it was with some relief that the road gave way to a descending grassy track at the end of which was a large old laverie with stone troughs and benches for washing. The GR65 carried on along a farm track towards Limogne, but the village of St. Jean de Laur lay just

Old farm buildings near Mas Ambeyrac

ahead at the end of a steep gravelly road. We climbed this to emerge in a village square but regrettably there were no facilities to enable a stop for refreshment.

It was now a case of looking at the map and deciding whether to head for Limogne via the GR65, which would involve a degree of back-tracking, or carry on down the D53 road. Road walking is normally anathema, but as the GR65 also seemed to involve a fair amount of road work, we opted for the more direct line to Mas Ambeyrac.

It was, in fact, quite a pleasant walk. The kilometres slipped by almost unnoticed as we passed large farms and numerous casselles in blinding sunshine, but with ameliorating cool shade provided by roadside trees. It was only just after noon by the time we reached the busy D911 from Cahors to Villefranche which we crossed to the minor road leading to the gite. Although it was early the welcome was sincere and a couple of beers revived the spirits. The gite was attached to a working farm which occupied a very rustic situation and the room was well-appointed if a trifle damp and musty. After changing and spending some time sitting in the sun, we went for a walk to the local village of Promilhanes to reconnoitre possible routes to Limogne as alternatives to the very busy D911.

We learned a little more about our hosts over dinner. There were no other guests so that conversation had to proceed by way of increasingly fluent 'franglais'. Pork was on the menu tonight and our host was at great pains to point out the provenance of the meal by indicating his collection of impressively well-padded pigs in the neighbouring field. Sometimes in Britain we lose the connection between our food and where and how it is produced. Here in deepest France any squeamishness was subjugated to practicality. We are not great meat eaters but could understand the sense of connection and pride. Mr and Mme Moreau had left Paris in search of a more amenable lifestyle and built up the smallholding as well as developing several gites to boost farm income. A distinct impression was gleaned that Mme Moreau, who was originally a Parisian, had reached the point where the rigours of such a life were beginning to tell and both recognised that they would soon have to downsize to something more appropriate for their advancing years.

In the morning Mme Moreau kindly gave us a lift into Limogne-en-Quercy, saving a long and tedious road walk. A dense ribbon of fog occupied the Lot valley above which the sun was shining strongly even though the temperature reading in the car was only five degrees celsius. In three weeks we seemed to have moved from high summer to the middle of autumn. Today was a 24 kilometres trek and the GR65 followed limestone tracks across the causses between dense stands of gnarled, dwarf oak. After an hour or so the village of Varaire was reached. This was an attractive place despite the fact that a busy D road ran through it. Coffee at the cafe overlooking the historic market square provided a welcome lift and it was interesting to note that in the local shop, (unusually a Spar), there were copies of the Sunday Times, no doubt testifying to the existence of a local English immigrant community. There would be worse places to emigrate to than this sleepy and tranquil place.

Walking out of Varaire there were some very attractive properties in the local vernacular style with dovecotes, towers and terracotta roofs with a distinctive change in pitch towards the base, all set in acres of land. They were often available, as we were to learn, at prices that would prove very tempting. The complexity of paths created some temporary anxieties as we carried on. Variants of the GR65 forked away from the main path and after consulting the map we followed one of these, which proved to be a fortuitous move bringing us out eventually back to the main road, the D19, at Vaylats. The village was sleepy and quiet but its cafe in the square was open so we availed ourselves of more refreshment before carrying on past a large convent. Directions from here were less than clear but we were guided by a young chap who pulled up in his car and pointed us in the right way. Splashes of red paint marked a sinuous path through woodland, which finally relented opening out into a landscape of ploughed fields and sheep pasture. A lane led to the evening's farm accommodation at Mas Ceres, an enchanting, historic place with a lovely room in the grounds.

It was nice to be in the company of genuine farming people with whom we endeavoured to converse over another splendid evening meal. Madame had a daughter in Australia and from her had learned some English, which enabled the conversation to flow more freely, although normally we would have done our best to speak in French. Les moutons coussenardes, we learned, were the staple breed in this limestone area and they could not have looked cuter with panda-like black rings around their eyes and a black nose and tail. We explained that in our part of the world Herdwicks were similarly dominant and when we returned to Cumbria we sent them a postcard featuring our local breed.

The final day dawned rather grey and cheerless but with only the last 26 kilometres to go we set off light of foot and energised. Our hosts had suggested the best way to re-join the GR65 and their instructions were followed as we walked along field tracks to re-join the main path after about an hour. This turned out to be the best part of a day that epitomised much of the route of the camino. Distance was not normally an issue. We could plod on at our own speed with reasonable confidence that the ground would be covered irrespective of the ups and downs along the way. The tiring aspect was the nature of the trail with its unrelenting adherence to hard surfaces that jarred, be they tarmac roads, gravelled farm tracks or, in today's case, lumpy limestone paths. It did not help that there few distractions to take the mind off the pounding that the feet were receiving. No villages were encountered and no cafes or places of historical interest that might have warranted a brief stop.

Kilometres passed as the GR65 wound its way around dry limestone valleys that seemed interminable. The consolation was that we made very good time, the first 20 kilometres taking just four and a half hours as we entered the hilltop village of Le Marchand. We had been advised that it would be downhill all the way from here to Cahors. It wasn't. Deeply dissected valleys vegetated by poor scrub and littered with weathered limestone detritus lay on either side of the approach to Cahors along the crest of a limestone plateau. But then, almost unexpectedly, Cahors lay beneath us, situated spectacularly on an incised meander loop of the River Lot. The final road descent into the town, like that at Figeac, was about one in three, sparing throbbing feet no respite. It was with considerable relief and no mean satisfaction that we crossed the main road bridge into town at journey's end. To celebrate we had a beer in the main square and found the Hotel Valentre within striking distance of the railway station. Nous sommes arrives!

At that moment, there was no sense of climax or fulfilment. That would come later as the daily rhythms and momentum of the last four weeks began to subside. In a strange way, the mind continued to urge the body to continue and it would have seemed more appropriate for our final day to see us crossing the river and continuing on the journey south towards St. Jean Pied-de-Port in the foothills of the Pyrenees. As it was, the final day was devoted to an exploration of Cahors. The promenade along the banks of the river Lot elicited some reflection on the fact that we had followed this river almost from its source to this point where it had become a stately and impressive

Pont Valentre, Cahors

river, bigger than the Thames. Bridging points were obviously of major significance and the oldest of these, the Pont Valentre, was an impressive structure with its soaring towers and elegant arches. The more recent functional railway bridge on the crown of the meander was then succeeded round the bend by the Pont Louis Philippe, the main road entry into the town.

The neck of the meander was crammed with the historic buildings of mediaeval Cahors including yet another very impressive cathedral. It was an interesting place even in the persistent morning rain that encouraged us to have an extended lunch in the market square whilst waiting for the rain to stop and the clouds to break, which they did in the early-afternoon. By now the ordering of a meal had become second nature and the idioms and cadences of French spoken 'properly' were beginning to embellish the simple vocabulary. An English couple who sat very close to us did not realise that we were English until we finished eating and began to use our own language. Ironically, they were all Lancastrians!

The highlight of our wanderings around the town was undoubtedly the Museum de la Resistance in the Place de General de Gaulle. This was not a pre-possessing building but inside it housed an interesting, sobering and insightful collection of documentary and photographic collection of the activities of the Resistance (and the SOE) during the

Second World War. It seemed that this area from Cahors to Figeac was the heartland of Resistance activities and having just walked across the landscape, it gave it an added dimension and perspective.

We had come a long way, not just physically but also in our understanding of the culture, history and traditions of rural France. En route we had met some interesting people, shared experiences, and improved the confidence to converse with them. From the volcanic heart of the Massif Central in the east to the broad open expanses of the granitic plateau of Aubrac and the limestone causses further west, there had been a fascinating relationship between geology, vernacular architecture, land use and history. There is no doubt that the journey had enhanced our appreciation of the frequently turbulent historical relationship between France and England and between this area and the rest of France.

In common with many isolated areas, this rural heart of France was almost certainly viewed by the Auvergnois as an island; conservative, Catholic and resistant to outside influences. It lacked the cosmopolitan feel of modern European cities yet was vibrant and confident in its own cultural traditions which provided a bulwark against ephemeral social and political ideologies. Nowhere can resist the inexorable advance of change, but one is left with a distinct impression that this part of France has absorbed change on its own terms, whilst having respect for its long history and deep-seated rural traditions. This was something in which one could feel a certain sympathy. It had been a very interesting insight and once again the concept of a journey had proved to be not only fulfilling physically but also emotionally and philosophically.

Journey's end, Cahors

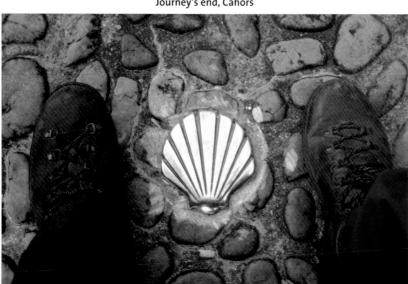

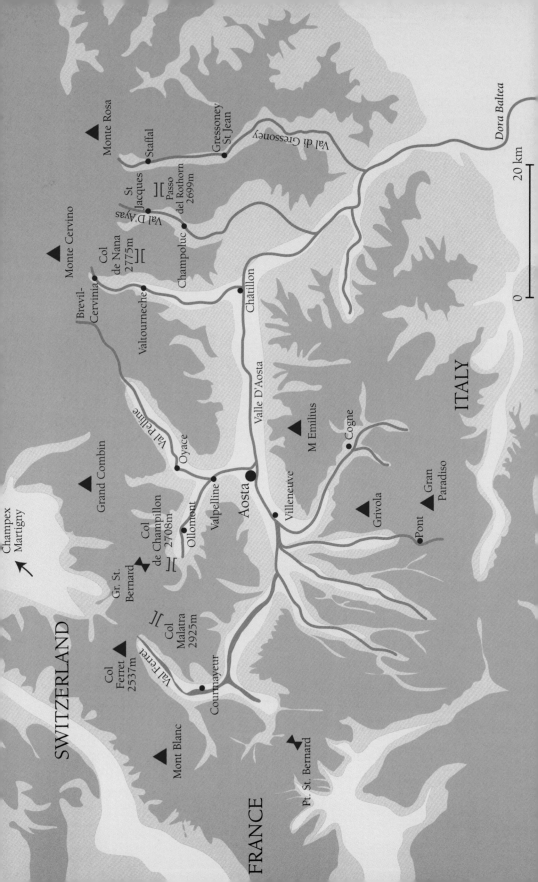

The Alta Via: Italian Alps

I F WE SUBSCRIBE TO the notion, however clichéd, that a physical journey has certain parallels with life's longer journey in providing us with challenges and even crises, it follows that, as in life, things sometimes go wrong. In life's broader tapestry it is the problems and difficulties we face that tend to shape us more, rather than the good times we tend to take for granted. Most of us at some time have had to contend with the inevitable pressures of work that sometimes seem relentless and overpowering, with domestic problems of caring for aged parents or fractious offspring and with medical issues that threaten to derail life's plans. As with life itself a journey throws up its own challenges. The sun does not always shine, the travel arrangements are not always smooth, illness can intervene, (sometimes in inconvenient circumstances), or it is possible to get lost.

The expeditions previously described were thankfully free of major incidents but the list of local difficulties over the years is extensive. Camping high up on the Biafo glacier in the Karakorum waiting for a three day blizzard to subside was intimidating; being rained on intensively in the Western Pyrenees for the first week of a four week trek along the GR10 was a literal dampener; there were Jennifer's strained ankle ligaments on the GR5 that necessitated walking over one col backwards; another three day blizzard in Val Roseg in the Bernina Alps during which the tent collapsed and we were forced to migrate to a nearby barn for two days where the sound of cowbells nearly drove us mad; diarrhoea in Nepal and India – things happen! As in life, it is how we adapt and contend with such difficulties that promotes self-knowledge. It is curious that when recalling a particular trek it is not necessarily the wonderful days that immediately stimulate the memory but the bad days, which, with hindsight, are recalled wistfully with a certain dark humour. We got by!

The above reflections are by way of introducing the journey across the Alta Via, the Italian long-distance path that skirts the southern edge of the alpine giants from the Dent d'Herens and Monte Cervino (Matterhorn) in the west to the Monte Rosa in the east. For good measure, the early stages follow the Tour du Mont Blanc and the latter stages offer an extension to the Gran Paradiso National Park to the south of the Aosta valley. It is a stunningly attractive but lesser known and travelled part of the Alps. Having traversed the GR 5 from St. Gingolph to Nice and the GR10 across the Pyrenees, it seemed appropriate to include on our trek list the Alta Via 1, or Giant's Way that runs from Courmayeur to Gressoney St. Jean across the northern side of the Valle D'Aosta.

The Italians have a somewhat capricious way of numbering their long-distance paths. Another Alta Via 1 crosses sections of the Italian Dolomites. It provides a degree of confusion that carries over into their system of way-marking trails that we were to find to our chagrin later. We should not have been surprised. In the early days of the Tour du Mont Blanc an insight into the national psyche of the various nations whose borders are crossed could be found in the mountain refuges used and the individual methods used to mark the route to be followed. The French huts tended to be somewhat anarchic but with a tolerant, laissez-faire attitude and excellent cuisine; the Italian huts were boisterous and very easy-going with little adherence to 'rules' and a collective volubility lubricated by copious glasses of red wine. The Swiss on the other hand were punctilious in the extreme. Everything was well-ordered, baskets were provided for outdoor gear and slippers supplied, lights-out and silence was strictly observed. The same characteristics could be said of their path marking and border controls. The French seemed to be exceptionally flamboyant with their use of red paint splashed liberally on boulders and prominent rocks – literally slapdash: the paths on the Swiss sections seemed to have been recently swept clear of debris and their red and white markings were fresh and perfectly geometric; the Italians on the other hand had a confusing arrangement of different colours to indicate regional and local paths that intersected with the main GR. In their case there was a penchant for multi-coloured modern art renditions where the path was obvious, but a singular lack of directional indicators where paths closely diverged. It all added to the flavour of such a long-distance trek!

Building on previous experience we decided to explore the Valle D'Aosta and the Alta Via 1, taking a tent to cover all contingencies should accommodation be found wanting. It is always helpful to have some knowledge of the local language. French, we could just about manage, German was less fluent, to put it mildly, and Italian was non-existent, despite both of us taking 'O' Level Latin at our small-town Grammar School in the 1950s. We got the distinct impression that Italian was the most vocal of languages, poetic in cadence, highly animated in delivery and punctuated by endearingly graphic manual demonstrations. We could manage the latter, along with stock phrases such as per favor, grazie, parla inglese, buon giorno/buona notte/buona sera and ciao! It comprised a pitiful list, but one travels hopefully.

With some preparation through maps and guide books, a flight to Geneva was booked and the train taken from here to Martigny in the Rhone valley where our variant of the Alta Via was to begin. Municipal camp sites are not always the most tranquil after a long journey and with adrenalin beginning to flow, it would be futile to pretend that a good night's sleep was had. The following morning, bleary and stiff, we caught the post bus to La Forclaz to begin the first section of the trek to Champex. It might have been an omen but it was one of those days when the glowering skies obscured most of the route, the clouds angry and dynamic. Occasionally glimpses of the valley beneath appeared through the boiling atmosphere revealing forests and valley fields, but this brief vista was then shut out again as we trudged on in the sticky humid heat of a summer's day. It was only as we entered the valley above Champex that the late watery afternoon sunshine appeared almost apologetically. The road to the camp site steamed and tendrils of smoky mist writhed through the woods. It was a typical first day to a trek in terms of aching shoulders and tired feet. The familiar routine of erecting our two-man tent seemed to amuse or impress our fellow campers ensconced in their large family tents, making our tiny shelter seem Lilliputian by comparison.

The power of the human body to revive after a decent night's sleep never ceases to amaze. The trail down to Le Fouly at the end of the valley follows the gushing river and the noisy road through woods and fields. Another cloudy and wet day did not dampen spirits and slight deviations were made to sample bilberry tart and strong coffee. We were heading for the high mountains and as the sky lightened the first glimpses of snowfields and glaciers appeared on our right beneath the arching corries and towering summits. By the time the second camp had been pitched at La Fouly beneath Mont Dolent, the sun was shining with burning intensity in a sky of deepest alpine blue. Sometimes the bad moments must be endured to savour even more intensely the good. With the scent of sun cream in our nostrils, the blaze of alpine flowers in the meadows around the camp site and the melodic chime of the cow bells, it seemed that we had come home. With the clearing skies the evening soon grew chilly and we sought the sanctuary of sleeping bags to harbour resources for the harder days ahead.

It is difficult to become blasé about the attractions of walking in high alpine scenery. The clarity of the air is like nectar and visibility becomes almost forensic, particularly in the early-morning. It was on such a pristine day that we packed up early, had a quick breakfast of muesli and coffee and began the first steep uphill section to the Col du Ferret and the Italian frontier. It is at this point that the route combines with the Tour du Mont Blanc and the way is well trod and well-marked. Watching shepherds in our native Cumbrian fells provides a good example of how to pace an ascent of rough ground. Rhythmic and measured without seeming to hurry, they cover the ground effort-lessly. We tried to do the same, gaining height slowly but steadily, losing sight of the valley as the path curved round to the west revealing the col ahead appearing deceptively close. From the screes came the high-pitched warning shriek of a marmot, an endearing sound and one that registered that we had now reached the higher, rockier ground.

It is one of the most satisfying feelings to breast a col. Part of it panders to the curious and exploratory; to see beyond the immediate and look ahead to the next objective. In that it mirrors many phases of

Pre-de Bar glacier, Col Ferret

our lives. The changing of jobs, the realisation of ambitions, the feeling that one has prevailed despite the challenges and obstacles confronted all relate to a place and a moment in our personal experience. At the Col du Ferret, the rewards were spectacular. Walking through a carpet of vivid alpine flowers; (saxifrage, gentian, orchid, campion, mountain buttercup, stonecrop, pasque flower, cranesbill and mountain avens) is an unforgettable sensory experience. The colours and the scents are ravishing. When this kaleidoscope is accompanied by mesmeric mountain views, it becomes almost overwhelming. At the Col Ferret, the pinnacles of the Grandes Jorasses dominate the view down the Italian Val Ferret, a classic glaciated U-shaped trough, but our eyes were drawn to the nearer foreground where the tongue of the Pre-de Bar glacier, which with its curved snout and sinuous moraines, is a text book example of a hanging glacier. With the sun shining from a clear sky, this was a place to sit and savour.

It is one of the blindingly obvious tenets of mountain trekking that what goes up must come down. For many people this is harder work, testing hips, knees and ankles that almost scream in protest at the strain. For many years we had observed alpine walkers with day sacs and trekking poles, judging the latter to be a Continental affectation beneath the dignity of the hardy, tough British, but one hip prosthesis later we learned the lesson. Adjusting the poles for descent takes an enormous amount of stress away from creaking joints and provides confidence to balance. From the Col Ferret to the valley is a good 800 metres, which with a loaded sac is enough for one day, particularly for the venerable and at the beginning of a trek. It certainly felt that way as we walked to the camp site at Lavachey. It is a spectacular setting beneath the outlying glaciers and ice fields of Mont Blanc whose ramparts rose almost vertically above the valley.

Camping provides versatility and there is no more comforting a

Grandes Jorasses from Col Ferret

feeling than to stretch out in a sleeping bag at the end of a hard day and give tired limbs a rest. Over the stove, preparing a simple meal and replenishing liquids via tea or coffee is the perfect end to a perfect day. Wild camps high in the mountains are often sublime with temperature inversions cloaking the valleys in mist while the evening sun pours its last warmth onto the upper slopes. When the weather breaks in frightening thunderstorms with only a thin skin of plastic between you and the raging elements, it is a different story, but there is also drama and spectacle in such wild ferocity. It is a reminder of how vulnerable and puny man appears in such an elemental setting as the lightning crackles and the thunder crashes, its sounds magnified and exaggerated by echoing reverberations amongst the crags.

As the years advance, the comforts of an auberge, refuge or dortoir with a solid roof, with meals provided and a proper sit-down toilet become increasingly compelling as the confines and relative insecurity of a tent become less attractive to stiffening limbs. Like so many things, we were reluctant to concede the passing of the years by accepting the ultimately inevitable, but camping, despite its unique attractions and symbolic significance, does impose certain constraints, chief amongst which is the loading. Our tent weighed just 2.2 kilos but with this comes the additional paraphernalia of cooking equipment and rations to last a few days as well as sleeping bags and spare clothes and rudimentary toiletries. Inexorably the weight to be carried begins to add up until we found ourselves carrying well over 15 kilos each. Being a gentleman, that was distributed in a more equitable fashion between the two of us, but it still means a fair amount to lug uphill and down dale. The packing of a rucsac becomes key, loading the heavier items, such as the tent, towards the top and trying to keep the rucsac as compact as possible to aid stability. It became a well-rehearsed routine and normally we could strike camp, have breakfast and be away within 30 minutes. As with all treks, a cumulative tiredness begins to take a toll after a couple of weeks, so that rest days become an important element in the planning schedule. At the start, a sense of anticipation and excitement fuels energy; towards the end the mirage of some luxury in the form of a comfortable bed and a good hearty meal sustains motivation.

At Lavachey, we officially joined the Alta Via delle Valle d'Aosta 1 (AV1) as it heads east towards the St. Bernard Pass. The initial climb is approximately 400 metres to the bench on which stands the cluster

Mt. Blanc from Vallone Malatra

of chalets at Malatra. The beauty of alpine paths is their wonderful grading that makes light of such height gain, meandering through woodland and meadows so that a steady pace can be maintained. In the morning shade, the air had a crisp, cool feel making such an ascent a real pleasure. The first rays of the sun bring an almost primeval relief, flooding the slopes with a richness of texture and colour and lifting the spirits. The emerging views of the Mont Blanc Massif only added to the beauty of such a moment, the glaciers glinting in the angled intensity of light.

We knew we were approaching Malatra as much by smell as by sight. To lovers of hard, nutty mountain cheese such as Gruyere or Emmental, this scent is unmistakeable. A number of small chalets were already busily humming with portable generators, dairy herds stood lazily by waiting their turn to be milked and sheets of muslin were hung over balconies to dry in the sun. In many parts of the Alps such traditional activities are struggling to survive in a world where big is beautiful but here it seemed perfectly in keeping with its surrounds. Long may it continue! Like people who live by the seaside but rarely cast a glance at the tide, the cheese-makers dressed in their bright blue overalls concentrated on their tasks whilst behind them was one of the great views of the Alps. Mont Blanc was clearly the monarch of this glen with its satellites the Aiguille du Geant and Les Grandes Jorasses soaring into the deep blue alpine sky above the trench of Val Ferret. Once again this was a view to savour before we hoisted rucsacs on our backs and set off climbing steadily towards the Colle Malatra at over 2900 metres.

The approach to the Colle Malatra was along a steadily rising basin that gradually steepened to a rocky cleft. Despite its altitude, the guides indicated that this was a perfectly negotiable col in most high summers, but nonetheless, we approached it with some trepidation. We turned for one last glimpse of the stunning views of Mont Blanc before concentrating on the immediate logistics of a very steep, rocky descent. Perhaps at this point it should be noted that of our many medical afflictions, Jennifer has a fear of heights, something that she has managed to conquer most of the time, but it means, for example that Striding Edge and Sharp Edge in the Lake District are definitely no-go routes. There is no rational explanation for such phobias. Mine is a fear of spiders that scuttle. They invoke an involuntary shudder. So it is with vertigo. Jennifer's strategy for dealing with it is to talk to the path where one exists, perhaps as a means of concentrating on the ground without sideways glances at the drop. It is not often that we meet people on such sections, but it must seem strange to come across someone so patently capable mumbling incoherently in an attempt to massage the perceived dangers away through such emollience. She is also doggedly determined not to let such things get on top of her and to overcome her real misgivings. I could see her approaching the col with some concerns and tried to reassure her with the fact that there appeared to be a zig-zag route through the snowy slopes that took the sting out of an otherwise vertiginous scree slope.

Fortunately, the ambient heat of the day had softened the snow so with care (and entreaties!) the descent proved less severe than it looked. The foot of the corrie bowl was shallow and alive with delicate soldanella, whose soft purple bells are the first to break through the melting snow. With the worst now over the descent of the Comba di Merdeux comprised a well-graded traverse above the deeply cut valley. About half way down we came across a small chalet where an elderly couple were tending their sheep and goats. They were solicitous in the extreme inviting us to sit down and share a cordial with them. This was communicated largely through sign language or basic French of which they understood even less than we did. Nevertheless, we were humbled by their kindness. All over the world we have been impressed by the generosity of people who patently have little material wealth but are only too willing to share what they have with us. It speaks volumes. On this occasion, the woman gestured to Jennifer to take off her boots so that she could anoint her tired and aching feet with some home-made soothing ointment. It was a lovely thing to do. How can you repay such generosity except to offer genuine and profuse thanks?

We stayed for 30 minutes basking in the sunshine and endeavouring to describe via the map where we were going to and where we had come from. If we had possessed sufficient linguistic skills we could have sought information on camp sites as we were now descending into a settled area at the foot of the St. Bernard Pass. A sweeping viaduct spanned the valley taking this major road through tunnels and contorted meanders back into Switzerland. After the solitude and serenity of the upper valley, the noise intruded. There appeared to be no municipal camp site nearby, so we took the plunge and sought refuge in the annex of a small country auberge where some English was spoken. A bed, fresh sheets, toilet facilities and steak and chips were a price worth paying. Even as we settled down for the night our thoughts turned to the elderly couple in their eyrie high above. Where would we rather have been?

It was fortunate that we had had a good day to cross the high col for the following morning was wreathed in cold, dank mist, but suitably fortified we set off early for what we knew would be a long and hard day. From the serpentine concrete coils of the road, the AV1 contours round the pastoral landscape of Saint Rhemy before descending to the

Descent from Col Champillon

adjacent valley of Val de Manouve. From here it is another 900-metre climb to the Col Champillon which gives access to the Valpelline. This would be our second successive Scafell Pike of an ascent with loaded sacs. It was one to take gently. Fortunately, the early mists dissipated after mid-day and we emerged into a landscape of high alpine meadows bedecked with flowers. The col itself was a tremendous vantage point, particularly to the south where the peaks of the Gran Paradiso National Park exerted a powerful, magnetic presence. With luck, we hoped to be among them in less than two weeks.

This was to be a literal and metaphoric high point. The day had been hot, and we had exhausted our water supplies. Such high pastures often contain wooden troughs supplied from adjacent streams by simple plumbing. Unfortunately, the only one we could find was liberally laced with algae, but the supply tap was near at hand and with a couple of rusty turns the water began to flow, albeit somewhat discoloured. We should have let it run longer, but thirst is more difficult to manage than hunger and Jennifer cupped her hands and drank. This was to prove a big mistake. I had resisted the temptation, having spotted a chalet a few hundred feet below, but by then the damage had been done as we were to discover the next day. The chalet was linked by a minor track that led circuitously to the small town of Valpelline and as we halted for a very welcome drink, we were offered a lift down to the valley. The driving was hair-raising, but the young man left us right outside the municipal camp site. It was another generosity well received.

Valpelline is an attractive place that could only be Italian. Its architecture and ambience were redolent of the Mediterranean and it did have a pizza restaurant that immediately focused our attention. Replete with pizza, reinforced with a couple of beers, we slept well on a fairly noisy site, but the morning brought its own problems. The new day started well enough with another unsolicited lift from our tent neighbour, a Scot, to drive us up to meet the AV1 at Oyace. It was not far but it took the strain out of the first 300 metres of height gain of the day. Packs loaded onto more protesting shoulders we set off on what would be a good two-day hike across wild unpopulated high country to the Valtournenche. It was not to be taken lightly. Unfortunately, the normally uncomplaining Jennifer requested a rest stop after about an hour and from her complexion it was clear that she was not well. Her colour had gone, to be replaced by a white sweaty pallor. Shortly afterwards she was violently sick.

The art of managing risk in the high mountains is to know when to turn back. This we promptly did and found a room at a local hostelry at Oyace, where she could clamber into a bed and hopefully sleep off the malaise. If the sickness persisted, we would have to catch the post bus back down the valley to Aosta and seek more expert medical advice. Was it the water? Was it incipient heat exhaustion? Was it simply too much, too soon, too old! We shall never know but it was patently clear that we could not carry on that day. Slowly the nausea and vomiting subsided and after replenishing lost fluids gently, she fell asleep. The room was quiet and simply furnished, cool and dark. It was not a bad place to hole up. By early-evening she seemed to have recovered some of her vitality and had some soup which stayed down. However, she was weakened, and our thoughts turned to the considerable challenge of the onward two days if we were to keep religiously to the plan to walk the AV1 in its entirety. We vowed to sleep on it and see what the following day brought.

It brought a thankfully re-energised companion but still 'woozy' with the after effects of the previous day's sickness. We had a continental breakfast, drank tea and water rather than coffee in copious amounts and considered our options. We were flexible in the sense that we were not committed on any day to a particular route, but the date of

Above the Crete Seche Refuge

the return flight from Geneva was a commitment we could not avoid. Losing one or two days now would mean some amendment of our plans. Mindful of the fact that this was not supposed to be an endurance test but an enjoyable physical holiday, we decided to give it another day, but to undertake a local walk without heavy sacs and see how the patient fared. With that in mind, we caught the late morning post-bus further up the valley to Bionaz and set off gently for the Rifugio Crete Seche, accessed via delightful flowery meadows heady with scent and

Col de Crete Seche

vivid in colour. Bees buzzed, myriads of butterflies fluttered, the force of the sun tempered by altitude and lingering light mist. It was nirvana! Whether it was the restorative benefits of such natural splendour or the light meal and drinks we enjoyed at the refuge cannot be determined, but Jennifer felt sufficiently strong to climb the last few hundred metres to the Col du Crete Seche that overlooks the Otemma Glacier and the Lac de Mauvoisin. From this superb vantage point familiar physical features encountered on the Haute Route from Verbier to Zermatt undertaken some years before came into view. In this world of ice, rock and sky the fecundity of nature still impressed. Brightly coloured saxifrage adorned the scree between large boulders, alpine buttercups flourished in seemingly inimical environments, streams gurgled, and marmots shrieked. We heaved a huge sigh of relief and satisfaction and made our way back downhill with confidence restored.

However, we had lost two days. Fortunately, the post-bus service here and throughout the Alps is extraordinarily efficient. We never cease to be amazed at the level of co-ordination that links the traveller in remote locations seamlessly with onward connections by rail or road. Why can't we do that in Britain? Our rural services have never been so poor and even the post-bus services we have used in north west Scotland seem now to have been axed. Over our evening meal it was decided to catch the morning bus down to Aosta and the forward connection to Cervinia at the head of the Valtournenche valley, picking up the AV1 again half way along near the village of Valtournenche itself. It was either this detour or the sacrifice of some of the most scenic parts of the journey.

The journey to Valtournenche took us to Aosta and then along a very busy valley where rail and road routes jostle for space in the crowded narrow space on either side of the boisterous Dora Baltea river. This is one of the main routes from the Italian side of the Mt. Blanc Tunnel linking the Chamonix valley with Courmayeur and eventually Turin. After the sweet air of the high Alps the general bustle and stench of diesel stuck in the craw. Thankfully, the bus connection took us only as far as Chatillon where after a brief wait, the next leg headed upwards to the north to rejoin the alpine world we had had to abandon for a couple of days. Just south of the village of Valtournenche we alighted with packs and headed for the camp site at Moulin delighted that we had regained acquaintance with the AV1. It was a cramped site but within striking distance of the mecca of Cervinia at the foot of the Matterhorn, which from this perspective looked rather more like a flat blade than a pyramidal peak. We vowed to use one more day to deviate from the long-distance path to walk up the valley to see it at closer range.

The approach to Cervinia was via the AV1 to the dammed Lago di Cignana on the shores of which was both an alpine refuge, (R.Barnasse),

Monte Cervino, Valtournanche

and a lonely chapel brooding over the dark water. It was an austere place, surrounded by tumbling crags and scree. The route to the head of the valley required a brief climb to turn an intervening spur before contouring along the western flanks of the valley where the full view of the Matterhorn and Dent d'Herens dominated a predominantly pastoral scene. Old stone barns whose roofs were tiled with moss spoke of the antiquity of farming in this area where scythe and sickle have been replaced with mechanical cutters. We did spot workers using wooden rakes to collect and spread the cut grass to enable the sun to dry it off into hay. It is a scene still replayed in many parts of the Alps where the scented hay is stored in barns or in stacks or laid across simple wooden poles. To some extent this tradition is governed by the nature of the environment that militates against the use of large machinery, but it certainly contrasts with the intensity of grass monoculture and silage production back in the UK. The grass is cut generally when the wild flowers are dying down and have seeded ensuring that the pristine environment is preserved. On a bright and sunny day with the Matterhorn overlooking this timeless scene, our emotions were torn between the idealistic romantic setting and the very hard graft that it took to make a living in this way. Many alpine farmers have found that younger generations do not share the same visions as their forefathers and migrate leaving an ageing rural population, a factor not uncommon even in our own country. Others, where possible, have milked the possibility of alternative uses of their land for tourism and, in particular, for winter sports.

As we approached Cervinia the price of such activities became evident. The Swiss seem to have greater empathy in the development of their suitable landscapes for downhill skiing. One only has to look at Val Claret in France or Cervinia to see that this sensitivity is not universal. The old vernacular buildings are now dwarfed by multi-storey concrete blocks that seem incongruous and indeed intrusive in this landscape. Skeins of steel wire and pylons identify the main ski runs and the bareness of the slopes testifies to the intensity of their use and the failure to reinstate the threadbare surface. Where this is attempted it seems to be mainly quick-growing single species grass. Gone are the flowers and gone are the butterflies; the melancholic cry of a marmot seemed to embody all that has been lost. That, of course, is the view of the romantic. Pragmatists understand that no landscape can be totally fossilised. People have to make a living from

Monte Cervino from Lago Goillet

the assets they possess and there is little doubt that winter sports have regenerated the economies of many alpine areas that only decades ago practised simple pastoralism. Winter sports have been extended into the summer months with the greater popularity of mountain biking and hiking. Lago Goillet, at the centre of the skiing area is a maze of tracks, increasingly the domain of daredevil cyclists who career down the gravelly trails in a blur of dust. For walkers who take their lives into their hands, the rewards are more simplistic. From the blue waters of Lago Goillet, Monte Cervino, the Matterhorn, stands supreme, one of the most iconic mountains in the world, beautiful but also deadly.

We sat by the lake and pondered the history of the first ascent by Whymper in July 1865 about which so much has been written. The tragedy of the fall on descent that took the lives of Michel Croz, one of the guides and the three Englishmen, Lord Francis Douglas, Rev. Charles Hudson and Douglas Hadow has now passed into history. Whymper was clearly obsessed by the Matterhorn but it is not as widely known that he had a great rival in his attempt to be the first to climb it. An Italian guide, Jean Antoine Carrel, from Valtournenche had been engaged by Whymper several times between 1860 and 1865 for the two of them to explore and attempt to reach the summit from the Italian south west ridge. For some reason, the two friends became rivals as Carrel focused on climbing the Matterhorn via the latter and Whymper switched his attention to the Swiss side. As Whymper and Croz stood on the summit at 2 p.m. on that morning of the 14 July, 1865, they peered over the precipice to see Carrel and his party working their way up the south west ridge. When Carrel saw Whymper and his party on the summit, the Italian group called it a day. Their disappointment must have been shattering. As we stared at the enormity of the Italian face we could only admire and respect the courage of those early climbers but also reflected on the obsessions that drive men to their deaths. It seemed almost paradoxical on such a beautiful summer's day.

It was time for us to move on along the AV1 towards the adjacent valley to the east, the Valle d'Ayas. Jennifer now felt fully recovered, which was just as well because the route now traverses two passes, the Col dei Croix at 2697 metres and the Col de Nana at 2775 metres. This would mean an overall height gain greater than Ben Nevis and, with loaded packs, the day called for a measured pace and a steady plod. We have come to respect the alpine paths. Often, they follow the line of old herders' tracks and all seem impeccably well-graded, ascending by well-designed meanders to maintain as even a gradient as possible. It is a pity that some of these throughout the Alps are being systematically degraded by thoughtless mountain bikers and walkers who opt for the more direct route downhill.

We picked up the AV1 again at Cretaz in the Valtournenche and headed steadily uphill through dense woodland with occasional clearings where clusters of chalets marked summer grazing pastures. It seemed an age but finally we broke through the forests at Cheneil where it was possible to buy a long aqua minerale and have a sit down. We do not tend to sit down for long. Regrettably, age confers increasing stiffness and with the sweat pouring off brows on the first ascent, we did not wish to lose the benefits of warming up the hard way. The AV1 continues its upward path from Cheneil across upland pastures where the sonorous chiming of cattle bells seemed the perfect accompaniment. The size of some of these bells is astonishing. There is apparently a hierarchy in which the senior 'queen cows' sport the largest bells. They must have neck muscles like steel. Our English upland meadows have their own profusion of wild flowers, but natural meadows are disappearing fast in favour of fast-growing monocultural varieties of grass that can be harvested several times a season for silage. In the North of England, the deterioration of upland pastures is testimony to the marginal character of much hill farming; bracken and sedges invade the land. It was therefore a delight to walk through an upland area awash with colour and scent.

The Colle dei Croix is approached steeply via a rocky basin cradled in the arms of imposing crags, but the 600-metre (2000 foot) climb from Cheneil along such a path did not seem draining. With a last backward glance at the trench of the Valtournenche and the obelisk of the Matterhorn, we paused for refreshment and headed on along a gently contouring path to the Col de Nana, the high point of the day. A chill wind greeted us at the top forcing us to huddle behind a large cairn as we took in the new vista to the north, where the glaciers spilling down from the Breithorn ground their inexorable way down towards the valley. I had climbed the Breithorn from Zermatt with a small party in the flush of early middle age and comparing slides taken from that era with the photographs taken today, the pace of glacial retreat is noticeable even after only a period of 40 years. The impact of climate change on the Alps will be profound affecting all aspects of the alpine economy and society. It is chastening to think that our grandsons may not be able to see and enjoy to the same extent the full majesty of the alpine landscape that it has been our pleasure to explore. In that sense, we have been very much a favoured generation.

The joy of surmounting an alpine col is difficult to describe. Emotions of relief and fulfilment compete with the delight of looking out across a different landscape. Part of the rhythm and tempo of alpine trekking is to stay high up above the crowds in alpine refuges or a tent, watching the elements play around you, for better or worse, see the colours change as day slides gently into night or the first slivers of an alpine dawn light up the horizon. If one subscribes to a religious experience, it comes close to what Buddhism would describe as the 'oneness of life'. It generates a feeling of being grounded and content, despite the anxieties of the future and the problems of today. Life assumes a different perspective. Meeting other like souls in an alpine refuge recounting their experiences in a Babel of languages, but thankfully principally in English, is to share a common bond. As one guardienne at the Schonbiel Hut above Zermatt once confided, 'you meet a better class of person the higher up you go'. She sold us a delicious apple tart a few moments later!

Our accommodation for the night proved problematic. We were

anxious to reach the valley head village of Saint Jacques, perhaps to use the official camp site or find cheap accommodation and enjoy a cooked meal sitting down at a table for a change. However, we seem to have hit Saint Jacques on the week-end of a public holiday. There was no accommodation available anywhere. Resigning ourselves to a rough illicit camp above the village, which would mean another traipse for tired limbs, a kindly Italian suggested that we approach one of the auberges and see if they would give permission to camp on their lawn. It was worth a try and a combination of sympathy for the plight of two geriatric, dust-stained walkers and the chance of enhancing their week-end takings, this was promptly agreed. We would pay a reduced charge, but have access to a bathroom and the dining room. The weather was changing, and the first objective was to erect the tent. This process had now become well-rehearsed. It needed to be on this occasion because it became clear that we had an attentive audience in the dining room. Soon other guests joined the throng to witness this strange and apparently compelling spectacle. We completed our task in near record time to a spontaneous round of applause. English, old and living in a tent – fame at last!

A bath was utterly restorative, a chance to wash hair (this did not take long in my case), and soak away the privations of the last few days. Waxing philosophically about the delights of elemental trekking, it is nevertheless supremely enjoyable to come back to civilisation and enjoy the simple pleasures that we all take for granted – a flush toilet that you can sit on, eating from a table, freshly laundered towels and in our case, this evening, splendid Italian cooking. We wandered back to our cramped quarters oblivious to its confinement and slept like logs swaddled in our sleeping bags. Breakfast was to follow, and we stocked up on food rather more than we would normally do: croissants, fresh-baked bread, honey and mountain cheese. It was to see us through what turned out to be an eventful day.

The route from St. Jacques turns south towards Champoluc and once again begins with a gently climbing forested section. We followed the well-defined path with its familiar markings emblazoned on large boulders. Perhaps we had become blasé, perhaps we had been spoiled by the previous day's good fortune, perhaps we were still recovering from a large breakfast and our brains were addled by the need for digestion, but when it came to a basic navigation decision, we made the wrong call. We came across a very large boulder at the confluence of paths liberally adorned with paint splashes and arrows. It was very decorative but not hugely helpful. We consulted the map and checked with a compass. The angle of divergence of the two main paths was narrow. The markings, we surmised, related to local paths as well as the main AV1 causing an element of confusion. The choice was made; the choice was wrong! There is no excuse. We are experienced walkers and have followed the maxim always to trust the map and the compass. More detailed scrutiny would have shown early that we had gone wrong, but by the time we realised the mistake, another decision had to be made.

To retrace steps and rejoin the AV1 just east of Champoluc and climb over the Colle di Pinter to Gressoney St. Jean would mean a major trek. This time we pored over the map much more diligently. To access the Gressoney valley it was possible to follow the trail we had erroneously stumbled on over the Passo del Rothorn to Stafal at the foot of the Monte Rosa. We analysed the route, glanced at the line of the path snaking its way to the col and decided to carry on. What a serendipitous choice this was rescuing us from a tiring long haul. It was an uneventful and scenic route. Descent from the pass was an unadulterated scree slope at the foot of which were a couple of tarns whose waters were ruffled by the mountain breeze. It was an austere spot and reminiscent of parts of the Lakeland fells. Except – the view! The head of the Gressoney valley was framed by a cascade of glaciers issuing from the Monte Rosa and Lyskamm, two alpine giants that we were familiar with from the Swiss side. Anyone who has travelled on the Gornergrat railway from Zermatt on a good day will be familiar with this world of ice and rock, moraine and sky. Linger and assimilate the primeval beauty of such a place! You have only to walk a few hundred metres to escape the hordes of tourists who seem to head inexorably for the cafe at the terminus. The view, however, is of the north-facing side of this sublime high mountain crest stretching from the Monte Rosa to Lyskamm, Castor, Pollux and the Breithorn where the glaciers are more shielded and therefore reach lower levels than on the south-facing side. On the Italian face, as with the Matterhorn, the perspective changes. How often in the Lake District have we found that simply undertaking a walk in reverse subtly alters perceptions of the landscape? With one eye on the unfolding view and one on the path we descended in a meandering fashion through a jumble of skiing paraphernalia to the tiny resort of Stafal where a very crowded camp site was to be home for the next two nights.

When you spend most of your days in splendid isolation in the mountain environment with its utter tranquillity, the trappings of civilisation seem to impinge all the more; the noise of traffic, the bustle, the litter! It was not the most comfortable of camp sites largely due to the noise and close proximity of fellow campers whose daily regime was clearly not our own. We had both had the privilege of spending our professional lives with young people whose energy and joie de vivre is infectious. Vicariously we shared in their high spirits on the camp site, lulled into sleep by their guitars and laughter. They took to us and we took to them like grandparents to rarely visited grand-children. In a curious way they probably regarded us mascots, a vision of their own futures, God help them! The camp site had the saving grace of a cafe and simple shop. The former served the most sumptuous apfelstrudel, the latter sold chunks of local cheese and baguettes. This was nirvana.

It was time once again to consider options. The goal ultimately was to head for Aosta and take a bus into the heart of the Gran Paradiso National Park to Pont or Cogne. If the weather held, this would give us enough time to explore fully, maybe even climb the Gran Paradiso again and still catch the flight from Geneva. If the weather broke we could

Head of Val d'Ayas near Stafal

simply spend more time in the Gressoney valley or in extremis, Aosta. It was good to have this degree of flexibility rather than be committed to a daily schedule. The first decision was to stay at Stafal for another night, gorge on apfelstrudel and explore this wonderful amphitheatre at the head of the Gressoney valley. Fortuitously, another long-distance path the AV3, part of the Grand Tour des Alpes, terminates just to the north of Stafal and we were able to gain height on this good track to obtain a closer view of this spectacular basin. Oh, to be young again and have the prospect of staying in one of the many mountain refuges that are situated at strategic points around these imposing mountains and embrace the camaraderie and the vitality of such places. We were simply grateful to be able to continue to enjoy the immersion in the mountain landscape amongst the flowers, the butterflies and the sonorous cattle, and dream young man's (or woman's) dreams.

Poring over the maps to orientate and locate various features, it was interesting to speculate on the provenance of language and culture in an area that at one point would be quite remote. As in the UK regional accents form variations on Standard English but even Glaswegian and Estuary English are vaguely comprehensible to the outsider. Along this southern fringe of the Alps at the convergence of the frontiers of Italy, France and German speaking Switzerland, the mix is a heady one. Linguists who know more about such things comment that Swiss German is unrecognisable from standard German or 'Hochdeutsch' and whilst Italian and French do have some common points of Latinate reference the admixture with a German dialect is distinctively parochial. In the past, of course, there have been elements of political tension along this border wall, for example in the Alto Adige/South Tirol provinces bordering Austria, but this area is much further to the east. The strategic significance of passes and cols through which we have walked sometimes give rise to striking political incongruities.

Trekking down the GR5 from Lake Geneva to the Mediterranean, a route that follows the spine of the Franco-Italian border, occasional crumbling remains of barracks and fortifications can be seen, testimony to man's folly. People living in adjacent valleys practised the same pastoral economies, lived similar lives, had the same social pre-occupations and cultural norms but a line drawn on a map determined that such groups should be set against each other. Where the GR5 commences its long journey south to the sun at St. Gingolph a river bisects the small town; east of the bridge lies Switzerland, west of

En route to Col Pinter

the bridge lies France. Within a few minutes of crossing this bridge into France a War Memorial is smothered in the names of the French fallen in two World Wars. There is no such testament to human loss on the Swiss side only a few hundred metres away. In 1944, the inhabitants of Montreux, a short sail away across the lake, watched as the retreating German troops razed the French half of the town, the intervention of a Swiss Army officer preventing further conflagration. Such are the more sombre reflections of trekking in the Alps. The mountains will endure.

Today Stafal is a tourist resort, not of the same scale by any means as Cervinia, but linked with the Aosta valley by a regular bus service. As we had unwittingly lost contact with the AV1, we felt it would be appropriate to link up for the last time by travelling down to Gressoney St. Jean. The early-morning service meant that the tent was pitched at the almost deserted municipal camp site south of the town by mid-morning. There was time to re-join the trans-alpine path by climbing steeply out of the valley, but this time with only day-sacs to burden. After a couple of weeks, we flew. Day after day of walking and climbing does eventually sap reserves of energy but there is no doubt that fitness accumulates. It was our final chance to savour the high peaks of the Italian Alps and to view a retrospective of our route. Sometimes, this is the best part; the acknowledgment that at journey's end we had made it without too much evident consequence and there in front of us was the evidence; Monte Cervino still impressively casting its precipitous south face to the glaring sun and nearer to hand a myriad of 3000+ metre peaks leading the eye to the Monte Rosa. It had been quite a traverse fully justifying its publicised attractions.

It was not yet over. We caught the bus down to the Roman town of Aosta, a lovely historic place, and walked up to the camp site that we knew above the town. The bus timetables indicated that we could catch a bus early the following day to Cogne, the main centre at the eastern edge of the Gran Paradiso National Park. The final leg of a somewhat disjointed journey was approaching. Italians have style, a certain brio and flamboyance. It can be seen in their design of fashion items and cars, the latter classic in design and performance but blighted in the past by rapid mechanical deterioration. Alfa Romeo, Maserati and Ferrari are not BMW or Mercedes. Italian bus drivers belong to the same idiosyncratic style. With peaked cap and shades many are surrogate racing drivers. They know the roads intimately and the protocol seems to be that all traffic gives way to the bus, partly because on a mountain road it takes up most of it and partly because the blaring of the horn regularly on blind corners signifies its priority of passage. The driver occasioned the odd raising of eyebrows but took us to the outskirts of Cogne unscathed but shaking. Paradoxically, as we set off walking up the valley towards Valnontey and the camp site a local peasant trundled by at walking pace at the helm of a Piaggio Ape three-wheeled truck, apparently oblivious to the queue of traffic fuming and gesticulating behind him.

The Gran Paradiso National Park contains the highest mountain region solely within Italy. It comprises the eastern section of the Graian Alps that extend from the Tarentaise in France via the Central Graians around Val d'Isere east of which the Col de la Galise leads down from the frontier to Pont on the western side of the National Park. A previous trek at the peak of my powers had been made from Pralognan in the Vanoise National Park in France to Pont. This had culminated in an ascent of the Gran Paradiso. Thirty years later, could this be repeated, or should it even be contemplated? The Italian National Park was the first to be established in Italy in 1922 and occupies the land formerly given over to the Kings of Italy as a hunting ground. It is, therefore, liberally supplied with good trails designed for men on horseback. It guards its present day protected status as a nature reserve diligently and is one of the few declining areas of the Alps where you can be almost certain to see herds of ibex and chamois as well as the ubiquitous marmots and choughs. Wolves and lynx are also present in small numbers. As a walking area, it is magnificent and surprisingly quiet outside the peak summer weeks. For climbers, the best-known peaks are the Gran Paradiso itself at over 4000 metres, Herbetet, La Grivola and Torre del Gran San Pietro. For walkers experienced in British winter conditions in the Lake District or Scotland, the Gran Paradiso itself is perfectly attainable by the standard route from the Vittorio Emanuele Hut.

All Alpine guides grade ascents according to a common standard. F (facile) in most favourable conditions means relatively easy. The route described is normally free of technical considerations that might deter the non-specialist alpine climber. It does not necessarily mean that it is straightforward in the sense that steep snow slopes and crevasses might be encountered, but the latter are usually well marked and flagged so that they can be avoided. However, 4000 metres is high when compared to even the highest peaks in the UK and some degree of acclimatisation is sensible. Rock outcrops tend to be negotiable via ladders or steps. The next grade is PD (peu difficile) which implies that the route can be technically demanding or awkward in places. How awkward depends on one's level of competence and confidence.

Ciarfaron from the ascent of the Gran Paradiso

Summit view from the Gran Paradiso

Sometimes the PD grading adds a + or –. PD– could be undertaken by the more experienced British fell-walker/climber under the right conditions. Any grading above this should be regarded with care and generally avoided by the everyday walker. There are three grades of 'difficile' ranging from 'assez' to 'tres' and the highest level of difficulty ED (extremement difficile) makes one blanch just to consider it. This is a young man's game. Rock climbs for those so inclined also grade from I (easy and moderate) to VI (very severe to hard very severe). Stay away walkers – this is not Jack's Rake! The ascent of Gran Paradiso is a good day's outing well within the compass of most accomplished British hill climbers and the view from it from Mt Blanc to the plains of Lombardy is well worth the effort. At its summit stands a statue of the Virgin Mary bearing witness to the expletives delivered by climbers jostling for a place on the limited and often crowded rocky crest. Most of the ascent after the initial morainic section is on snow and is well marked by the thousands of feet that pound up it in most seasons. Crampons are helpful, and an ice axe offers some protection, but the only real difficulty is the bergschrund just beneath the summit that is usually filled in and does not normally present a hazard.

For now, however, we were content to dawdle to the camp site that stood on an elevated grassy bench above the shallow bowl of Valnontey. Coffee brewing on the stove, we relaxed and looked towards the plunging glacier of Ghiacchio della Tribolazione, its various icy tongues separated by rocky arêtes. The roar of the melt water streams

Vittorio Emanuele Hut, Gran Paradiso National Park

could be heard in thunderous spate. With the rest of the day to explore, we followed the path along the Valnontey to the foot of the polished rock barriers below the main glacial snout. These were glistening with water and forming miniature rainbows as the light refracted on the water droplets. Marmots screeched their warning signals from the depths of the scree and a herd of chamois padded noiselessly across the higher rock slopes. We returned down the valley to an evening meal cooked at a local auberge as our recidivism to the good life continued.

The main refuges of the National Park lie at opposite sides to the Gran Paradiso. The Vittorio Emanuele to the west is a hugely impressive building, a futuristic domed construction in dazzling aluminium as well as a collection of humbler stone buildings. I had been here in the past when packs of mules carried essential supplies, such as crates of beer up from Pont, the muleteer hanging on to the tails of the most convenient beasts of burden. Today, of course, it is supplied by helicopter that clatters in almost daily. It is a very large hut, almost akin to a hotel, is fully staffed and serves meals. At its busiest climbers and walkers sleep in the corridors or wherever space can be found. In an earlier existence, the upper floor of the main building had a single long sleeping mattress. You crossed your fingers and on a good night might find an attractive signorina at your side; more often you would try to sleep by the side of an inveterate snorer. It was stifling below the aluminium roof and climbers usually started their day at intervals after midnight so little sleep could normally be counted upon. The second main refuge is the Vittorio Sella above Valnontey, which again has a warden, staff and full meals service. Both originated as hunting lodges. The Vittorio Sella was to be our next day's destination.

Supplying the Vittorio Emanuele Hut, old-style

The alpine refuge is about two and a half hours from Valnontey and is approached by a motorway of a track that testifies to the frequency and intensity of its use. The trail zigzags above the left bank of the Lozon stream easing to a gentler basin, before rising again in a series of broad meanders to reach the gently sloping glacial plain in which the buildings are situated. It was on one of the crowns of these meanders that we spotted perhaps the largest, fattest marmot we had ever seen. It did not even stir itself into a vertical position to issue a warning cry but flopped on the grass totally undisturbed by our presence. It had chestnut fur turning white and scruffy, an appearance for which we had a certain empathy, but it was obviously used to passing walkers and treated them with utter disdain. The Vittorio Sella is a solid looking group of buildings in an impressive setting. There is a route from here that traverses the rocky slopes over the Colle Lauson before descending sharply from the col at nearly 3300 metres to the trench of the Valsavorenche (and Pont) to the west, but this is a long and

Roman Gate, Aosta

Central Piazza, Aosta

challenging route. The alternative attractions of spaghetti bolognese and a beer proved irresistible. Almost to justify this self-indulgence we spent the afternoon walking to the vantage point above the hut, the Lago del Lauson, where the shimmering glaciers of the Gran Paradiso were reflected in the blue waters of the tiny lake. When we returned the marmot was still there and condescended to give us a grunt as it finally scurried away to its burrow.

Any plans to migrate over to Pont and the Vittorio Emanuele were well and truly scuppered that evening when an almighty thunderstorm broke over the valley, the crashing of thunder magnified by the mountain amphitheatre. With this intervention we had run out of time. On a dull and somewhat forlorn morning, we reluctantly conceded our final amendment to well laid plans to spend our last full day at Aosta. It is a good place to hole up in bad weather, rich in Roman remains and with an architecturally interesting central piazza. It was at a bookshop in this square that a fortnight's linguistic exposure was given its ultimate test. I asked for a particular 1:25000 map to complement the 1:50000 map we had been using and which by now was very bedraggled. Choosing words carefully and endeavouring to adopt the poetic cadence of French I arrogantly thought I had done well. The assistant replied in English spoken in a broad Yorkshire accent. She had apparently spent a couple of years as an au pair in Bradford. Ten out of ten for trying she averred. How did she know we were English I responded, little realising that the English abroad are readily recognisable by their demeanour and deportment. Even in scruffy mountain walking gear our attempts to go native had failed abysmally. There was enough confidence left to order coffee and croissants in more halting Italian before we set off to explore the Roman features of this very Italian alpine town. That evening we played cricket on the camp site armed with a tennis ball we had found with an ice axe for a bat and a rucsac for a wicket. It was minutes before we were joined by a crowd of amused campers wishing to participate in this quaint English pastime.

All that was now left was to dawdle down to the bus station to catch the bus for Orsieres over the St. Bernard Pass, the lower end of which we had walked under aeons ago. Our driver was an endearingly jaunty facsimile of the one that had taken us to Cogne a few days previously. Perhaps he was the same one! With his face hidden behind shades we would never know. Once again, the degree of co-ordination of bus and rail services across the Alps struck us forcibly, reaching its apotheosis in Switzerland. In this case, the bus delivered us via engineering marvels of hairpin bends and tunnels to the waiting train to Martigny at Orsieres with immaculate timing and with a minimum of hassle. We made our flight home from Geneva comfortably.

If each trek provides learning experiences, what had we learned from this adventure? Basically, we had learned the humility to adapt to circumstances and to recognise that we could no longer press on regardless which, with the impetuosity of youth, we might well have done. There are certain things which demand full attention as you get older. 'Do not overdo it' becomes a common mantra; easy to say, but far harder to do. Be aware of your body's responses. If you are tired take a break, if you feel the draining caused by sequential days of high exertion, have a rest day. Go with the flow might be the 'hippy' expression but it makes perfect sense. But, always aim high, not to recapture the ambitions of youth but to make new ones more fitted to venerable health and strength. Do it – *carpe diem!*

Having established the above, the learning curve also suggested that in our mid-60s we should no longer be heaving heavy sacs about and, much though we enjoyed the singular delights of camping, a bed and a roof would henceforth be the norm. We would exchange independent travel for supported long-distance walking where payment is made to take the strain and walking can be done with just a day sac. Sometimes, despite our English reserve and aloofness, it pays to copy our Continental friends and jettison the old adage that there is 'no gain without pain'. How dated and Spartan a philosophy this can be! In future we would enjoy and explore the high mountains using refuges and dortoirs. For the aged this is a much more civilised way to travel. We have earned it and fully deserve it!

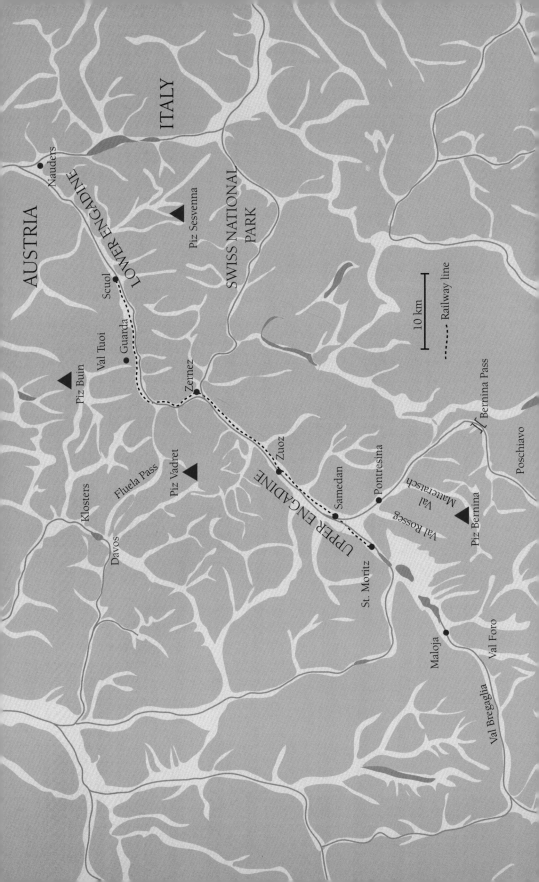

Old Dogs, New Tricks: Snowshoeing

'YOU CAN'T TEACH AN old dog new tricks'. 'You're never too old to learn'. Two diametrically opposed sentiments, both containing glimmers of reality in their underlying premises. Certainly, most specialist and refined skills, such as learning a foreign language or developing high grade musical proficiency are more readily and fluently undertaken whilst the brain is at its most receptive and learning has the confidence and agility of youth. That does not mean to concede that such learning is the prerogative of the young. Indeed, there is much to be said for always striving to learn something each day as we pass through life. There is no feeling quite so rewarding to watch vicariously as young people develop their talents and to have had a small part in their evolution from childhood to maturity. It is the reason why people devote their lives to teaching. It certainly isn't the pay or, despite common misconceptions, the work-load!

After 50 years formally engaged in education, I am a firm believer that old dogs *can* be taught new tricks; it sometimes takes a little longer than in the primacy of youth, but the satisfaction derived is, consequently, that much greater. Retirement is often the catalyst to provide such opportunities if only because motivation to achieve quiescent ambitions re-awakens, unfettered by day-to-day preoccupations. Indeed, there is much clinical evidence to suggest that those that continue to exercise their brains and have ambitions still to achieve live longer and more fulfilling lives. You need luck also to be on your side!

After decades of physical activity, there was one thing missing from the catalogue of outdoor pursuits – *winter sports*. Most winters were reserved for classically English winter sports, most of which seem to involve copious amounts of mud and frozen extremities. Rugby and field hockey, cross-country running and cycling seemed to fill free winter hours until the warmer theatre of the squash court was preferred. Mountain Leadership courses, which developed skills of ice axe and crampon work, winter navigation and survival, opened up more challenging aspects of winter fell walking and climbing that graduated to nervy ice climbing in the gulleys of Great End or longer glacier traverses in the Alps. For the latter activities confidence and balance are necessary and both suffer from the degradations of ageing. However, the mountains in winter can be a paradise and it was time to rectify the omission when the first retirement took effect.

The first attempts to teach the old dog new tricks were frankly embarrassing. Despite a hip that was clearly on the blink, the prospect of downhill skiing seemed one way to realise hidden ambitions. A few months after early retirement in my mid-50s, I was invited to join a school ski-training group on the artificial slopes of Pendle Hill. Surrounded by ex-pupils who sought desperately to conceal their amusement, the old dog went through the motions of learning how to strap on the skis and snow-plough, in short how to stop. This was spectacularly unsuccessful. Launched onto the beginners' slope with exhortations to bring the skis together into a 'V', co-ordination failed, and with a cry of exasperation I careered over the boundary onto the main downhill slope scattering more proficient youngsters. Landing in a very undignified heap and with skis now separated from feet, a tedious climb back up to the button-lift was required. No-one had said a word about how to use the button-lift! At the first attempt to clamber astride the ball as it rattled upwards, I fell off, only to suffer yet more indignity as struggling to my knees, the next ascending ball cracked me on the back of my head. Even I could see the funny side of this, but the youngsters were hysterical at the sight of someone who until so recently had given the outward impressions of being calmly and totally in control reduced to a shambling wreck. A good dose of humility followed.

Disconcertingly, this was a new trick that would take more application and resolve. Perhaps the more expedient course would be to learn to snowshoe instead. A few years previously we had ventured out in the Alps to undertake a winter walk armed with crampons and trekking poles. It was a beautifully crisp and cold day when the only sound was exaggerated breathing and the comforting crunch of crampons biting into the hard-packed snow. We reached our destination at a col, leant back to enjoy the warm winter sunshine and have refreshments before setting off back. In the three hours that it had taken the intensity of the sun had done its work. The hard crust had softened so that it only briefly took our weight before it collapsed, precipitating us frequently into thigh deep soft snow. To struggle on under these conditions was gruelling work. As we rested, sweating and frustrated, an old guy, (i.e. someone our age) padded noiselessly and effortlessly past greeting us with 'bonjour, ca va?' His trick was to use snowshoes.

Like most sports, technology has changed the nature of the game. The old gut-strung squash racket has been replaced by carbon fibre; tennis rackets fire the ball at twice the speed. Would the exquisite skills of a Laver or a Borg match up to the relentless hammer blows of the ball emerging from the racket of a Djokovich, Murray or Nadal? Thankfully we shall never know so that our illusions can remain untainted. Snowshoes have not escaped such advances. Most people have the misconception that these resemble giant old-fashioned tennis rackets that were strapped laboriously to the feet before padding through the Nordic or Canadian forests and tundra. Today lightweight plastics and modern ski-style bindings mean that snowshoes can be fitted to normal walking boots within minutes. They look and feel like plated crampons but unlike the latter they do spread the weight so that under soft snow they bed down, but do not sink. It means that winter mountaineering and trekking does not necessarily depend solely on skis. In fact, as misanthropy seems to be a growing feature of ageing, the prospect of enjoying the peace and serenity of the mountains in winter away from the whoops and yelps of the downhill skiers as they race past was a decided bonus. As we observed the winter scene in the Alps it became clear that while some downhill skiers were decidedly heavy in build, we rarely came across an overweight cross-country skier or snow-shoer. They all seemed to be built like whippets, spare of frame. Many were also older than us. Indeed, some were positively venerable! It was time to teach the old dogs some new tricks.

After some amateurish experimentation, hiring snowshoes as needed, we decided at the beginning of my eighth decade to sign up for a winter snowshoeing course in Chamonix. There were only four of us, which may hint at the eccentricity of such an activity and we were comfortably the oldest. Our instructor was a charming young lady who could not have been more solicitous. The snow that week lay deep and crisp and even, burying some chalets on the higher slopes. It was apparently ideal conditions for learning how to snow-shoe properly if only because there would be soft landings. The first moves were ungainly and precipitous. Fastening on snowshoes one has to remember to walk differently, to raise the knees rather more and above all to walk with the legs splayed apart slightly to avoid tripping up over the base plate. It is something that comes naturally after the first few attempts ended in ribald laughter from our fellow trainees. One learns new words, some of them not expletives. Within hours we were walking over the roofs of buried chalets and contending with downhill manoeuvres designed to avoid descent by uncontrolled 'bum-ski'. It was all huge fun. Now that's an expression not often used in one's working life!

As the week advanced we grew more confident, even 'cocky' as we graduated to longer expeditions that normally culminated in an objective which had a hot chocolate at the end of it. It was hard work, but the camaraderie of young and old learning together made nonsense of the generation gap. Our instructor was a delight and we teased her unmercifully. When she announced that the day's walk would be an undulating one, and as we climbed relentlessly upwards for a couple of hours, we did mention good-humouredly that the semantics of 'undulating' implied that there would be ups – and downs. As we grew more proficient and ventured forth into more remote areas it was necessary to rehearse avalanche drills and rescue techniques using transponders and probes. Having established with serious intent the rudiments, there was some resort to adolescent pranks when transponders were buried for us to find. Under a glorious winter sun in the most majestic of landscapes where better to draw on the child-like enjoyment of learning once again, even involving some puerile mischievousness?

Snowshoeing opened up the more remote areas of the Chamonix valley where even cross-country skiers do not often frequent, mainly because prepared pistes are not provided. The silence and abundance of wild life testified to the absence of other winter sports enthusiasts and our decision to opt for snowshoes rather than skis seemed thoroughly vindicated. This was an area of the Alps that we knew well, but in winter it was completely transformed. Familiar views of the Chamonix Aiguilles, remembered from summer visits, became more austerely impressive. The world of alpine colour was replaced with a dazzling world of glistening white set against a sky of deep azure blue. Our 'training' did not begin in such a romantic idyll. For the first two days it snowed almost continuously as we padded around nervously on our spiky plastic plates around Montroc and Vallorcine, near the Col de Montets, slowly getting the feel of tramping through deep snow without the need to brace the knees against the anticipated shock of breaking through the crust. Snowflakes the size of small plates filtered down through the trees and covered the chalets with a 'Hansel and Gretel' mantle of white. It was every child's dream world of imagining. It was not a threatening malignant blizzard but a soft accumulation that deadened sound. This soft powder snow was ideal for plodding through, providing that someone else was breaking the trail! A perfect winter playground for people old in years but young at heart! We walked over roofs, across small lakes and through forests which had the capacity to dump large clods of snow on the unwary to childish shrieks of delight.

For the skiers, this was to become nirvana as the new deep snowfall covered the pistes in the valley. For us overnight frost, clear skies and ideal conditions for snow-shoe trekking meant that we could begin to hone new-found confidence and skills away from crowded pistes. The new day dawned clear, bright and cold. The Chamonix Aiguilles sparkled in the clear morning light and the pillar atop the Aiguille du Midi seemed closer than its height suggested. As we headed south of the Chamonix valley, we emerged from frozen shade into a blazing winter sun, which was the perfect foil to the dazzling new snow. Even near Chamonix areas off the beaten track are not hard to find. We followed the road to Servoz and meandered upwards towards Plaine Joux, where we disembarked and strapped on our snowshoes

Pristine conditions for snowshoeing, Chamonix valley

to find our way through the forests towards the towering craggy scarp of Fiz. Beyond here lies the Col d'Anterne, fondly remembered from our trek along the GR5 some years previously. Winding through the coniferous trees hung heavily with snow became an exercise in 'dodge the dump' as the slightest nudge of a branch precipitated a fall. As the sun generated heat, great blobs of snow cascaded down through the trees to much hilarity and amusement, particularly if they landed on the head or shoulders of other members of the group.

By the time we emerged from the forest we were already warmed up, but the intensity of the winter sun made a mockery of the freezing

Climbing to Plaine Joux

temperature. Out on the open mountain slopes, which in summer would be pastures awash with flowers, chalets lay silent and abandoned for the season. Many were buried up to their eaves in snow and only the tops of way-marking posts jutted out from beneath the blanket. Across the valley to the south the white dome of Mont Blanc dominated the horizon, a banner of icy cloud billowing from its summit. A posse of choughs emerged from the forest with their excitable clamour on the expectation of tit-bits as snacks were consumed on a snow-free bench. Their insistence was hard to ignore. Like the shriek of marmots, the chattering of choughs is one of the most distinctive sounds of high places in the Alps and their collective antics and aerobatics never fails to raise a smile. They were not the only living things to inhabit this winter wilderness. Tracks of deer and fox dotted the snow and as we turned back a lonely ibex traversed gently across a deep snow gully in front of us. All this and complete silence! It was an excellent introduction to the possibilities of snowshoeing.

Having satisfied our instructor that we were reasonably capable despite our advancing years, the next two outings were to prove more challenging. The first took us to the slopes above Sallanches where we practised steep descent techniques, not always successfully as bodies piled up in the snow to much childish hilarity. Descent, of course, also implies ascent and in the clear invigorating air at nearly 6000 feet, a rhythmic well-graded climb of 2000 feet was thoroughly enjoyable. Like Robinson Crusoe, we looked back at our solitary zig-zag tracks through the white as evidence of passage, raising our heads occasionally to assimilate the pin-sharp view of Mt Blanc and its satellites. In Megeve one summer the Meteo (weather forecast) at the Tourist Office put the freezing level that day at 4500 metres. In other words, only the top thousand feet or so of the highest mountain in the Alps was not melting that afternoon. In the era of climate change this was a sobering thought, but today the glistening iciness did a little to allay anxieties. The air was crisp and clear, the snow deep and crunchy beneath our plastic pads, and with stupendous views and wall-to-wall sunshine plus a natural sense of bonhomie, this was turning into a real eye-opener of a trip.

Ambitions became literally more elevated as we then climbed some 2300 feet to the summit of Mont Truc overlooking the Chalets de Miage above the Contamines valley. This brought back many memories of an expedition in the early-1970s in the first days of the establishment of the

Mont Blanc

Tour du Mont Blanc, when our first day's camp was near these summer chalets. In those days of breeches, Smash dehydrated potatoes and TVP (textured vegetable protein), packet soups, cheese and baguettes, gas stoves and heavy Vango tents, we somehow contrived to lose a stone of weight in a 14-day trip. The cluster of chalets lies below the imposing Aiguille de Bionnassay and the Glacier de Miage. Today the summer

Winter Paradise

Honing descent skills

hamlet lay completely dormant. The scent of glacier cream was so evocative in helping to revive such memories and was certainly necessary as the sun's intense radiation reflected from the crystalline icy surface. We were joined at the summit by a French party who were both surprised and delighted to learn that we were English and in the traditions of mountain hospitality offered us some celebratory refreshment from their

Exchanging notes above Sallanches

flasks. I had expected hot chocolate but instead tasted the most delicious liqueur which was passed round with typical Gallic fervour. The French do have style and we left them to enjoy the view as we made our way less certainly down the snow slopes, our meandering route only partly down to the need to ease the gradient.

Throughout our training the camaraderie of the group, young and old, had been something to savour and it did not seem possible that we were nearing the end of the week which had started with our first hesitant and gawky steps on snowshoes and was ending with a reasonable level of proficiency. Our instructor was obviously impressed and laid on an ambitious last day when we climbed Mont l'Arpille near La Forclaz on the Swiss side of the Chamonix valley. This was another pristine day, culminating in a wonderful panorama of Mont Blanc, the Chamonix Aiguilles and the Rhone valley. To the east lay the distinctive fin of the Grand Combin and the complex of peaks around Arolla including the Weisshorn and Mt. Blanc de Chaillon. Below, nestling on its terrace above the Rhone valley, Verbier was bathed in light and the trench of the Rhone, with Martigny at its head, bisected the mountains to north and south on its linear course towards Visp and Zermatt. What a view! It was sufficient to sit back and take in this winter scene of Europe's highest ground, which prompted reminiscences of summer treks, when joints were nimble and energies unconstrained.

Another memorable day was coming to a close and we descended reluctantly mindful of the fact that this was our final day. We had been fortunate in the cohesiveness of the group, its collective humour, its capacity to adapt and its desire to pull together. Our young instructor, Julia, had been a fount of knowledge and experience and occasionally the butt of some adolescent humour. She had taken our high spirits with commendable tolerance and equanimity. Sometimes it is good to roll back the years and the carapace of respectability we adopt in the pursuit of our professional lives. Letting off steam should not always be the prerogative of the young. With Julia, we had learned a great deal, laughed a lot and suffered little. The dark horse of the group was Russell, who had a wicked sense of humour and uncanny luck at evening games of cards. On this last day, he called in at the French-Swiss border post and its inevitable gift shop to purchase a singing marmot. This was to join his 'tat' exhibition at work. Apparently, prizes were given for the most tasteless contributions to the Office 'tat' display and it would have been entertaining to see his colleagues' reactions to the constant happy refrain of his singing marmot. It would be doubtful whether it would survive more than a day. Ann, the final member of our quartet was researching the trip on behalf of the trekking company and was quietly competent and effective with a genuine empathy and cheerful demeanour. We liked her a lot. In short, we all got on exceptionally well considering that we had been thrown together as strangers only a week ago. The fact that we were of a different generation counted as nought. It had been an extremely enjoyable week and now we were ready to go snowshoeing on our own.

Compared to skis, snowshoes are relatively cheap to buy or rent. We chose to buy on the premise that, having spent hard-earned pension funds on the purchase, we would be much more inclined to recoup the investment by using them at every opportunity. Ironically, the first opportunity came in our native Cumbria which had received a hearty snowfall that brought communication in our sheltered valley to a halt. Traffic moved on the dual carriageway to Barrow at the foot of the Lyth valley but there was no prospect of even reaching the minor road some 100 metres away without a 4 X 4 or a tractor. It was a splendid opportunity to clip on the snowshoes and pad down to the village shop for supplies which occasioned a great deal of interest and much native Cumbrian wit. This was just before Christmas and buffered by the security of having our own water supply, cooking gas and a good stock of candles should the electricity fail, we prepared to sit it out until the County Council got around to clearing and gritting the minor roads. Basic utilities sorted, we then discovered that on Boxing Day we had run out of milk. With no powdered milk or old-fashioned condensed milk to fall back on, we resigned ourselves to tea without milk. After a day, this resolve collapsed, and we enquired whether the garage shop on the road to Newby Bridge was open and had any milk in store. The answer was affirmative. The only problem now was getting there. The garage lies several miles away and we could either make our way there via the now deserted road to Gummers How or strap on the snowshoes and walk over Cartmel Fells to Newby Bridge. On a bright, sunny winter's morning this latter option seemed ideal.

So it was that a couple of hours later we staggered into the garage to ransack the depleted shelves like hungry squirrels raiding their reserves. It was only when we came to pay that a real problem presented itself. My wallet had been left at home; we had no money! I offered to trudge back and return before nightfall leaving my wife there as collateral, but the garage owner took one look at Jennifer and refused point-blank. There seemed nothing for it but to wander back empty-handed. We rifled through pockets to try to find any spare cash but then Jennifer discovered some spare coins in the lid pocket of her rucsac, secreted there just in case she was caught short on one of our local Lakeland walks. We found enough loose change – just – to pay for a container of milk and grumped out into a deteriorating day of glowering shower clouds. The blizzard struck en route back over Gummers How but at least we could now enjoy a real cup of tea, thanks to snowshoes!

Within weeks we were in the Lower Engadine in Switzerland to give our snowshoes a more conventional outing. Switzerland is expensive, but unrivalled in the provision it makes for tourism in general and winter sports in particular. It does things well. Busy skiing resorts would be anathema and we have long had a particular association with the Lower Engadine in south east Switzerland. The Engadine is a particularly interesting part of Switzerland for a number of reasons. It lies within the large canton of Graubunden and extends from the Italian border in the west to the Austrian border in the east. It comprises a

Lower Engadine from Guarda

linear trough drained by the infant river Inn that flows from the lakes occupying the broad glacial basin near St. Moritz. Half way down the valley the gradient steepens, and rock barriers form a natural divide between the upper broad valley near St. Moritz and Pontresina and the lower more deeply incised section that comprises the Lower Engadine. This part of the Engadine is dominated by sharp dolomitic peaks to the south which present a formidable frontier wall with Italy. To the north, contrastingly, rise large smooth-sloped mountains of around 3000 metres. The area also contains Switzerland's National Park to which access can be gained at Zernez.

The whole of the valley is serviced by the efficient Rhaetian railway linking St. Moritz in the upper valley to the railhead at Scuol in the lower valley. As in all Switzerland the timetables are scrupulously kept and link impeccably with local bus services. The railway company enjoys the distinction of World Heritage status for the spectacular engineering that has been deployed in linking the valley with Chur to the north and Poschiavo, via the Bernina, to the south. In the past the main connection between the Engadine and the rest of Switzerland would have been via the Fluella Pass to Davos and Klosters, at nearly 2400 metres, fine in summer but difficult to nigh-on impassable in winter. Characteristically, the Swiss resorted to tunnelling to resolve this frequent hiatus and the 19,000 metre Vereina Tunnel now connects Klosters directly with the Lower Engadine at Sagliains.

The Engadine is also the main bastion of Switzerland's fourth language, Romansch. German, French and Italian all feature within the various regional cantons and it is remarkable how train company officials break seamlessly from one language to another as they cross cantonal boundaries. Romansch is spoken by only one per cent of the population, (about 60,000 people), most of whom are concentrated in the Engadine. To the outsider it has an almost lisping soft susurration that makes it readily distinguishable from the more overtly flamboyant Italian with which it shares some Latinate roots. School children in the valley are taught Romansch as their first language before moving on to German and, thankfully, English. Like many world minority languages, Romansch is under pressure but is seen locally, like Welsh or Gaelic, as reinforcing cultural traditions and distinctiveness. Standard phrases soon become adopted: 'Allegra' is the common greeting, 'Bun di' – good morning and Buna Sera – good evening. Information boards normally are phrased in both Romansch and German and for someone who did Latin 'O' Level, the Romansch seems instinctively the easier to translate.

The 'posh' part of the Engadine is undoubtedly the upper part of the valley centred on St. Moritz where most of the skiing and the Cresta Bobsleigh run are situated. In St. Moritz the fur coats are real, shops do not display prices (how common would that be?) and a cup of coffee is made to last whilst observing the moneyed folk strut by. The Lower Engadine could not be more different. It is quiet and classically alpine with a variety of outdoor options to attract the more discerning. In summer, the upper meadows have to be seen to be believed. The natural displays of alpine flowers are a sensory delight, luxuriant, colourful and sweetly scented. In winter, there is some downhill skiing at Scuol, but this is mainly an area for langlauf (cross-country) skiing, snowshoeing and winter walking. It is sublime.

Unlike the English, the Swiss expect snow in winter and deal effectively with it. On returning from the Engadine one winter an overnight snowfall of over a metre occurred. It would have paralysed English communications and we were fearful of not making our connections home. We need not have worried. The post-bus down to the valley railway halt was on time but the train was nearly three minutes late for which profuse apologies were offered! Within hours of snow falling on the surrounding slopes mechanical equipment clears and levels the snow, slicing double grooves into its now compacted surface for the cross-country skiers to use and preparing the local snowshoeing routes, which are normally marked with directional arrows and pink snowman signs. Inevitably most of the signed routes follow relatively gentle gradients but there is abundant scope to go off-piste as well. With air temperatures below freezing, but in brilliant sunshine and a complete lack of wind, it does not feel like winter and with the scent of sun cream and lip salve assailing the nostrils, it becomes a glorious way to explore winter mountain landscapes.

It would be difficult to cover all the snowshoeing routes that the Engadine offers, but the availability of frequent and reliable public transport enables the full riches of the entire valley to be experienced. Our preferred base is Guarda, two stops down the line from the Vereina Tunnel between Sagliains and Scuol. It is a lovely village, characterised by its sensitively restored mediaeval buildings embellished with decorative plaster work called 'sgraffiti'. There are a couple of hotels and some hostels. The place sits idyllically on a south-facing bench at an altitude of 1600 metres and has an old-fashioned feel to it. The smell of real hay, redolent of summer meadows, drifts over the one cobbled street; ancient troughs and wash-basins are decorated with icicles and the church clock rings out the hours with gentle peals. It forms an excellent base.

A variety of snowshoe routes begin in the village itself of which two are classics; the first is the four-hour walk along a high-level balcony that connects villages such as Bos Charl and Ardez with Scuol lower down the Inn valley. The second is the more challenging proposition of climbing up the spectacular Val Tuoi to the mountain refuge of Chamanna Tuoi, that stands on a ledge below the shark's fin peak of Piz Buin. The former follows the northern side of the valley to Ftan above Scuol and looks out over the dolomitic spires to the south that form the Italian border and across to the ancient redoubt of the castle at Tarasp, that guards the main route up the Inn valley from the Austrian border. The latter is sometimes barred because of avalanche risk but, in most years, it is possible to venture as far as the high alpine chalet of Alp Suot. Our first visit to this area was in summer when we camped at Scuol and the area exerts an almost mesmeric influence. Seeing it in winter offers an entirely different but equally attractive perspective. It was almost as if we were seeing the area for the first time.

To re-acclimatise winter-starved limbs to the rhythms of snowshoeing, the walk along the balcony to Scuol is an excellent first day's outing. Even after the heaviest snowfall, the track carries a little local traffic, including the school bus, so it is always impeccably cleared. It winds across embayments on the slopes with gentle ascents and descents between walls of snow. Black squirrels scamper up the trees, choughs congregate on the chimney pots above wood fires and shy deer sidle among the tree trunks. Tracks in the snow point to the passage of chamois and fox. The eyes are drawn ineluctably to the spectacular serrated mountain wall to the south. The trail passes above Ardez and its elegant church spire, the village huddled astride the valley and the railway, and follows the summer line of the Via Engadina, an ancient trading route. Photographers are spoilt for choice such is the magnificence of the panorama. For the weary, the larger village of Ftan offers both refreshment and a bus service back down to the valley, but most would want to carry on to Scuol, the main town of the lower Engadine, nestling in its constricted valley. It is only on the latter part of the day's walking that skiers are encountered. On numerous occasions we have halted at Ftan to watch the cross-country skiers engage in competition or training. Once an international competition was being held including teams from Russia and the main alpine nations. These are athletes! Seemingly without breaking sweat they glide effortlessly along, up and down slope with rhythmic efficiency. It looks very easy, but such a degree of proficiency must take years to perfect. For the more venerable, cross-country skiing becomes more of a soft shoe shuffle, but they still cover the ground and to a ripe old age!

Scuol is the antithesis to St. Moritz at the opposite end of the Engadine. It has a functional bustle about it without the same level of pretension. As the railhead in the Lower Engadine it has a constant procession of trains arriving from Klosters, Landquart, Chur and Samedan, where the line divides for St. Moritz and Pontresina. As in all parts of Switzerland passengers are met by a phalanx of post buses connecting the station to the many villages that surround it. All are timed to link with train arrivals so that waiting for an onward connection rarely takes more than a few minutes. It begs the question

Tarasp Castle, Lower Engadine

of what might happen if the rail timetable were to be disrupted. We once sat on the station at Geneva waiting for a departure at 1535 only to find that at 1540 the train had not moved. Even Swiss trains apparently do break down sometimes! Consequently, we missed our post bus connection from Sierre to the Val d'Anniviers south of the main Rhone Valley. The railway guard moved swiftly down the train establishing in the appropriate language of each group of passengers if any forward destinations had been compromised. We explained our position and at Sierre station the SBB had laid on a Mercedes taxi as substitute for the post bus, which we passed en route to the destination. It cost them over 80 Swiss francs. Comparisons with British railway companies need not be made!

Scuol does have tourism credentials in a more down-to-earth manner than its more famous counterpart at the other end of the Engadine. In the season, skiers disembark for the only major ski-lift in this part of the valley, clunking their way over the platforms to reach the lift only 100 metres away. Ski-boarders are a different breed, predominantly young and wearing their distinctive 'uniforms'. With boys, it is the jeans casually allowed to fall well below hip height so that they are in danger of dropping off; for girls, the bare midriffs. All carry their multi-decorated boards with casual nonchalance, the epitome of cool! Commercial traffic by-passes above the town en route to the Austrian border only 20 minutes away, leaving the old heart of the place peaceful with its narrow, cobbled streets and sgraffiti-decorated mediaeval buildings. Corners are tight for modern vehicles and many buildings bear the scars of close brushes with trucks and buses. Grand hotels line the main street as a legacy of busier times past, when the hot springs gave it a reputation as a spa town. The thermal baths remain, but faded hotels suggest that in terms of traditional tourism the best days may have been some time ago. Nevertheless, it is a busy place and there is much new residential development. The town is a major bridging point of the River Inn and commanding the bridge on an elevated outcrop stands the main church, very much in the local vernacular style.

Bustle does not really apply to Guarda; its attractions are exactly the reverse. However, it does come to life in at least one week during the winter when the World Economic Forum meets in Davos, not too far away by train. When our visits have coincided with the latter we have had many interesting conversations with the lower rank attendees who seek to escape from the fever of Davos and its high expense. We met a banker from Frankfurt, who many years before Brexit predicted that the EU was suffering from 'mission creep' and would retract into a compatible core of six or so like-minded industrial nations. His predictions have become uncannily true. With hindsight, we should have placed a few pounds on them. However, he also, more importantly, taught us some useful Swiss German phrases, none of which was more useful than the term for 'shandy' (panache), subsequently used on many occasions thereafter at mountain refuges. Regularly we meet up with an American couple who spend the winters here. Both are well versed in international financial matters and their assessment of economic developments has again proved frighteningly accurate. Well before 2008 they suggested that the world financial systems were in crisis and they had converted their clearly substantial reserves into gold and Swiss francs. If they knew something was afoot, why didn't we? It is a different world!

The finest snowshoe trail from Guarda is to climb above the village and enter Val Tuoi at the head of which stands the spectacular shark's fin peak of Piz Buin, of sun cream fame. The trail is normally prepared

Piz Buin and Alp Suot

Val Tuoi in summer

in winter, but for only a certain distance, making snow shoes imperative if progress is to be made. The track climbs steadily to the summer chalet at Alp Suot, the view from which back down the valley is magnificent. In summer the meadows are a blaze of colour. Cattle are kept off the pastures until the flowers have seeded, a policy supported by most of the village communities in the Lower Engadine, maintaining a famous visitor attraction in June and July. In the muted colours of winter, valley streams are subdued and both chamois and ibex inhabit the lower slopes. Golden eagles and buzzards quarter the ground and choughs gather in excitable squadrons. This is the alpine landscape of Heidi. At the head of the valley stands the refuge of Chamanna Tuoi that opens its doors in late June, but which in winter offers a welcome balcony and seats. When brushed clear of snow these allow the snowshoer and skier to rest weary limbs after the 800-metre climb and gaze on the awesome sight of the wonderfully aesthetic peak of Piz Buin. Sunshine at this altitude is a winter balm, a harbinger of warmer days to come. It is remarkably therapeutic.

It was on one such walk that we looked down from the Chamanna Tuoi to see one figure making slow but steady progress towards us across the sea of dazzling white. It turned out to be an 80-year old

Snowshoeing in Val Tuoi

Swiss chap who plodded on to join us looking the acme of health. Strangely for a Swiss, his English was limited but, somehow, we managed to exchange pleasantries. He lived in Zurich but spent as much time as possible in the Engadine either cross-country skiing or snowshoeing. It was on his recommendation that we first travelled up the valley to watch the cross-country skiers in their thousands moving silently like a procession of ants across the frozen lakes west of St. Moritz. His creased bronzed features testified to a lifetime spent in the outdoors and advertised the benefits of maintaining physical activity as long as possible.

It takes about 45 minutes on the regular train service to reach St. Moritz with all its glitz and ostentation. There is an abundance of downhill skiing runs near St. Moritz and it is also, of course, the home of the Cresta Run, but this journey up the valley opens up a range of superb snowshoe routes, two of which are absolute classics, Val Roseg and Morteratsch. Again, it helped that we had been here before in summer, so we had some knowledge of the mountains of the Bernina Alps. In 1981, I had led an expedition over the Fuorcla Surlej into Val Roseg where we camped before intending to move up the next day to the Tschierva Hut prior to attempting to climb Piz Morteratsch at nearly 3800 metres. We were fit, young and acclimatised having already climbed several peaks in the western part of the Bernina complex. The air was heavy by late-afternoon and soon began to crackle with menace. The first rolls of thunder preceded a violent alpine storm. Lightning

Track into Guarda

flashed, droplets of rain hammered down and within an hour these had turned to sleet and then to snow. The size of the snowflakes and the intensity of the blizzard meant that within a couple of hours the tents were buried and some had collapsed. There was nothing to it but to strike camp and drag belongings down to a semi-derelict stone barn some 800 metres down the valley. It had decent walls and some roof

Piz Bernina

although many timbers had collapsed. It was also occupied by about 20 cows that looked mildly bemused by this invasion. As best we could we spread ourselves out on the rough cobbled and earth floor, found a section of roof, through which the snow had not fallen, and hunkered down until the storm abated. Little sleep was had. Cowbells are melodious in their normal setting and redolent of the Alps, but here in the confines of the barn every movement of the cows' heads set up an un-orchestrated peal from which there was no escape. It stopped snowing at about noon the following day by which time over a metre of snow blanketed the valley. Any higher-level climbing was now out of the question. Instead we helped the farmer carry bales of hay to his beleaguered cows in exchange for his inadvertent hospitality. We were imprisoned in the barn for the better part of three days before the track down to Pontresina was cleared and we were able to stagger down the valley to the camp site at Morteratsch in welcome silence.

Val Roseg is approached via a well-maintained track that in winter is used by horse-drawn sledges to carry tourists up to the Hotel Roseg, a hotel restaurant with one of the finest views in the Alps. The head of

Upper Roseg valley

Piz Bernina and the Tschierva Glacier

the valley is an amphitheatre of ice and snow dominated by the shapely peaks of the Bernina Alps, including Switzerland's most southerly 4000-metre giant, the Piz Bernina. The hardened track can be walked but snowshoes and skis are separately provided for in trails that wind through the forests before the valley opens out into a broad, flat glacial basin. It takes nearly two hours to walk up to this point from the station in Pontresina, but throughout the walk the wild life continually captures interest. Snow muffles sound and in winter herds of chamois and ibex descend from the more exposed slopes towards the more accessible lower pastures and are often oblivious to human presence. Black squirrels scamper and the bird life is astonishing – Alpine jays, woodpeckers, crested, marsh and willow tits, finches and pheasants all congregate near the many feeders replenished daily. The woods are alive.

It is a justifiably popular walk, as is the Hotel Roseg as a refreshment stop, and most people avail themselves of tasty but pricey food and drink and then return via the same route. For cross-country skiers and snowshoers, however, the best is yet to come. It is about four kilometres to the beginning of the jumbled moraines of the Tschierva Glacier, where the going in winter becomes tough, but this is a splendid extension. The curved lateral moraines of the glacier betray its existence, despite the fact that the whole of this mighty river of ice is blanketed in snow. Small Arolla pines, which are normally the first trees to colonise this glacial desert of rubble, stand out from the snow like hundreds of Christmas trees decorated with icy baubles. Soaring into the brilliant blue of an alpine sky are the main Bernina peaks of Piz Bernina, Piz Roseg and Piz Scerscen, all at or slightly below 4000 metres. It is jaw-droppingly beautiful and spectacular. We do not often in this world just take the time to stop and stare, to assimilate the natural beauties all around us. The head of Val Roseg is one such place where this becomes almost obligatory, when scenes and sights become seared on the memory for a lifetime. At the back of one's mind, however, is the fact that the return journey is likely to take the better part of three and a half hours but, despite a train to catch, this is not a journey to hurry.

Pontresina is also the starting point for the second snowshoe classic – the Morteratsch valley. One of the engineering marvels of the Rhaetian Railway is the Bernina railway line that climbs to nearly 2300 metres near Alp Grum before descending in a maze of tunnels

Morteratsch valley

Upper Morteratsch valley

and hairpins to the warmer plain at Poschiavo and Tirano in Italy. It is a miracle that this line is kept open punctiliously all year through the heaviest of snowfalls, and it has become a well-subscribed tourist destination on the Glacier Express route. In winter, it is a busy line as far as Diavolezza where the skiers disembark to take the gondola up to nearly 3000 metres, before a variety of runs whisks them back down to the Bernina valley. For walkers, or those with snowshoes, the stopping place is just up the line from Pontresina at Morteratsch, where a station and restaurant were built in the late-nineteenth century to cater for visitors who had taken the train to gaze at the glacier snout within a couple of hundred metres of the railway. The Morteratsch Glacier is the largest in the Bernina Alps and its melt waters drain into the Inn and thence to the Danube and the Black Sea. In the last 130 years the ice front has receded by two kilometres. The rate of melting has increased in the last 50 years and the speed of recession has accelerated to the order of 30 metres per year. This is a chastening testimony to the impact of global warming and the location of the ice front is marked by notice boards at regular intervals up the valley to the present snout. Significantly, the intervals between the posts measuring the scale of retreat have shortened over time.

Winter sunshine, Morteratsch valley

With its ease of access and the stunning views that await walkers, the Morteratsch valley is undeniably popular and whilst most keep to the main track there are abundant off-piste options. Skiers disembarking at Diavolezza are able to ski down the glacier to the Morteratsch valley to complete a spectacular loop back to the railway. Cross country skiers have various prepared pistes to choose from which separate them from walkers, and for those with snowshoes, it is possible to explore the full environs of the glacial outwash plain as well as returning to Pontresina by snow shoe track through the forest.

The head of the valley with its collecting basins and its glistening, shapely, icy peaks must be one of the finest panoramas in the Alps. In winter, the intensity of the low-angled sun requires good quality sun glasses to avoid squinting, but the light effects are quite literally dazzling. From Piz Bernina to the west to Piz Palu in the east, this amphitheatre could quite easily justify the description of 'the throne room of the Gods'. Piz Palu, with its distinctive triple snow-clad ridges, is aesthetically one of the finest peaks in the Alps and resembles Blencathra in its architecture, give or take a few hundred million years. For those who wish to obtain a bird's eye view of the

Lac Cavloc

Morteratsch Glacier and its mountain fastness, it is a great end to a day's snowshoeing to take the railway up to Diavolezza and take a brief walk on this high snowy crest. You will share the cable car with hundreds of skiers on the way up but be in splendid isolation on the return journey. The view from this 3000-metre bench fully justifies the additional expense.

Val Forno

Each time we travel to the Engadine it is possible to find new snowshoe routes. Beyond St. Moritz the frozen lakes are mainly the province of legions of cross-country skiers, but there are numerous ways of avoiding the crowds by taking the hourly bus to Maloja where the road drops down steeply to the Italian-speaking Val Bregaglia. From Maloja, winter paths, often virgin, allow snowshoers to walk back to Sils St. Maria or Silvaplana on undulating trails along the lake margins to the east. Our favourite, however, is to head due south to Lej Cavloc and then to traverse round to Val Forno. This is a relatively quiet valley normally free of other winter walkers or skiers and its charms are abundant. The closed mountain restaurant on the shores of the lake is a good place to rest and bask in the surroundings and to feed the hordes of marsh/willow tits that descend magically from the adjacent conifers. The route round to Val Forno, like so many of the routes described in the Engadine, is transformed in summer by the sheer profusion of alpine flowers. Even in winter when the colours are more limited, the picturesque blue-shaded ice-bound waterfalls catch

Pre St. Peder above Vna

the eye and herds of ibex look down from the rocky ramparts above. Val Foro itself is a narrow, constricted avalanche-prone valley, but again a discreetly placed seat allows for rest and the assimilation of some pristine mountain views.

We have met few people on this route but many of those have proved to be discerning and interesting people. A venerable lady teaching her middle-aged daughter to cross-country ski met us once on a bend in the track and bemoaned the lack of vim in her trainee. The mother must have been in her late-70s at least and left us with a whoop of delight on a straight downhill section, leaving her daughter to negotiate the section as best she could. An Italian man was even older. He spoke perfect English and spent some time in conversation with us bemoaning his country's travails at the hands of Silvia Berlusconi. We could have countered with our own assessment of the British political scene but left him to carry on in his typically animated Italian fashion. He revealed that he was 83 but did not look 60. Suddenly his diatribe ended, and he just threw back his arms and commented that the main reason he spent time in the mountains was to restore sanity and perspective. He had such an obvious love of life and a palpable inner contentment that it did us good just to give him time to explain his love of the outdoors. Well into our 70s, he regarded us as striplings. He strapped his skis back on to return to Maloja, wished us 'buona fortuna' and with a final 'ciao', sped off back to the valley like a demented leprechaun in a haze of glittering ice crystals. Moral to this story? – you're never too old, or to return to the theme of this book, CARPE DIEM!

Since learning to snowshoe another facet of mountain exploration has been revealed. Joints creak, muscles ache but nothing that a hot bath and, in extremis, a couple of pain killers cannot resolve. The rewards are enormous. To sit down at a refuge listening to a babble of languages at the end of the day sipping a hot chocolate and consuming apfelstrudel or tarte myrtille and to look out on exquisite mountain landscapes with the sun on your face is heavenly. It is one of life's inestimable pleasures.

Regrettably, winters in Cumbria do not afford the same opportunities. Winters here, like so many other things in life 'ain't what they used to be'. We have, however, found an alternative use for snow shoes in the winter. They make excellent lawn aerators when the rains turn the grass into a swamp!

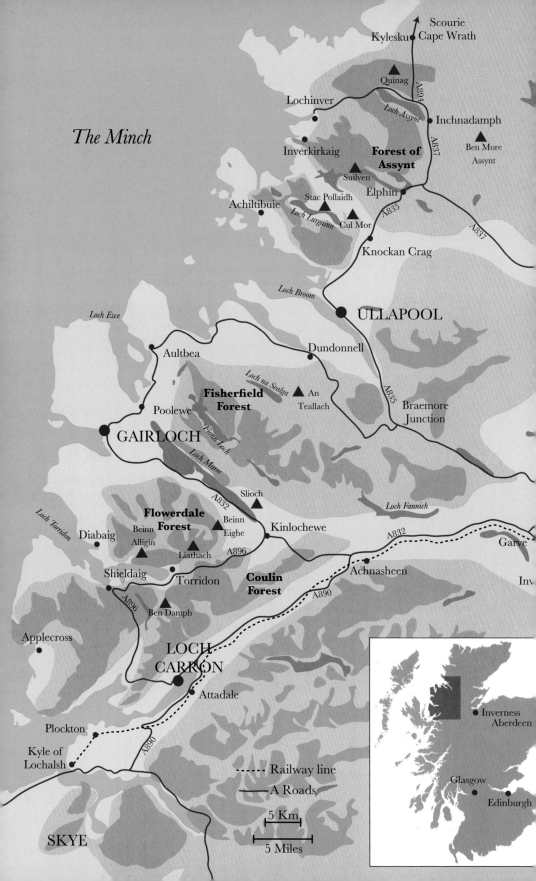

Forays in the Forests

THE OBSERVANT READER WILL have noticed that there is a notable
omission from these accounts: no mention has been made of the
UK! All the accounts to date have focused on treks undertaken in the
author's seventh and eighth decades when the mind is willing, but the
flesh becomes inexorably weaker. What about the ninth decade? There
is an increasingly reluctant acceptance that extravagant treks to exotic
places may now be beyond us, but we have seized the day so far, despite
a growing litany of medical issues. Much of our lifetime's experience of
outdoor activity has inevitably been undertaken in the UK which offers
so much variety to the adventurous. It seems appropriate, therefore, to
finish on a British note.

The question often asked as part of the lecture circuit I have given
over many years is 'What has been your favourite trek?' It is, of course,
an impossible question to answer. The most dramatic was probably
the traverse of the Karakorum from Skardu in Northern Pakistan to
Hunza, for the sheer scale and ambition of the undertaking (it does

not feature in this book because it was done alone as part of a small party of four when my wife was still working). The most enjoyable was probably Spitzbergen, but the competition in this category is stiff. The most colourful could include any variety of summer alpine treks; the most emotional was probably the trek to Gokyo Lakes in Nepal and the first sight of Everest. The categories could go on!

If asked to nominate our favourite part of the world, loyalty suggests that, as adopted Cumbrians, the answer should be the Lake District, but if pressed harder the answer becomes a contest between Norway, Scotland and New Zealand. The more perceptive will have gleaned a common thread in this choice. All are characterised by mountainous areas in close proximity to the sea. It is a compelling juxtaposition. Is there anywhere in the world to match the peerless scenery of the Lofoten Islands in Arctic Norway, where granite obelisks rise like dragons' teeth from the turbulent North Atlantic? The devotee of Scotland would respond by nominating the Cuillin of Skye. Is there anywhere in the world with the sheer sense of space and the kaleido-scopic variety of landscapes as New Zealand? Well, again the response might well be the north of Scotland. It is, of course a very subjective matter.

All three have emotional connections, which perhaps swings the balance. My maternal great grandfather was a non-English speaking Gael who came down from Scotland to work on the Nottinghamshire coalfields. My father was a Royal Marine who was assigned to the Royal New Zealand Navy in the early days of its inception. Part of his service career was spent at Scapa Flow in Orkney on HMS Repulse and the Iron Duke. It was from here that a flotilla of destroyers mounted the raid on Narvik in 1940 to prevent German access to Swedish iron ore. To walk the coast of the Lofotens islands or northern Norway is to flick back through the pages of naval history. To see the lonely fjords where the Tirpitz holed up before its eventual destruction by the RAF in a fjord near Tromso, brings history to life and with it a degree of empathy for those 'in peril on the sea'. To walk the quay at Bergen and see a discreet and easily missed memorial to the 'Shetlanders', who maintained vital links with Norway during these troubled times is to begin to understand the close links that bind Scotland to Norway. Looking down Loch Ewe in north west Scotland where the Arctic convoys and their escorts used to gather prior to setting out on their hazardous journey to Murmansk or Archangel inevitably engenders a degree of melancholy when imagining young sailors looking back on the wonderfully scenic mountain landscape of Wester Ross and Sutherland. For too many this might have been their last glimpse of land in this life.

Therefore, if we are to choose somewhere in the UK to begin our account as we enter the ninth decade, it has to be where so much began – Scotland! To our minds there is little doubt that, given the right weather, there is no finer place on earth than the North West Highlands. To those that contend that there is no such thing as bad weather just bad gear, I would refer them to north west Scotland. The Eskimos are reputed to have 39 variations on the word 'snow'. There must be at least as many terms to describe the qualities of mist and rain. Many years ago, I taught a student whose father was a GP and who had grown up on Lewis. For most of his early years he spoke mainly Gaelic. Having examined Ordnance Survey maps of the Highlands in some detail, the Gaelic language fascinated me. To gain deeper insights, I asked him to teach me some Gaelic and to that end purchased a 'Teach Yourself Gaelic' book. It is not the easiest of languages to pick up, but it is interesting to learn basic vocabulary to begin to understand some of the place names that feature on Scottish maps. The 'Teach Yourself Gaelic' first exercise is to learn basic Gaelic vocabulary: nouns include iolair (eagle); achadh (field); taigh (house); uisge (water); beinn (mountain); monadh (moor); cnoc (hill); obhair (work). The adjectives are even more illuminating: Lesson one – fuar (cold); fliuch (wet); sgith (tired); trang (busy). It paints a revealing picture! There is a poignancy about Gaelic, its cadences vibrant with a poetry that stirs the soul. Gaelic music and culture is permeated with a sense of melancholy and loss. One has only to look at this austere and unforgiving landscape, the abandoned crofts and silent shielings to recognise how marginal life could be. It was a situation exacerbated by the infamous Highland Clearances during which crofting families were forcibly evicted from their land. Many emigrated to Canada, Australia or New Zealand leaving their homeland to seek a better life abroad. It was a shameful episode. Only recently has the issue of absentee landlords been addressed and many crofting communities, as in Assynt or the island of Eigg, have begun the process of restoring the land to its indigenous people.

As well as the weather, there are the midges! Lake District midges can be a nuisance, Scottish Highland midges are voracious. There is no real answer to them although Highland outdoor workers swear by Avon Skin So Soft. We stumbled on this secret as were being eaten alive in Torridon. Highland road maintenance workers seemed oblivious to midge predation whilst we were lathered in jungle strength insecticide. They had their sleeves rolled up and bare flesh exposed; we had as much skin covered as a humid sticky summer's day would allow. We asked if they were not bothered by the swarms of midges gathering above them with evil intent. From their packs, they took out the Skin So Soft and plastered it all over their muscular arms and rugged faces. It does not kill them they suspected, but midges stuck to it as in a Venus flytrap and therefore could not exact their bite. The real answer to avoid midges is to go to Scotland early (May/June) or in autumn (late September/October) when the frosts wreak havoc on the 'wee beasties'. Alternatively pray for wind or walk quickly!

Despite all these apparent deterrents, north west Scotland has a magnetic pull. In Torridon, aesthetically sculptured plum-coloured mountains, capped by white quartzite, rise sharply above the sea, resting on their beds of ancient gneiss rocks like so many Palaeolithic beasts. To mountain lovers, Liathach or An Teallach are universal objectives, challenging or frightening according to disposition. In Sutherland, the mountains are lower but equally dramatic. The first sight of Suilven from either the landward or the seaward side, or of the irascible porcupine-spine of Stac Pollaidh, is unforgettable. My first visit to Torridon from North Lancashire before the days of motorways took 14 hours; today with a following wind it takes only about six hours from South Cumbria. Despite this improvement in access the North West Highlands still exude an air of isolation and detachment.

It is perhaps relevant at this stage to explain the derivation of 'Forest'. The term conjures images of commercial plantations, probably of uniform conifers, but in the context of the Highlands, 'Forest' normally means a large area managed for deer stalking and shooting. This hunting connotation is shared with many upland areas in Britain which are paradoxically often treeless. In Cumbria, Stainmore Forest and Milburn Forest near Cross Fell, Sleddale Forest and Fawcett Forest spring to mind, whilst just to the south in North Lancashire is the Forest of Bowland. In north west Scotland, the deer estates or Forests are often in prime locations for the outdoor enthusiast and give access via superb stalker's paths to some of its finest mountain scenery. A word of caution is necessary. The Forests are actively managed for deer and whilst landowners are normally quite amenable to walkers using such paths a certain amount of give and take is required, particularly during the main hunting season, which is usually between July and October. There have been tensions in the past but all that is needed is for walkers to note and abide by requests to stay away from designated areas between certain dates. As in all walks of life it only takes one or two incidents to poison relationships, so that the majority of sensible and considerate trekkers and climbers are tarnished with the same brush. 'Take only photographs; leave only footprints' correctly emphasises the Country Code.

The Forests of Assynt: Inchnadamph, Inverpolly and Drumrunie

Assynt is technically a parish in the south east part of Sutherland, for purposes of immediate identification located between Ullapool in the south, Kylescu in the north and Lochinver to the west. It contains some of the most stunning landscapes in the world, shapely mountains, glittering lochs and magnificent coastal scenery. Above all, despite the link of the main A835 road, it still conveys an atmosphere of

Ullapool

Assynt landscape from Drumrunie

remoteness and isolation. Most explorations begin with a reconnoitre up the A835 and on our last visit in late April the weather could not have been more perfect, sharp and clear with a penetrating easterly wind. Heading north from Ullapool, by far the largest settlement in Assynt, the eyes tend to veer to the west to assimilate the emerging panorama of the Assynt mountains rising from their glacially eroded hummocky platform studded with lochans, like so many fossilised primeval monoliths. From Ben More Coigach to the south via Cul Beag, Stac Pollaidh and Cul Mor to Canisp, Suilven and Quinag to the north, these Torridonian towers comprise one of the most distinctive and spectacular areas in Britain.

Against this background, it is all too easy to miss the small parking area about 10 miles north of Ullapool that gives access to Knockan Crag. This place is of huge geological significance and had a monumental effect on the understanding of plate tectonics. It was analysed over a number of years by two 'amateur' geologists, Peach and Horne, who could not understand how the ancient Lewisian gneisses had come to overlay the younger Cambrian rocks of Moine Schists, Durness limestone and Torridonian sandstone without envisaging some lateral movements of the earth's crust. Peach and Horne were carrying on in a long tradition of geological research that began in Scotland through James Hutton, who in the mid-eighteenth century walked the Scottish landscape armed with a lively mind and an inexhaustible sense of enquiry. He saw that even in the oldest rocks veins of quartz had been injected by forces he could scarcely imagine. Strata was folded and tilted, fossils of sea shells could be found on top of some of the peaks and the mountains were quite evidently being worn down by the forces of erosion. The apparent permanence of the landscape we see now, he surmised, was merely an illusion, our understanding limited by our own puny life spans. Hutton's work was carried on by other scientists, such as Humphrey Davy, in an age when the sense of scientific enquiry reached a new intensity, challenging not only accepted orthodoxies, but also established religious views. Another Scottish geologist, Charles Lyell, carried on this work in the early-nineteenth century and in three volumes of 'The Principles of Geology', he laid out with both clarity and elegance the argument that the key to understanding the earth's past is to analyse the processes currently at work in shaping the landscape. In doing so, he developed the notion of the 'abyss of time'. Soon afterwards, the young Charles Darwin marshalled a similar catalogue of facts and reasoning to explain some of the geological features observed during his visit to South America on HMS Beagle. How could sedimentary deposits be uplifted thousands of feet to form the Andes unless there had been enormous forces at work over a vast period of time?

Peach and Horne's examination of the Knockan unconformity was very much in vogue with developing geological insights which were beginning to cast doubt on certain established understandings. It had been argued that if sediments and rocks are laid down sequentially, the oldest at the bottom and the youngest at the top, it followed that any exposure should conform to this principle. But here at Knockan the reverse was the case; older rocks sat on top of younger. This acknowledgement revolutionised the embryonic geological sciences and advanced our understanding of the earth on which we live as a dynamic and mobile construct. The mechanisms of earth movement were not fully understood until the mid-twentieth century but the age of plate tectonics had arrived. It is certainly an interesting place to examine and well-documented explanatory notices accord the site its historical and scientific significance. Climbing up to the actual site of the Moine Thrust at Knockan, to place hands on this world-famous plane and gaze across at one of the oldest landscapes in the world is to reflect on the ephemeral nature of human existence. How does one grasp the concept of billions of years against the measure of human evolution of only several million? In geology, the scale of time is as difficult for the human mind to assimilate as the concept of distance and time in astronomy. Against the immensity of both we are but mere transient specks of dust.

In real time and space, it is useful to reconnect with the present by walking amidst this ancient landscape. Having completed our geological tour, we set off to climb nearby Cul Mor, initially along a well-made stalker's path, branching off after a couple of miles to climb steeply upwards guided by well-sited cairns to a pronounced bench at the foot of the steep quartzite pyramid that constitutes the last few hundred feet of the mountain. By now, however, we were being subjected to a very uncomfortable battering by a gale-force, blustery easterly wind and as the hazy conditions became even more limiting, we decided to cut our losses and finish at the foot of the final scree slope to obtain a full view of the Suilven ridge and the ruffled waters of the lochans as far as the coast at Lochinver. Years ago, we would have pressed on regardless but at our age we have nothing left to prove and so we retreated with heads bowed into the howling wind back to Knockan Crag.

We headed now for a cup of tea and a cake in the convenient tea-room at Elphin, run in those days by an émigré couple from Yorkshire. In common with many parts of the North West Highlands, English people have settled here for a whole variety of personal reasons. On such a gorgeous late April day, it was chastening to note that we were the only customers despite the ravishing view of the perfect pyramid of Meall Meadhonach, the eastern summit of the Suilven ridge. The Yorkshire couple, like so many others had been so entranced by this place that they had made the decision to uproot and develop an old crofting complex into a visitor attraction, but they conceded that the winters were hard and trade even in summer insufficiently consistent to guarantee a sustainable regular income. For this reason, they were also engaged in part-time stock-rearing. All around their reinstated buildings lay the shells of abandoned crofts and barns, testimony to the fact that even the most ravishing views in the world do not necessarily generate income. It was sad but no real surprise to note that some years later the tea rooms at Elphin were for sale. It had clearly been an unequal struggle. One felt for them.

Suitably refreshed, we turned back to the single-track road to Achiltibuie and the Summer Isles and passed gently along the shores of Loch Lurgainn, leaving the car to the east of the main Stac Pollaidh car park near Linneraineach. This gave us immediate access to another stalker's path that wound its way up the hillside through a belt of gorse and Scots pines to emerge at the col at Lochan Fhionnlaidh. The unmistakeable stump of Stac Pollaidh rose to the west above the drab, winter-bleached moorland. Stac Pollaidh may be the miniature sibling of the Assynt hills, but it exhibits all the attractive features of its more imposing neighbours; a base layer of Lewisian gneiss, grey and dour; a pavement of wild moorland studded with lochans nestling in the glacially scoured hollows of the impervious gneiss and finally a spiky, pinnacled summit ridge composed of Torridon sandstone. Unlike its neighbours, Cul Mor and Quinag which have a white quartzite cap that protects the sandstone from erosion, Stac Pollaidh has no equivalent protection so that the forces of nature have produced a series of crumbling towers. In anthropomorphic terms, it resembles an adolescent's Mohican haircut and exudes a cheeky impudence. On this occasion as time was pressing, we resisted the temptation to climb up to the summit ridge and traverse the crags by means of a well-made footpath that skirts the pinnacles from east to west.

We continued down towards the Doirie Dhubh by the loch of the

Loch Lurgainn and Stac Pollaidh

same name past groves of birch and holly woodland. In this sheltered embayment primroses, violets, wood anemones and celandines made a welcome splash of colour. The vivid greens of the emerging leaves of the gnarled birches provided a startling contrast to the severity and austerity of the glacially scoured landscape. It was an enchanting place and easy to imagine that this could well be the lair of wild cats and pine martens. Above the ancient woodland rose the towering Torridonian buttresses of Cul Beag, aprons of weathered rock spilling down to Loch an Coire Dubh, which was itself connected by a narrow strait to the highly indented and complex geography of the much larger Loch Sionasgaig. The stalker's path ended here so we took in the ambience of this remote, attractive but melancholic spot before heading back the way we had come.

The all-pervading silence of the last couple of hours was broken by the incongruous wailing of the siren of an emergency vehicle, which turned out to be a fire engine racing down the single-track road to the main A835 road. Its destination soon became obvious. All afternoon we had noticed the plumes of smoke rising over the hills to the south and being whisked along in the strong wind towards Loch Broom. As we drove back to Ullapool it appeared that the hillsides inland from Strath Canaird were ablaze. In an area noted for its heavy rainfall, the recent spell of drying easterly winds had made the desiccated ling tinder-dry and a controlled burn had clearly got out of hand in the blustery, capricious, gale-force conditions.

The following day as we headed north again, the damage wrought by the moorland fires was plain to see. The hillsides were still smoking, and the acrid smell of soot pervaded the morning air. However, it was another gorgeous day to continue geological explorations, the immediate destination being the small car park at Inchnadamph to explore the valley of Glen Dubh. This has a major outcrop of Durness Limestone, one of the oldest limestones in the world, with ancient caves occupied by Palaeolithic man. For the first mile or so we followed a dusty, gravelly track past Inchnadamph Lodge to the renovated shepherd's cottage at Glenbain. The view ahead was of the shattered quartzite slopes of Conival and Ben More Asssynt, the highest peak in Sutherland, but we were heading up the River Trailligill (Troll's Ghyll in Norse) that tumbled down over, and often under, the exposed beds of Durness Limestone. A small forestry plantation sang in the wind, which was now becoming quite ferocious, but in the lee of this shelter, with heads down in the blustery gale, we came across an adult adder on the track. It was distinctively marked, fully two feet in length and not at all intimidated by our presence. In fact, it raised its head, 'sniffed' the air and adopted a vaguely menacing posture. We detoured sharply around it but spent many minutes admiring its characteristic diamond-shaped markings before watching it writhe sinuously away down the dusty track.

A confluence of streams saw us cross a small wooden footbridge and make our way steadily uphill to a distinctive line of crags where we hoped to find the caves marked on the map. The first of these was very spectacular, an angled defile through which the River Tralligill thundered boisterously from a spring. Higher up still we came across a second broader cave beneath an arch in the limestone, which offered immediate protection from the scouring wind. Remains of bones from lynx, bear and elk in this cave have been carbon-dated from 7000 BC and it was not difficult to imagine small family groups of Palaeolithic hunters capitalising on these natural well-protected shelters. Once again, we were treading in the footsteps of history both on a geological and a human timescale.

The savagery of the wind precluded further exploration higher up the valley but retreating down we did pause to examine the point at which the tormented waters of the river quietened, its bubbling cascades disappearing in less than 20 metres as the river seeped away into the gravels. However, we were not yet finished with the Durness Limestones. With curiosities aroused, we decided to explore the parallel valley to the south, the Allt nan Uamh, where caves have again yielded evidence of man's early settlement on the retreat of the ice sheets some 7000–9000 years ago. This was serendipitous and engaged us in an entirely different valley walk. Initially the Allt nam Uamh resounded to the gushing, cascading waters of the river but after a kilometre, and within the space of a few metres, the sound was replaced only by the sighing of the wind as the waters disappeared completely. Above the impressive spring feeding the river, the river bed became a jumble of boulders and the eyes were led to a dominant projecting crag that constricted the width of the upper valley. The path crossed the dry valley and snaked upwards towards this limestone buttress. The caves at its foot were reached by a stony, stepped path and were well worth the effort involved in reaching them. Excavations have revealed the existence of bones from bear, lynx and elk as well as human artefacts.

Allt nan Uaimh valley

It was fascinating to rummage around in them. All sorts of questions assailed the mind. Hunting such animals must have taken a degree of social organisation and the employment of language /communication. Would this valley have been forested 7000 years ago; would the climate have been as challenging; was there contact with other Palaeolithic peoples; where did they come from? Would they look out at the same

Caves in Durness limestone

landscape that we were observing with any sense of aesthetics or with more basic practicality? One suspects the latter.

The two distinctive and dominant peaks of the northern part of Assynt are Quinag and Suilven. It requires good weather over a couple of days to do them justice. The starting point again was Inchnadamph where the road to Lochinver follows the shores of Loch Assynt. On another blustery morning, white-crested waves ruffled its blue waters. The gaunt ruins of Ardvreck Castle, at the head of the loch stand as stark testimony to the troubled history of this area. Troubles of various kinds have persisted to the present day, albeit of a less violent nature. We parked just beyond Assynt Lodge to explore a newly established trail constructed by the Assynt Foundation that gives public access to the formerly private land of shooting moor and fishing lochans. It was a very well-made footpath, traversing a series of reed-fringed lochans set in the midst of wild ling-covered moorland with clumps of naturally regenerating birch and Scots pine. This area, like so many others, has a fascinating social history. For many years the land was held by large landowners, many of whom became effectively absentee landlords. The plight of the crofter in this quasi-feudal relationship was often overlooked. Little security of tenure and virtually no influence

High-tech toilet, Assynt

on the development of the land on which they had lived and worked for generations engendered an understandable sense of grievance and bitterness, particularly where the landlord-crofter relationship was characterised by neglect and a lack of empathy, understanding and investment. In recent years, legislative changes have allowed associations of crofters such as the Assynt Foundation to purchase their land back when estates come up for sale and to manage it for the benefit of all. This happened in June 2005, when the Foundation, on behalf of the community of Assynt, bought over 44,000 acres of the Glen Canisp and Drumrunie Forest under the provisions of the 2003 Scottish Land Reform Act. This has led to the development of local hydro-electric schemes, the growth of local industries and advances in farming, forestry and fishing that formerly may have been vetoed. Tourism is clearly a main focus of this economic regeneration and the Culag Trail is part of this initiative.

The first section of the path led to a small jetty and a wind-powered, solar panelled public convenience, which was certainly an interesting novelty. Quite what the wind was powering remained something of a mystery! A few hundred metres further on is a second public

Quinag

convenience, a turf-roofed, well-constructed shelter and a convenient picnic table where we stopped for refreshments. Clearly, environmental considerations weigh heavily in such recent developments. Occasional viewpoints look out across a landscape of glittering pools and rocky, dun-coloured ling moorland towards the ramparts of the long ridge of Quinag to the north. In the other direction, the steep bulbous face of Castel Liath at the northern end of Suilven loomed out of the wind-borne haze. It is unquestionably a very scenic walk and on our visit its attractions were enhanced by the sound of the first cuckoo of spring.

It was mid-afternoon by the time we reached Lochinver and rather than rush our planned walk up to the foot of Suilven, we opted instead to drive round the rocky peninsular road to Kylesku via Drumbeg. This is a narrow and incredibly beautiful scenic route crossing headlands and skirting vivid blue bays interspersed with inland sections of lonely lochans and wooded birch/alder filled ravines and gulleys. The road clings to the coast but sometimes opens out in to broader sandy bays such as the one at Knockancross. The Stoer peninsula looked bleak, although from past experience its headland and bird sanctuaries are well worth visiting. We carried on past the lineated crofting settlements of Drumbeg and Nedd to finally emerge on the main A894 road near Kylescu. Even for someone who relishes the serenity of wild and lonely places it must take a particularly resilient and adaptable character to live in such a remote area throughout the year. Late in life we have been tempted to join such communities but then the inevitable practical questions begin to nag away – how far to the nearest doctor/dentist? Where is the local pharmacy? Where is the nearest hospital? (Ragmore in Inverness is a good two hours away!). These are old folks' questions! If these thoughts pass through your mind you have already made a decision.

Kylescu in times past was another ferry point in the journey up the west coast of Scotland that made such a journey an expedition in itself. Ballachulish was the first to be encountered, then Strome ferry across the mouth of Lochcarron and finally Kylescu. All have now been replaced by road detours or bridges. The ferry at Kylescu formerly took vehicles north to Scourie, Durness and Cape Wrath, but has now been replaced by an aesthetic curving concrete bridge very similar to examples we have seen in Northern Norway of which this glorious landscape is so redolent. The bridge spans the waters of Loch Gleann

Dubh and Loch Glencoul that drain vigorously through the narrows here into the open Atlantic. On a sunlit evening with a glass in hand from the excellent Kylescu Inn that occupies the head of the old ferry slipway, it is a heavenly place to be. The drive back to Ullapool in the radiant evening light was embellished further by the scents of gorse, rowan and hawthorn. Ullapool itself, with the deep blue waters of Loch Broom penetrating for miles inland, nestled in a bowl of scented gold.

The circuit of Quinag left Suilven, the most iconic and charismatic of the peaks of Assynt. Rather than driving direct to Lochinver via Inchnadamph again, we took the narrow road past Stac Pollaidh and Loch Lubnaig towards Achiltibuie, diverting from the latter onto the narrow coastal road to Inverkirkaig. This was a wonderfully scenic detour, offering different perspectives on the now familiar individual outlines of the Assynt skyline. Inverkirkaig is strung out around the indentations in the coast south of Lochinver but the main attraction is the walk up the forested valley of the River Kirkaig to the waterfalls. Despite its thoroughly warranted popularity, there were very few people about on a late spring day and the walk itself was quite enchanting. The valley is clothed in native birch, the fresh green leaves contrasting

Traverse to Fionn Loch

Fionn Loch and Suilven

with the more austere upland slopes. The under storey of the woodland was dotted liberally with spring flowers – primroses, violets, milkwort, lousewort and butterwort – and the place was alive with the sound of birdsong, the most persistent being that of the cuckoo. There is some evidence to suggest that cuckoos are becoming relatively rare in mainland England. Certainly, in Cumbria their calls have become later and rarer. However, the Highland cuckoos seem plentiful and in good voice.

The Falls are about three kilometres from the car park, the river Kirkaig plunging some 20 metres or so from its turbulent moorland tract into a classic plunge pool. Most walkers turn back at this point, but we carried on in splendid isolation towards Fionn Loch at the foot of Suilven. Deep in the birch forests of the Kirkaig valley, there is no view of this majestic hill, but within 15 minutes the full scale and grandeur of Suilven was revealed over a crest in the encircling moorland. It is one of the few mountains that create an instant impact on first sight. (It would be interesting to compile a list of the others – the Matterhorn, Ama Dablam in the Himalayas, Mt. Cook in New Zealand etc.) The distinctiveness of Suilven lies in the constantly changing perspectives it offers and from the fact that it rises like a Palaeozoic galleon breasting the waves of glaciated Lewisian gneiss below it. Suilven is yet another hill that makes a mockery of the Munro-Corbett lists that classify according to mathematical height rather than aesthetic and emotional appeal. The former is clinically objective but when has the exploration of the natural world been entirely objective and not engaged deeper and more subjective emotions?

From Fionn Loch, the great bulbous cone of Castel Liath looked impregnable giving way to the castellated turrets culminating in the sharply pyramidal Meall Mheadonach at the eastern edge of the ridge. However, even such a formidable looking crest has its weak spot. From the north the rocky col, (Bealach Mor), that separates the two main summits of the hill gives access to either end of the ridge. In previous years of 'derring-do', this proved to be a good line of ascent, still not for the faint hearted, but perfectly manageable for those with good balance and a secure head for heights. On that occasion, Bealach Mor was approached from the north via Glencanisp Lodge that lies east of Lochinver. An estate track leads from here to the bothy at Suileag and carries on to a bridge over the outlet stream flowing from Loch na Gainimh. It was a blustery day following a night of heavy rain and the loch was being tormented by a savage squally wind. Curtains of spray hurried down the loch and columns of water spiralled some 50 feet into the air into the air, the whirling waterspouts flecked with foam. The gusting wind howled and roared. It was not the best of omens as I set off climbing by meandering through tough ling moorland to reach the base of the rocky chimney that leads to Bealach Mor. Although rough and certainly steep, a line up has been created by the passage of many boots and the subsequent climb to the top of Castel Liath over terraces of Torridonian sandstone is relatively straightforward. The summit is in fact a broad and open plateau from which the view across the water-studded landscape to the sea is stunning. The eastern end of the ridge that appears as a sharp pyramid from Elphin is much more of a daunting proposition with a sense of real exposure in places. Descending from the sharp summit back to Bealach Mor was something of a trial and it was with a sigh of relief that I regained the path across the moorland back to Glencanisp Lodge. It seemed a long day and with hindsight it would have been better not to have gone alone.

Today sitting on the shores of Fionn Loch listening to the sighing of the wind and the lapping of the waves against the pebbles, reflecting on past glories, we could have been the only people on the planet. It was paradise. To make the day complete we watched a large pale-coloured bird with broad powerful wings and the hooked beak of a classic raptor fly low over the loch. It lowered its talons, kissed the water and rose again fluently with its prey securely held in a vice-like grip. It was an osprey. Ospreys now return to the Lake District every year to breed but although that is a success story, the downside is that we seem to have lost our only golden eagle. The North West Highlands remain their sanctuary and sightings of this imperial bird come almost as a matter of course in the more remote areas. Torridon is one of their fastnesses but perhaps the most unforgettable experience occurred further south on Beinn Sgritheall (Sgriol) above the shores of Loch Hourn. On a clear and cold late February day two of us climbed the peak and rested in the rough shelter on the summit. As we huddled there a blizzard of snow buntings passed overhead. Just as we were pondering the reasons for this apparent flush of activity, a golden eagle soared majestically above us from the adjacent corrie wall unconcerned at our presence. With its forensic eyesight, it could hardly have been oblivious to us. We hardly dared to breathe. Every detail of its plumage and its stately flight became seared on our consciousness. Minutes later to our surprise, it was joined by another. The pair rose effortlessly into the late winter sky, touched talons and cascaded separately down before rising again to repeat the aerobatics. These are experiences that thrill and delight. It is to be hoped that one day golden eagles will return to the quieter parts of the Lake District to join our growing numbers of red kites and ospreys.

Fisherfield and Letterewe Forest, Wester Ross

Fisherfield Forest, south of Ullapool, is often referred to simply as 'The Great Wilderness'. Inevitably, in these days of mass communication, to ascribe such an epithet attracts interest in it and increases its popularity. The 'Wilderness' is not what it was some 50 years ago but nevertheless it remains a challenging proposition and the traverse of this area is one of the great British expeditions. For 'Munro-baggers', Fisherfield Forest contains some of the most remote 3000 foot+ peaks, such as A' Mhaighdean and Mullach Coire Mhic Fhearchair. The classic

An Teallach

route begins or ends at Dundonnell on the shores of Loch Broom and crosses some of the wildest, most dramatic and most inaccessible parts of Scotland before emerging at Poolewe or Kinlochewe. The shorter of the two main routes is about 23 miles, which normally means an overnight stay. Fortunately, good camp sites are easy to find and there are conveniently placed bothies as an alternative.

One of the most frequented of these, Shenavall, lies near the beginning of the walk from Dundonnell. As an introduction to the Forest there is a good one-day circuit via Shenavall from the parking area at Corrie Hallie, about four kilometres south east of the Dundonnell Hotel on the main A832 road to Ullapool. Corrie Hallie is also a popular starting point for the ascent of An Teallach from its southernmost peak of Sail Liath. A good estate track climbs steadily south through clumps of hardy birch and alder by the deeply incised valley of the Gleann Chaorachain burn. The gradient slackens, and the track enters a gentler valley where the burn is bridged. A short steep section follows to a pronounced stone cairn on an obvious col where the track reaches open moorland. It is here that the first views appear into the giant corrie of Toll an Lochain below the pinnacles of An Teallach. This is a view to take the breath away, both awesome in its grandeur and intimidating at the same time. For many climbers, it represents the most formidable traverse on mainland Scotland and is respected and feared in equal measure. The exposure from Sgurr Fiona and Lord Berkeley's Seat is only for the most experienced. A path of sorts takes the walker on a safer traverse to the west of the main pinnacles, but even this is not for the faint-hearted. In winter, An Teallach becomes a very serious proposition and has claimed many lives. I managed the traverse from Sail Liath as a young man in a small party when the summit was wreathed in mist. This may have been a blessing in terms of exposure but made route finding more tortuous. The full round from Dundonnell is a long day's outing, best done in late spring or early autumn when the hours are still long and the pinnacled ridge less likely to be shrouded in mist.

For us, it was just enough to rest by the col, gaze into this enormous ampitheatre of plum-red Torridonian sandstone and reflect on the forces of glacial erosion that had sculptured this into what many regard as the most dramatic mountain architecture in Scotland. Tracks divide at the col. The main 4 X 4 track carries straight on down to Achneigie; a less distinct path forks right towards Shenavall and the

Beinn Dearg Mor from Sail Liath col

Shenavall and Beinn Dearg Mhor

beginning of the ascent of Sail Liath. We deviated from the latter across the bone-dry, brittle, ling moorland with its hidden lochans enclosed within outcrops of Torridon sandstone and continued upwards to reach the foot of the white quartzite slopes. From here it was possible to obtain a full-frontal view of the perpendicular crags overlooking Loch Toll an Lochain. Morning spring light emphasised the colour of the rock and the fine detail of these immense precipices. Its counterpart in Torridon itself is probably Coire Mhic Fhearchair at the south-western end of Beinn Eighe, but this always seems a darker, broodier and more foreboding place. Awesome applies to both. Sometimes to be lost in awe and wonder can be a quasi-religious experience. We encounter such insights only too rarely in our busy everyday lives. Assimilating the drama of this landscape takes time. Each visit conveys its own atmosphere depending on the season and the prevailing weather. For lovers of mountain scenery, it is magnetic and absolutely unforgettable.

The descent to the bothy at Shenavall has become more eroded in the 50 years since first acquaintance. It has become very boggy in places and the final steep descent that leads down to the marshy plains of Strath na Sealga can be bone-jarring. It is a poignant place to stand and stare. Shenavall is surrounded by a legacy of crumbling stone walls and abandoned biers and shielings. It looks out on the dramatic crags and wonderfully scalloped corries of Beinn Dearg Mor to the south. The bothy itself is well maintained. It has a sound roof with new skylights and its upper sleeping chamber and connecting staircase has been quite recently refurbished. Downstairs is cosy. It would make an excellent port in a storm and is conveniently sited for the second leg of the crossing of The Great Wilderness. Outside the bothy, the rowans continue to withstand battering from the wind and are protected from deer predation by stone abutments. It is an enchanting spot, full of romance and interest, but for the original shepherds and stalkers it would have represented an entirely different proposition, its isolation and the practical problems associated with it proving difficult to bear. It is always something of a self-indulgence to view such places through the rose-tinted lenses of an aesthetic romanticism rather than the harsher pragmatism of daily survival. At Shenavall, Wordsworth would have no difficulty in investing poetic drama and licence in the scene, but the reality is more prosaic.

The house was built as late as 1891 by Colin MacDonald, a local crofter, fisherman and stonemason who had been appointed stalker on the Dundonnell Estate. The family arrived by boat from the head of Loch na Sealga on a November morning, their possessions including a few trunks, some bedding and a wheelbarrow. The walls were unlined, but by spring 1892, these had been plastered and faced with wooden linings and an upstairs bedroom had been added. Mrs MacDonald had four children to look after, three of whom were born at Shenavall. The midwife came out from Dundonnell on a pony. The pony also brought half-yearly supplies of meal, sugar, tea and paraffin. The children were taught by a pupil-teacher who stayed with the various families in the locality in exchange for board and lodgings. In this last decade of the nineteenth century there were other occupied houses at Achneigie and Larachantivore. The MacDonalds had four cows, the milk being made into butter and cheese. Sheep supplied wool, spun by hand and knitted into socks and pullovers. A walled garden provided fresh vegetables in season and both venison and trout were available from the estate. It may sound idyllic, but it was a harsh existence. Late in December 1895 a heavy snowfall blocked the exits from Shenavall for three months. It was a place for the hardy and resilient. Colin MacDonald eventually moved south to Dollar in Clackmannanshire, where he was apparently still a very fit and vigorous man in his mid-90s.

Today on a lovely late April morning only ghosts remained. The view across the strath to the 'Corbetts' of Beinn Dearg Mor and Beinn Dearg Beag graces many calendars and is justifiably regarded as one of the finest mountain views in Scotland. For people about to cross Fisherfield Forest from the north or seeking shelter at the end of the traverse from the south, Shenavall is an oasis. It was one of the first bothies to be taken over by the Mountain Bothies Assocation (MBA) and elementary maintenance work began in the summer of 1966. We talked to a Dutch walker who had just squelched his way across Strath na Sealga who, in the perfect English the Dutch always seem to possess, rated this walk the highlight of his life. It changes people. Its aura is well expressed in a poem written by one of the MBA's early volunteers, Jim Baillie. With the MBA's permission, I reprint it here:

> In winter here, no heart could mourn for summer, nor spring,
> No blemish or sickness or deformity see,
> In anything that grew upon the earth
> On all the land there was no stain.
> Though hiking days are gone,
> And dull and grey the sky
> In memory still lives on,
> Days on mountain high.
> Of days stilled in twilight calm,
> And fires that flicker in the evening breeze,
> The mountain river sang an evening psalm
> Someday, perchance, we will return to these.

Along the Strath na Sealga in late April the river was quite low, but its crossing in spate would be a serious undertaking. There is no bridge between Shenavall and Larachantivore, the only other visible dwelling across the river with its small clump of trees and decaying stone walls enclosing a small patch of flat land. For those carrying on up the Gleann na Muice to the next bothy at Carnmore on the shores of the giant inland Fionn Loch, there is no alternative to wet feet. Keep your boots on and carry fresh dry socks! For those content to complete the more local circuit there is another option. A track leads from the foot of the strath near Shenavall to the estate cottages at Achneigie. Cottages would be a handsome description. Achneigie was once a much larger building with three sets of chimney pots servicing two

Achneigie

separate semi-detached dwellings. Of these the western side is falling into disrepair, but the eastern side is still reasonably well maintained with a locked door that implies that it is still used by the estate. Old gate posts and rotting fences are indicative of longer term decay and the place has a melancholic air.

From here it is a long trudge back to Corrie Hallie of at least six miles of hard walking and climbing but a more direct line up the hillside can be found via an old pony trail that leads to the 4 X 4 track followed in the earlier part of the day. Within an hour the col below Sail Liath and An Teallach is regained and it is mainly downhill all the way back to Corrie Hallie. This circuit is still a fair walk for limbs that have seen better days, but it does have the advantage of a shandy at the Dundonnell Hotel at its conclusion to sharpen resolve. Even this reduced introduction to Fisherfield Forest becomes a memorable experience. Glorious views and isolation so profound it assails the senses! The sounds of silence save for the sighing of the wind and the trickling of the burns are something rare and precious in our increasingly frenzied world. In such an environment, we remember what it is to really feel alive. Silence can be manna for the soul.

Torridon and Flowerdale Forests, Wester Ross

In the early-1960s, many of the roads in the North West Highlands were single-track with passing places. The route up the west coast was utterly beautiful, but punctuated by a number of vehicle ferry stops and the route up the east coast via the A9, which was then largely single carriageway, involved a detour to Beauly to bypass Inverness and the neck of the Moray Firth. Today a sweeping, elegant bridge carries the road west over the Moray Firth and the A9 will shortly be all dual-carriageway. The interest in Torridon was provoked by the SMC Guides and the illustrated books of W.A. Poucher. There was no internet, few mountaineering magazines and photography was relatively primitive. There was, however, a growing cult of the outdoors fed by the exploits of early climbers – Hamish MacInnes; Chris Bonnington,

Liathach and Loch Clair

Sunset over Loch Torridon

Tom Patey, Joe Brown, Eric Shipton, Dougal Haston, Don Whillans – whose exploits in the golden age of mountaineering inspired countless youngsters. It was also the age of books that provided further fuel to the imagination and ambition. One of these, that has now assumed the patina of any venerable, well-thumbed book was 'The Torridon Highlands' by Brenda Macrow, who spent extended periods in a cottage in Inveralligin. Her descriptions, not only of the mountains, but also of the way of life of her crofting neighbours generated an enthusiasm to visit this part of the world. As with so many other young people, I also drew inspiration from two of my teachers, who introduced an impressionable lad from the backstreets of Fleetwood to a brave new world of mountain challenge and excitement. One of them was a keen climber and had taken his ancient Ford car up to Torridon during a summer holiday. He came back, as so many do, eulogising about this magnificent mountain landscape. A love affair was born.

There are many ways to describe heaven. It is a sense of place and time, something deeply etched into our consciousness. It is more than just a religious or metaphysical concept. It is somewhere we all aspire to be when the travails of everyday existence fade away and assume a rightful perspective. Great minds have wrestled with the notion of heaven. To Henry David Thoreau, 'heaven is under our feet as well as over our heads'. CS Lewis in 'The Last Battle of Narnia' expressed a view that many of us would share: 'I have come home at last. This is my real country! I belong here. This is the land I have been looking for all my life, though I never knew it till now'. For me that place is Torridon. It is a place that exerts a hold, it captivates and mesmerises. The first views across Loch Torridon to Beinn Alligin or the classic view of Liathach from Loch Clair create a lasting impression for the outdoor enthusiast. In all its various moods, Torridon is heaven.

The usual approach to Torridon is via Inverness and the much-improved road to Kinlochewe. At Achnasheen, the road diverges to the right down Glen Docherty and it is from here that the first glimpses of Loch Maree can be gained. This is often described as the most beautiful loch in Scotland. Looking down on the blue waters of the loch which is studded with dark and ancient wooded islands to a maritime horizon would be memorable in itself, but the loch is also framed by wonderfully aesthetic mountains that gently enfold it. Of these none is more impressive than Slioch. From Kinlochewe, the anticipation intensifies as the now single-track road leads down Glen Torridon. Rounding a bend in the road the first sight of the mural precipices of Liathach never fail to excite and impress. It broods over the

Evening light over Coulin Forest and Loch Torridon

Beinn Damh over Loch Torridon

tightly constricted valley for the next five miles, unfailingly imposing, sometimes sinister and often lit by patterns of light and shadow that play on its terraces of gently tilted ancient rock. Gradually, the glen broadens as the upper reaches of Loch Torridon come into view. This is a hugely scenic expanse of sea water. In sunlight, it becomes a Mediterranean blue; when the wind disturbs the waves, flecks of foamy silver appear. The scent of salty seaweed fills the air, strands of kelp float like satin ribbons; mussels hang like grapes on the limpet-encrusted rocks. Along with the gentle lapping of the waves there is the keening of gulls, the piping of oyster catchers and the crooning of eider. Razor bills and guillemots bob on the water and cormorants fly purposefully past like dark arrows. It is a soothing introduction to this special place.

The traverses of the summit ridges of the Torridon peaks are some of the most exciting expeditions on the Scottish mountains. Both Liathach and Beinn Eighe are serious outings, each involving some exposed scrambling. Beinn Alligin is another to set the pulse racing. From the earliest days, clad in Army and Navy surplus gear and a gas cape for a waterproof, that whipped up in the summit winds to give a passable impression of Darth Vader, these major Torridon objectives exercised both mind and body. But with greater maturity and experience some of the 'lesser' peaks were undertaken. By 'lesser', of course, we mean that these are not classified as 'Munros', with summits over the requisite 3000 feet. Beinn Dearg and Beinn Damph are attractive and challenging, even if they fail the Munro classification by only a few feet. Then there are the lonely sentinels in the vast expanses of the Flowerdale and Coulin Forests. I once sheltered against the bitter wind howling across the Helvellyn plateau on Raise with a distinguished looking elderly gentleman who could not get his mobile phone to work. In conversation, he remarked that the phone company had certified that his password had the highest level of security and was unlikely ever to be hacked. Never using a mobile phone, cheekily I asked him what it was. His reply was a phonetic 'Bosh-venn'. With immense smug self-satisfaction, I asked him if he meant the Gaelic Baosbheinn, a shapely isolated peak in Flowerdale Forest? He was astonished that his secure password should be rumbled quite so quickly. It transpired that he was a retired Professor of Geology at Oxford University who had also fallen under the spell of Torridon! We talked at length about our shared passion for this hallowed part of the world before going our separate ways.

The main Torridon peaks are for confident and experienced walkers and climbers and it is with huge regret that the advancing years have consigned many unforgettable days in their company to memory. As balance and confidence ebb away, however, Torridon can still be enjoyed by the vintage walker using the many well-maintained stalkers' paths that give access to this superb mountain terrain. With each visit the attraction of these routes increases, opening up some of the more remote areas of the Torridon and Coulin Forests, providing new perspectives on familiar peaks and offering revealing insights on mountain flora and fauna. In this way new chapters of exploration unfold. The list of possibilities is large but three favourite excursions are detailed; Coire Mhic Nobuil, Drochaid Coire Roll and Coire Lair.

Coire Mhic Nobuill is perhaps the most popular valley route in Torridon. The NTS parking areas above Torridon House to the west or further east along Glen Torridon at the foot of the Coire Dubh Mor both represent obvious starting points for the traverse of one of the most impressive glacial glens in Scotland. In the past, a post-bus service from Diabaig was available to link the two but this seems to have been the victim of recent 'cuts'. We normally begin at the western end above Torridon village and walk through to Coire Dubh Mor to rejoin the Glen Torridon road to the east. It is quite a long traipse back

Western crags of Beinn Dearg

to Torridon village, but we have in our advancing years relied on some kindly soul at the eastern car park to take pity on us or stagger down the glen in a somewhat exaggerated fashion with thumbs at the ready to elicit sympathy from any passing motorist. It has worked so far!

The setting of Coire Mhic Nobuil is majestic and the route passes by a quartet of the most iconic Torridon peaks: Beinn Alligin, Liathach, Beinn Dearg and the final western ramparts of Beinn Eighe. It is never less than memorable. The trek starts gently enough with the climb from the car parking area by the side of a deeply cut gorge through which the waters tumble musically. Stands of older Scots pine give way to more recently established birch and rowan, until abruptly the woodland ends and the open glen beckons at a large deer-proof gate. In this initial leisurely climb along a well-established path the eyes are inexorably drawn to the main architectural features of Beinn Alligin's profile; the turrets of the Horns of Alligin, the great gash of Sgurr Mhor and the final dominating terraced slopes of Tom na Gruagaich. Approaching 70, my son nudged me along this exquisite traverse of the mountain, nursing my ankle ligaments that had recently been sprained for the umpteenth time. Walking in the Lakeland hills where most

Baos Bheinn, Flowerdale Forest

excursions begin with a little height gain, one needs to remember that the Torridon ascents begin at close to sea level adding more demands on ancient legs.

Just as the full wonderful amphitheatre of Beinn Alligin is revealed the bustling burn is met by a tributary stream crossed by a sturdy footbridge. Shortly afterwards there is a clear divergence of paths. To the north, following the tributary stream, a well-defined route heads for the Horns of Alligin across pronounced ribs of the ancient sandstone towards the beginning of the summit traverse. A variant for the valley walker is to carry on along this path briefly almost to the foot of the 'Horns', where a cairn signals another route to the Bealach a' Chomhla, the rubble strewn valley separating the eastern slopes of Beinn Alligin from the western crags of Beinn Dearg. It is not the easiest track to follow in places, the general advice being to keep as near the edge of the rocky slopes of Beinn Alligin as possible to avoid seductive but ephemeral tracks that beguile the unwary into the maw of the boggy valley. We speak from experience! The view from the col is of the watery, lonely expanse of Flowerdale Forest, where large inland lochs are overlooked by the classic Torridon peaks of Baosbheinn, Beinn an Eoin and Beinn a' Chearcaill. This, however, is an all-day excursion in itself. From the footbridge the Coire Mhic

Nobuil path veers off to the right following the line of the main stream through a chaos of giant boulders and hummocky glacial debris. It is a route that commands attention and retains interest. To the south the precipitous pinnacles of the north-facing ramparts of Liathach exert a powerful intimidating presence. This is mountain grandeur at its most prepossessing. So deep is the valley and so perpendicular are the crags that the spiky turrets of Am Fasarinen are not fully visible but, nevertheless, one is aware of this truly awesome mountain wall. In spring, the snow clings to the crags long after the general snow melt on the peaks has finished; in autumn, the sounds of stags reverberate around its rocky hidden corries.

The path continues to meander through a jumble of glacial hillocks and peaty depressions humming with midges on a still late summer day, before a necklace of small lochans marks arrival at the col of An Drochaid below the imposing bulk of Sail Mhor, the western arm of Beinn Eighe. A short detour from the col provides vistas of the almost lunar landscape of Flowerdale Forest. A second detour, well worth the diversion, is to carry on briefly to link up with the path around the prow of Sail Mhor to the magnificent Corrie Mhic Fhearchair. This

View north up Coire Mhic Nobuil

is a text-book corrie enclosed by a crescent of precipitous crags that embrace a large lochan. We have been here on wild days when the wind funnelling into this amphitheatre has been so strong that the falls issuing from the lochan have been blown back upwards. On more mellow days it is a good place to stand and stare and wonder at the forces that created such a spectacular natural feature.

From the lochans the main route of descent via Coire Dubh Mor to the parking area in Glen Torridon is relatively straight-forward. There are some occasions in bad weather when this descent has been to palpable sighs of relief that give way to satisfaction at completing this classic valley traverse. In more clement conditions, our experience has been enhanced by the sight of golden eagles soaring effortlessly overhead or by herds of red deer that glide noiselessly away at our approach. Mountain flora speckle the floor; cotton-grass, sundew, purple ling, blue butterwort, yellow tormentil, with numerous sedges and rushes, none as flashy as their alpine cousins, but in this setting demonstrating nature's capacity not only for momentous destruction but also healing restoration. Often the weather creates patterns of light and shadow that glide over the landscape; clouds gather and mists writhe. It is a truly elemental scene.

One of the many distinguished mountains that lie in the inner fastnesses of Torridon is Beinn Damh. It is distinguished not because it has been accorded the status of a Munro (at 2960', it falls short by 40'), but because it is such a commanding sentinel providing expansive views across Upper Loch Torridon, not only to the major Torridon peaks but also, on a clear day, across the Hebridean Sea to the mountains of Harris. Its western slopes drop steeply down to Loch Damh, but its eastern flanks comprise a series of formidable crags and high corries. In Gaelic, Beinn Damh means the mountain of the stag and in autumn the noise of the rutting stags provides a constant accompaniment to the walk. One of the finest shorter walks in Torridon is to take advantage of the well-worn stalker's paths that encircle Beinn na h'Eaglaise to the east of Beinn Damh and which provide insights into the wilds of Coulin Forest. The starting point lies just above the Torridon Inn on the road to Shieldaig, where a small lay-by provides parking for a couple of cars. Alternatively, we have found the Torridon Inn itself a very welcoming and relatively inexpensive place to stay for a week in Torridon. The adjacent Torridon Hotel with its imposing Victorian turrets and its commanding view across Loch Torridon to Liathach is for the better-heeled!

The initial climb is up a beautifully graded forest track by the side of the Allt Coire Roill waterfalls. A few years ago, the lower slopes were heavily vegetated with rhododendron, but this was rapidly becoming an invasive scourge. Much has now been cut to allow the native pines and birch to regenerate freely although at present the white skeletal remains of the rhododendron trunks and branches look something of an eyesore. It takes only 30 minutes or so to climb through the forest to emerge on the open moorland with a marvellous retrospective view of the length of Beinn Alligin. Few people passing by on the road to Shieldaig can resist the temptation to stop at the lay-by on the crest of the road above the Inn to take a photograph of Beinn Alligin across Loch Torridon. In spring the immediate foreground is awash with the colour and scent of gorse; in late autumn the first snows of winter

Retrospect of Beinn Damh

Coulin Forest from Beinn Damh Forest

provide added glamour and drama. It is a wonderfully aesthetic and photogenic view.

Reaching the open moorland, the main track leading to the summit of Beinn Damh branches off to the right and it is very tempting to follow it. However, the stalker's path crosses the stream at this point on the left. It seems that at one time there would have been a simple bridge, but that has long gone although it is perfectly feasible to cross the stream by boulder hopping to join a faint path that slowly becomes more defined along the western side of Beinn na h'Eaglaise. This becomes a delightful route, winding its way around benches of plum-red sandstone and crossing small burns, many of them bridged by large slabs. Such stalker's paths have been used for years to bring deer off the hills by pony and their course follows a line distilled from intimate knowledge of the landscape. As a means of accessing these remote mountain areas they are invaluable. With height gained the precipices that line the eastern flanks of Beinn Damh become more apparent until the path describes a contouring crescent towards the head of the valley at Drochaid Coire Roill. Here, beside a ruffled mountain lochan the first views of the dramatic peaks of the Coulin Forest can be obtained. The bulbous dome of Maol Chean Dearg is the closest and the most spectacular, but there is a splendid array of lonely isolated peaks such as Sgorr Ruadh, Beinn Liath Mhor (both over 3000 feet) and An Ruadh-stac. This largely treeless country is the haunt of eagle, raven, and red deer. It has an austerity about it and a wildness that is almost melancholic in its effect. It has the capacity to make humans feel small and insignificant.

Below the col the main stalker's path now veers downhill above the broad and often boggy Strath a' Bhathaich towards the southern end of Loch Damh. This is a long and tiring route but the walk back along the shores of the loch to the Falls of Balgy is facilitated by a 4 X 4 track that runs half the length of the loch on its northern side. The far more scenic option is to track cross-country north east around the head of the strath to Loch an Eoin. There is no defined path and it is about a mile of rough country dotted with sandstone boulders and hidden vegetated gulleys. On a clear day, there is no problem for the experienced map reader and navigator; in misty weather, the potential to go wrong is considerable. Keeping high along the steeper ground that lies to the south east of Beinn na h'Eaglaise is the recommended course. This is a chance to rehearse old skills, orientating the ground by reference to a map, determining a course to follow, fixing a bearing and taking a deep breath. In the Lake District, it is nigh on impossible for the experienced fell walker to get lost, although the Mountain Rescue organisations would probably take a different view. Here in the wilderness of Torridon, a basic mistake could lead at least to a long detour or at worst to complete disorientation in misty conditions.

Beinn Alligin and Torridon village

Mullach an Rathain, Liathach

Eventually if all has gone according to calculation, you will emerge on a flat boggy col with numerous peaty hags looking down on the dark waters of Loch an Eoin. This occupies a shallow basin at the foot of Maol Chean-dearg and always seems an atmospheric place to stop. Rocky spurs on the water's edge carry small, gnarled rowans whose bright red berries in autumn light up what can appear a morose and austere setting. Around its shore a path is joined linking Coulags in Strath Carron to the south with Glen Torridon to the north, and another stalker's route clambers across the rocky sandstone slabs to the Bealach na Lice that leads into Coire Lair and thence to Achnashellach in Strath Carron. Despite this nexus of paths, we have never had company on any of these routes, enjoying the serene solitude in solitary splendour. Recently, however, we have noticed that the Coulags path has become a preferred route for mountain bikers for whom this must be an exhilarating and challenging expedition.

The descent is long and stony, crossing streams by means of giant stepping stones, and passing numerous picturesque lochans. There is no difficulty in following this superb stalker's path, whose final reward is the angled view down Glen Torridon and the relentlessly steep terraced slopes of Liathach's southern flanks. At sunset in the evening light the sandstone benches glow a deep plum colour. The final delight is the view of Upper Loch Torridon, the lineated white

Beinn Eighe from Loch Clair

cottages of the village strung like pearls around the sheltered blue bay. In the background are the familiar outlines of the Torridon giants. It is a view to take the breath away. Above Annat, the path finally contours round to descend to the main road by a cottage built into the rock face. This must be one of the finest one-day wilderness walks in Scotland.

There is no finer iconic image of the Torridon landscape than the view of the shapely, dominant prow of the eastern end of Liathach mirrored in the pine-fringed waters of Loch Clair. It graces many a calendar. At any time of year this is a splendid view, but our favourite time is autumn when the colours are resplendent. Spring is also lovely as the snows persist along the summit ridges and the new growth begins to soften the harshness of the winter drabness. A taxing walk is to traverse Coulin Forest from Loch Clair, 26 kilometres or so, which with height gain and loss is enough for ancient legs. There are two ways of doing this, both superb and both entering the heart of this more inaccessible Torridon country. Both involve walking beyond Loch Coulin and climbing up the tributary stream of the Easan Dorcha following a finely graded stalker's path to Drochaid Coire Lair. At this point one alternative is to continue to climb up to the higher col of Coire Lair from which a long descent can be made to the Ling Hut on the main Glen Torridon road. The other alternative is to drop down into Strath Carron just above the railway station at Achnashellach and return via the Coulin Pass. Both are estimable routes.

There is a small parking area at the end of the estate track to Coulin Lodge where both routes begin. Loch Clair is an enchanted place. At its western rim a bank of Scots Pine perfectly frames the imposing sight of Liathach rising sternly over 3000 feet from the valley floor. In spring, we have watched utterly beguiled as black-throated divers pile in with a splash and begin their distinctive courtship wails. In autumn, the surrounding cloak of birch trees change colour to russet and orange and the moorland heath and ling turns bronze. The track soon reaches a bridge that turns right into the Coulin Lodge estate buildings, but also carries straight on towards Loch Coulin through ranks of silver birch and past limpid pools in the briefly sluggish river. These carry the reflections of the trees and the mirror image of Sgurr Dubh that rises in the background. There is much forestry plantation around Loch Coulin, or to be more precise, there was when we first undertook this route. Over the last decade much of this has been cleared. The landscape around the broad basin of Loch Coulin always seems to support a variety of ducks and geese. It is clearly stocked with brown trout and must be a fisherman's paradise. At the eastern end of Loch Coulin it is possible to swing off the main 4 X 4 track onto a loch-side path that takes a short cut to the cottage at Torran cuinn. This is a holiday let and the last time we visited we were greeted by its then occupants, a couple from Cornwall, who had driven up the full length of the country in relays. They come each year. Such is the pull of Torridon! Until recently this point marked the entry to a world of quiet stalker's paths and grassy estate tracks where only the sound of cascading streams punctuated the silence. Our last visit, however, changed perceptions drastically. We passed the cottage to the thump of diggers and the rattle of heavy machinery working higher up the glen. The grassy estate track had turned into a harsh, broad stony road, a broad swathe of rubble wide enough to support heavy construction equipment that was busily excavating deep runnels that form the basic infrastructure linking hydro-electric generating plants. At the time, it felt like an intrusion of noise and modernity into an otherwise pristine landscape, but it is all too easy to take this selfish, simplistic view. One of the great resources that the Highlands possess in abundance is water and the Coulin scheme is one of many hydro-electric projects we have observed recently in more remote parts of the North West Highlands.

Coire Lair

South of Loch Carron at Attadale lies another multiple hydro scheme, where one of the chief contractors and engineers is the local Kendal firm of Gilkes that specialises in hydro generators. So not only is a valuable Highland resource being harnessed, local Cumbrian employment is also being safeguarded. Eventually the scars will soften, the noise will subside, sensitive reinstatement should follow, and the glen should return to its quietude. Change is endemic and to rail against it is to sanction the retention of a fossilised landscape. We were visitors; others must make a living from this harsh and unforgiving land.

At the old stone bridge that spans the confluence of the River Coulin with its tributary stream of the Easan Dorcha, the broad stony track continues but is replaced shortly by the former stalker's path to Coire Lair. It passes a deeply incised valley lined with hardy pines and birches through which the water gathers momentum. Hidden around a bend in the path is a small wooden bothy, known locally as 'The Teahouse'. It is where guests of the estate used to be taken for tiffin and remains a good place for a break. It resembles a large garden shed but is kept scrupulously clean and has sufficient space to allow a handful of people to shelter overnight if need be. Like many of these bothies it contains a book to register comments of people who have stayed or rested there. It is revealing to observe that many comments are from overseas visitors, some of whom have travelled a long way to savour the attractions of this Highland landscape. Unlike some equivalent books there are no graffiti or lewd offensive comments, quite the reverse. Most eulogise the peace engendered by such a place; some wax eloquently philosophical.

It is hard to tear oneself away from such an idyll, but the path continues its gently meandering way up to the Drochaid Coire Lair across moorland studded with large boulders. Whoever designed these routes knew what they were doing! The col lies at the foot of the eastern slopes of Beinn Liath Mhor which forms the northern rim of Coire Lair. Its southern boundary is marked by two shapely hills, the 'Munro' of Sgorr Ruadh at the far end of the valley and the distinctive pyramidal crags of Fuar Tholl. There is a substantial cairn at the col that marks the parting of the ways – north west up to head of Coire Lair and the descent to the Ling Hut or down to Achnashellach. Given the state of the construction works along the River Coulin, we were tempted to take the former route, but it is long and the weather was slowly deteriorating. It is a superb route when time and weather are favourable. We have rarely met any fellow walkers on these routes but those that we have encountered have proved invariably to be kindred spirits. Huddling by the small tarn at the head of Coire Lair on one occasion, heading for the Ling Hut, we were joined by a formidable group of elderly ladies out for 'a stroll' over Sgorr Ruadh. We chatted for a while and were impressed not only by their physical vigour but also by their mental positivity – 'mens sana in corpore sano', as our Latin teacher used to extol (a sound mind in a healthy body). All of us were well into our seventies and all trying as best we could to uphold this ancient virtue. On a more recent occasion we bumped into a chap from Aberdeen with the shaggiest Shetland sheepdog ever seen, called Jasper. He, too, was sheltering against a biting autumn wind on the col and gallantly offered to accompany us down to Achnashellach where his car was parked. Whether this kindly gesture was out of sympathy for a couple of old wrecks or whether he welcomed our company we shall never know. There is an old saying that dogs reflect their owner's looks and personalities. Jasper certainly did. His owner was bearded and wild-haired and with a lively but gentle demeanour. Jasper was just wild. Both were in their element.

We headed down the steep but well graded stony path towards

Beinn Alligin sunset

the upper limits of the coniferous plantations of Achnashellach Forest that spread for miles along this northern side of upper Strath Carron. It seemed incongruous for the silence to be interrupted by the familiar blare of a train horn, but we had descended almost to the station where trains from Kyle of Lochalsh to Inverness and reverse run several times daily. By this time Jasper, with canine intuition, sensed that the car was parked nearby and was off in a jiffy down the plantation track. His owner had other ideas, calling him back to accompany us on the climb back up to the Coulin Pass. After a long downhill section, the hardest part is to muster energy to regain height, particularly as the clouds were now gathering with malicious intent. It was a kindly gesture; we enjoyed his company as another 'hill man' and relished Jasper's boundless energy and entertaining antics. Breasting the col late in the afternoon on this autumn day, we could see Loch Coulin in the distance and at least the estate track in the upper reaches of the Coulin glen had not been affected by hydro works. It was a delight to walk on a softer trail. On both sides of the valley stags bellowed and roared but remained largely inconspicuous until a movement betrayed their camouflage and revealed their whereabouts. By 5 p.m. the evening light was starting to fade, and we hurried through the estate grounds back to Loch Clair just as breaks in the cloud allowed glancing rays of golden sunlight to reflect on the mists spilling over the summits of Liathach and Beinn Eighe. It seemed that molten waterfalls were cascading down the ridges and billowing over the rock pinnacles. By the time we reached the car it was 6.30 p.m., almost too close a call for comfort. It had been a long nine hour day but surprisingly after a shandy and a hot shower, joints and muscles did not protest unduly. The following day was another matter!

Torridon is a mountaineer's nirvana. There is so much for the vintage walker to do. It would be presumptuous to list or describe more. Half the joy of exploration is to uncover secrets for oneself without preconceptions of what to expect. Hopefully the general tenor of this unique mountain area has come through. Its attractions are infinite. From Loch Maree to Lochcarron lies a concentration of some of the best scenery in the UK. Most of it accessible to walkers of indeterminate age. Walking in this landscape revivifies and reminds us why we took to the hills in the first place, not only to assuage a need to explore and escape and for the physical challenges presented, but also for the spiritual refreshment that is the balm of our frenzied existence. The day may come when, finally, we can only stand (or sit) and stare and recall with fondness days of yore when we strode with the vigour of youth over these and other mountain areas. Memories are the amalgam of experience; wisdom and contentment are their legacy. We have seized the day!

Appendices

THE GESTATION OF ALL the treks and walks listed begins with a sense of exploration and adventure, but this would in itself not be enough to enable sound planning to be undertaken. For those who might contemplate emulating some of the treks or designing their own adventures, the following Appendices should prove helpful. Please bear in mind that the writers are of a certain vintage, characterised by their reliance on maps and guides as well as more technological modern aids that are now available for research and information. It is also useful to bear in mind that in the areas covered by this book, great changes may have taken place in routing, way-marking and in geographical, economic and political circumstances. We have been heavily reliant on trekking agencies and on the assistance of local guides and portage, particularly in the Hindu Kush. Both here and in Spitzbergen individual trekking can be fraught with difficulty and, sometimes, danger. Trekking agencies used are identified where appropriate. Similarly, transport arrangements used may in some cases date back nearly twenty years but the companies used are mentioned and reference to the internet will provide up-to-date routes available, timetables and prices. Accommodation in many instances was ad hoc, based on alpine refuges, which are also identified, although camping wild was the norm for many journeys. Reference to guidebooks was a pre-requisite for effective planning. For each section, helpful guide books used are specified but further information is now available via the internet.

With these obvious disclaimers, read on!

Section 1: Hindu Kush

This trip was undertaken in 2000 when we were in our early 60s. Trekking in this area of Northern Pakistan fringing the border with Afghanistan only became possible due to an amelioration in political circumstances and, sadly, these have now deteriorated again. It is an area where the employment of local guides is imperative. The major British trekking agencies, including the one we used, no longer organise trips to this area, although many do still operate in the K2 area of the Karakorum.

Recommended guides
- Trekking in the Karakorum and Hindu Kush: John Mock & Kimberley O'Neil: Lonely Planet series.
- Karakorum Highway: John King & Bradley Mayhew: Lonely Planet series.

Background reading
- The Gilgit Game: John Keay: Oxford University Press.
- Three Cups of Tea: Greg Mortenson and David Oliver: Penguin Books.
- Among the Mountains: Wilfred Thesiger: Harper Collins.
- A Short Walk in the Hindu Kush: Eric Newby: Secker and Warburg.

Maps
Maps of sufficiently detailed scale are thin on the ground; the best are probably the schematic maps included in the guides listed. This is a sensitive political area subject to controls. We have used adapted military maps that rely on satellite imaging but these tend to be on too large a scale. Leomann Maps do produce a series of 1:200,000 maps that cover the mountainous border areas of Northern Pakistan. Sheet 1 in the series covers Gilgit, Hunza, Rakaposhi and Batura. Do not expect

these to be of Ordnance Survey detail! However, they do include the main trekking routes and suggested treks.

Transport

Islamabad was the first destination. We used PIA from Manchester but many airlines now fly this route from the major British airports. From Islamabad there is an internal airline service to Chitral, but like its counterpart to Skardu, the normal starting point for Karakorum treks, the service is subject to the vagaries of the weather and other factors. Trekking in both the Hindu Kush and the Karakorum, we have travelled there and back via the Karakorum Highway, a rugged journey and an adventure in itself. To reach Chitral by road requires the hiring of local jeeps but the route via the Swat valley and Dir over the Lowari Pass would probably now be considered a dubious proposition for Westerners.

Trekking agencies

For many years, we used our local agency based in Keswick – KE Adventure Travel – through whom the trip described was arranged. They were, and are, first class. Within Pakistan itself, the services of Waljis was used to arrange for jeeps and guides. It may still be possible to arrange individual trekking trips through them. Their sirdars have impressed us. The local address is: Waljis Travel; 10, Waljis Building; Khayaban-E-Suharwardy; PO Box 1088; Islamabad: Pakistan. Tel. 05811-455895/6/7 or info@waljis.com.pk

Accommodation

In Islamabad, Chitral and Gilgit, good hotel accommodation was organised by KE Adventure Travel. Otherwise, this was entirely a camping trip.

Section 2: Spitzbergen

This journey was undertaken as we reached our early 70s in 2010. Svalbard has become a much more accessible Arctic region, mainly due to the opening of the airport at Longyearbyen that takes modern aircraft. Travelling in Svalbard is subject to certain controls. It is a sensitive environmental area and the Norwegians are anxious to maintain its pristine qualities. Guides and group travel are normally employed. Individual trekking is possible but not recommended. All parties normally include a nominated person(s) capable of using a firearm to deter predatory polar bears. Attacks are rare but there have been sufficient fatalities to warrant extreme caution and adherence to sensible protocols.

Recommended guides
- Spitsbergen-Svalbard; Rolf Strange; May 2009; info@ spitzbergen.de. This is a superbly comprehensive guide that includes the history and geography of the archipelago as well as detailed coverage of fauna and flora.
- Norway; Anthony Ham & Miles Roddis; Lonely Planet series pp 352-367

Maps
For large-scale geographic outline we used the 1:1,000,000 map of Svalbard published by the Norsk Polarinstitutt, Tromso 2003, which also produces a range of more detailed topographical maps on a 1:100,000 scale as well as some excellent geological maps.

Transport
Svalbard is accessed by air to Longyearbyen from Oslo or Tromso. We flew from Manchester to Oslo via Copenhagen with SAS and caught the connecting flight from Oslo to Longyearbyen, also with SAS. In the last decade a range of other services have become available. Norwegian is now a major competitor and offers a regular direct service from London Gatwick to Tromso. Swiss operate from Birmingham to Longyearbyen and Lufthansa run services to the latter from Glasgow and Edinburgh. A civilised, but more expensive alternative, would be to travel from Bergen to Tromso with Hurtigruten, the Norwegian coastal ferry

service, a wonderfully scenic journey and a splendid introduction to Arctic lansdscapes. (see hurtigruten.co.uk/Spitsbergen).

Trekking agencies

A number of companies operate coastal sailings but to include a trekking option our advice would be to look no further than the main agency on the islands, Spitzbergen Travel. Their experience and employment of local guides/experts was of the highest order. Through them, or Hurtigruten, bookings can be made on MV Expedition or Nordstjernen, small cruise ships that sail round the islands but also drop people off at Raudfjorden and/or Blomstrand, where camps are established. Further information can be obtained via info@spitsbergentravel.no or via PO Box 548, 9171 Longyearbyen, Norway - Tel +47 7902 61 00. The Tourist Office in Longyearbyen is also a useful source of information- www.svalbard.net.

Accommodation

Camping! However, the sites used were pre-erected and featured some home comforts in the form of a mess tent, or yurt, and a stove. At the end of the season in mid-August, the last trekking group, which we were, is responsible for dismantling the site and storing kit for the long Arctic winter. This is not onerous but, conversely, a thoroughly social activity! At Longyearbyen, there is a range of accommodation available. We stayed in Longyearbyen Guesthouse, which was perfectly comfortable, but there are also more expensive and luxurious alternatives, including Radisson SAS Polar Hotel and the Spitzbergen Hotel.

Section 3: The Camino St Jacques

We undertook this trek across the Central Massif in 2014 when we mustered a combined age of 150. We had some previous experience of the main Camino route from its normal starting point at St. Jean Pied de Port in the foothills of the Pyrenees, following it for a short distance before deviating east to walk the GR10, the long distance Pyrenean trail from Hendaye on the Atlantic to Banyuls sur Mer on the Mediterranean. The standard well-publicised Spanish Camino heads west to finish at Santiago de Compostela and Cape Finisterre. We opted instead to walk the French section across the Central Massif from Le Puy to Cahors, following the GR56, principally because we thought it would be scenically more diverse, culturally interesting and quieter. We were not disappointed.

Recommended guides

- Cicerone publish an excellent guide, 'The Way of St. James' by Alison Raju, which contains clear maps and extensive historical and geographical information.

Background reading

- Any history of mediaeval England will include sections on the relationship with France, but for a concise summary we used 'A Traveller's History of France' by Robert Cole, published in 1988 by Windrush Press, simply because it happened to be on our bookshelves. For those interested in more modern background, some reference to the role of the French Resistance and SOE during the Second World War will have passages that include areas of the central Massif, which was the heartland of resistance. The Rough Guide series 'Dordogne and the Lot' gives a brief summary of the Camino (pp290–302) and has a useful bibliography of history and geography.

Maps

The Cicerone guide contains excellent schematic maps but for real detail the Institut Geographique National (IGN) publish a 1:100,000 series (Sheets 156 and 155 cover most of the Camino route with part sections on sheets 154 and 162. Even more detail is supplied by the Cartes de Randonnee series at 1:25000. Relevant sheets can be identified by accessing www.ign.fr. (eg: the sheet covering the opening section of the GR56 from Le Puy-en-Velay is 2739. We used the 1:100,000 series simply because of the length of the trek.

For those who wish to carry something more concise and practicable, the Federation Francaise de la Randonnee Pedestre (FFFP) publish guides with integral maps covering each Grand Randonnee (GR). 'The Way of St. James from Le Puy-en-Velay to Figeac' by Wilfrid Alexandre (Editions de Felin)is also published as a Paperback Mini.

All the above can be obtained from Stanfords in London or via Amazon to which reference should be made.

Trekking agencies

Having backpacked for many years, we decided that the time had come to arrange for our main baggage to be transported on each day to the following destination to allow us to carry day sacs only. The agency we used was Mac's Adventures (Tel 0141 530 8886; info@macsadventure. com). They organised both nightly accommodation as well as forward transport of baggage. The French agency delegated the responsibility for seeing that all went according to plan from Le Puy to Conques was: La Pelerine, Randonnees et Voyages a Pied, Place Limozin, 43170 Sauges, France Tel 33(0) 471 74 47 40 – www.lapelerine.com). From Conques to Cahors the responsibility for luggage transfers was delegated to Transbagages, Hameau de Chanteruejols 4800 Mende – Tel 04 66 65 27 77. Both proved to be very smooth operations.

NB. The downside of planning such an arrangement is that walkers are committed to reaching the onward accommodation each day. It is easy to underestimate timings when there are abundant cultural, historical and gastronomic distractions en route and also easy to discount the draining effects of sequential stages of over 25kms per day, particularly in searing heat likely to be encountered in summer. Sometimes it is better to divide successive long sections into two or plan a rest day (Conques is ideal).

Transport:

Flights were booked to Lyon via Gatwick (Easyjet), returning from Toulouse. There is an efficient tramway link between Lyon airport to Gare Part Dieu, from which a regular train service goes to Le Puy via St. Etienne. An alternative would be to use Eurostar to Paris and then travel to St. Etienne by TGV. From Cahors, there is a regular train to Toulouse or to Paris (Austerlitz).

Accommodation

This consisted of gites d'etape and chambres d'hote, the French equivalent of B&B. Breakfasts are continental; further sustenance may be needed en route. It is a good reason to halt for a while and enjoy some local cuisine. Evening meals favour the carnivore; vegetarians may need to order in advance. Only at Cahors was a hotel used.

Section 4: The Italian Alps –AV1 – The Giant's Trail

Mention is made in the text to idiosyncratic waymarking and route identification. The AV1 (Alta Via), that runs along the southern edge of the Alps from the Matterhorn (Monte Cervino) to the Monte Rosa is often confused with a more frequently walked AV1 in the Dolomites. Both, however, adopt the standard AV way-marking of a central white oblong flanked by two vertical red bands or by a red triangle with the AV number painted within it. Confusions may arise when prominent rocks also feature different coloured markings and numbers that denote local footpath routes (Itinerari nei Communi). Sometimes, paint splashes can seem over-exuberant and rock markings become versions of modern art! You may need to keep your wits about you.

Guide books

The AV1 Across the Dolomites is well-covered by Cicerone; the Giant's Way is less well-publicised. Our initial inspiration came through reading an article in a trekking magazine. We did not use a guide simply because we could not find one that covered the route in the detail we wanted. We undertook this trek in 2001 in our early 60s before internet search engines were as highly developed; today the most comprehensive information can be obtained from the web-site of Valle d'Aosta Tourism.

To the south, the Gran Paradiso National Park is well documented. West Col Productions publish Alpine climbing guides; the one on Graians East features the Gran Paradiso, providing a summary of climbing routes as well as details of huts and transport. One of the best general guides is again by Cicerone – Gran Paradiso by Gillian Price, that features the AV2 together with 28 day walks in the National Park.

Maps

Most of the AV1 is covered by the 1:25000 series published by the Instituto Geografico Centrale (IGC). The relevant sheets are 115 (La Valpelline – which is on a scale of 1:30000!) and 108 Monte Cervino-Breuil-Champoluc). The eastern boundary of the route is covered by Sheet 109 (Monte Rosa – Gressoney). To the south, where the AV1 becomes the AV2, the Gran Paradiso-Cogne area is covered by sheet 101. All the above can be obtained from Stanfords, who are exceptionally helpful, or via the internet.

Trekking agencies

This was an independently organised trek . However, the local Tourist Office in Aosta does organise guided treks within the region (see web-site).

Transport

We used Easyjet to fly to Geneva and Swiss Rail (SBB) from Geneva to Martigny. The local post-bus services are superb and link impeccably with the train schedules. In Switzerland, details of destinations and services may be obtained from www.postauto.ch/en. From Aosta, local bus services connect the main Valle d'Aosta with all the adjacent valley destinations. The main services used included those run by SAVDA to Chatillon that run every hour (line 376) and cost about £6-£9. This connects with the valley service to Valtournenche-Breuil, leaving Chatillon every four hours at a similar cost. The line 17 service from Aosta to Cogne is operated by SVAP, leaves every three hours and costs about £2. There are twice daily SAVDA services (391) to Martigny from Aosta costing £9-£13. All services tend to be co-ordinated making onward connections relatively straightforward. For example, we left a camp site at Valnontey by early morning post bus to Cogne with an onward connection waiting to Aosta (SVAP). After a short wait, the bus from Aosta to Martigny over the Grand St. Bernard Pass (SAVDA) connected seamlessly with the Swiss rail service to Geneva Aeroport.

Accommodation

This was the last of our wild trekking/camping trips. Camping confers flexibility and some of the ad hoc sites used in the mountains have been memorably scenic and atmospheric. However, the attractions of supported trekking increase with age!

Section 5: Snowshoeing

Guide books

There are instructional books on snowshoeing, but most tend to be North American. Snowshoes are now easy to attach to boots and almost fool-proof to use. Our advice is to do just that. Get used to them on gentle ground such a cross-country skiing pistes, preferably with some instruction, before trying them out on sloping ground. Essentially, just do it!

We attended a snowshoeing course in Argentiere organised by KE Adventure Travel. Some of the routes described in the text are listed as summer walks in the Cicerone publication 'Chamonix Mountain Adventures' by Hilary Sharp. Probably the best source of winter snowshoeing routes would be the Chamonix-Mont Blanc Tourist Office, which produces copious skiing and winter sports information, including schematic maps. Guide books to the Engadine, where many of our snowshoeing adventures have been undertaken, are legion. Most relate to summer walking options, such as the Cicerone guide 'Walks in the Engadine' by Kev Reynolds, and again the best winter option would be to visit or contact the Tourist Offices in St. Moritz or Scuol. In our experience all the snowshoeing routes detailed in the information are immaculately prepared and maintained. On the ground all are identified by pink snowman signs. Courtesy requires that you avoid the grooved langlauf tracks that are the province of the cross-country skiers.

Maps

It is probably sufficient to rely on the maps published by the Tourist Offices but to provide context the following may be additionally helpful:

Chamonix Valley:
IGN 1:25000 series Sheet 3630OT Chamonix-Mt. Blanc + Sheet 3531OT Megeve.

Engadine:
Kummerly+Frey - Wanderkarte 1:50000 - Oberengadin

Kummerly and Frey – 1:60000 – Unterengadin

Landeskarte der Schweiz – 1:25000 Sheet 2524T – Scuol-Guarda-S-Charl

Details of the above and adjacent sheets can be obtained via www. swisstravelcenter.ch or from Stanfords.

Transport

For the Chamonix valley, numerous budget airlines operate services to Geneva, such as Easyjet. From the airport, regular shuttle services, both public and private, operate to Chamonix valley destinations. It is probably advisable to book these in advance by researching on the internet.

The Engadine lies in the far south-east of Switzerland but can be accessed in a number of convenient ways. We have used cheap flights to Geneva and then purchased a return SBB transfer pass rail ticket to Guarda. This is a long train journey via Zurich and Berne, with connections at Landquart for Klosters and the Engadine, but it never loses interest. SBB, the Swiss main line operator is famously punctual and efficient. From Landquart the regional company, Rhatische Bahn (Rhaetian Railways) takes over and is responsible for communications within the canton of Graubunden. It runs a regular service along the length of the valley from Scuol to St Moritz and Pontresina. Part of its operations is the UNESCO World Heritage Albula-Bernina line from Chur to St.Moritz. Its reputation from both an engineering and scenic point of view is fully deserved. This section forms part of the Glacier Express route and carries on from Pontresina over the Bernina Pass to Poschiavo in Italy.

Alternatively, Swiss run flights directly to Zurich which shortens the journey but is marginally more expensive. From Zurich the connections by rail operate as above. For travellers averse to air travel, there is now the option of using Eurostar and its linkages to Geneva.

Post bus services in the Engadine are regular and highly efficient, linking all main centres and rail halts with outlying villages. Timetables and destinations can be obtained in advance if required via the main Tourist Offices: www.myswitzerland.com/en/scuol.html and www. myswitzerland.com/en/st-moritz.html. For all these services in the Engadine it is possible to purchase a Graubunden travel pass that greatly reduces overall costs and is good value for money.

Accommodation

A huge range of accommodation options exists in the Chamonix valley and its surrounds. We used the chalet in Argentieres provided by KE Adventure Travel through whom we booked our training week. In the Engadine the centre we use most frequently is Guarda, but other options exist at Zernez and Zuoz. Switzerland is not cheap! We have adopted the Hotel Meisser in Guarda simply because it occupies a beautiful position in the Lower Engadine, where many of the snowshoeing routes are situated.

Section 6: Forays In The Forests

Background reading

It is difficult to separate romance from reality in any documentary accounts of the North-West Highlands. For historical references, the following provide useful insights:

- Highland Clearances: John Prebble: Penguin Books
- The Highlands and Islands: Fraser Darling and Morton Boyd: Fontana New Naturalist series published by Collins. This was first issued in 1964 but remains a major source of information on fauna and flora, geography, geology and history. It reminds the reader of what we are in danger of losing.
- The Torridon Highlands: Brenda Macrow: Robert Hale publishers: first issued 1953 but gives an interesting insight into this iconic area before it became well known.

Guides:

For walking, climbing and trekking guides, the following are highly recommended:

- Cicerone Guide to Northern Scotland: Graham Uney.
- Cicerone Guide to Torridon: Peter Barton.
- The Northwest Highlands: D.J. Bennet and T. Strang: Scottish Mountaineering Club District Guide series.

Two pictorial guides are worthy of mention:
- Scotland: W.A. Poucher: Constable London: published 1980
- Scottish Mountain Drawings: Volume 1 Northern Highlands: A. Wainwright: Westmorland Gazette, Kendal. (The master craftsman on good form!)

Maps:

Look no further than the Ordnance Survey. In the 1:25000 Explorer Map series, Torridon and Fisherfield Forest are covered by Sheets 433 and 435. Sheet 442 covers the area between Inchnadamph and Lochinver. Alternatively, 1:50000 series, sheet 15 Loch Assynt, provides a broader overview of this part of Sutherland.

Transport

This is an area where the flexibility and practicality of the car is required. Driving up to the Northwest Highlands is no longer the endurance test it once was, thanks largely to the improvements made to the A9 and the bridge over the Moray Firth at Inverness. There is a rail link to the latter, including a sleeper service. From Inverness, a rail connection can be made to Achnasheen and Kyle of Lochalsh, but services along this beautiful section of line are infrequent (normally four a day in each direction). Alternatively, Inverness airport is served from other British hubs and a car can be hired from there.

Within the Northwest Highlands local buses do operate but again the services are patchy. With the best will in the world, a car is needed.

Accommodation

An abundance of B&Bs, hotels and holiday cottages are available but it pays to book in advance, particularly in peak periods. The authorities on Skye recently advised visitors to stay away in July and August unless they had prior bookings. Skye is full was the message. Far better to stay outside the peak holiday months. The weather is usually better in spring and autumn and the midges lie low if there is a hint of frost in the air.

Notes on the Authors

CLIVE DARLEY WAS FORMERLY Headmaster of Clitheroe Royal Grammar School. He retired early to pursue his mountaineering ambitions between fulfilling various roles as education consultant at the Universities of Cumbria and Lancaster, where he worked until final retirement at 75. He has been involved in the organisation and leadership of a large number of expeditions and participated in many more to all parts of the world including the Himalayas, Karakorum, Hindu Kush, New Zealand, Iceland, Norway and Spitzbergen. For many years he led Alpine trekking expeditions to the main European mountain ranges. Since 'retirement' the couple have trekked several times a year both at home in the UK and abroad as well as continuing to engage in fell walking in Cumbria and Scotland. He had a hip replaced in 1999 and a cardiac pacemaker implanted in 1997.

Jennifer Darley retired from a senior position at Hutton Grammar School near Preston in 1997. Like her husband she was heavily involved in the Duke of Edinburgh's Award Scheme and was a keen sportswoman, playing hockey and squash. Although suffering from vertigo, she has accompanied her husband on all the vintage walks and treks documented. Despite their combined age of 156, both are firm believers in retaining a sense of adventure through their advancing years.

Both went to the same school and both graduated from the same University. They have lived in South Cumbria since 1997.

Acknowledgements
Both Clive and Jennifer would like to place on record their appreciation of the companionship of so many people, young and not so young, who have accompanied them on their adventures over many decades; former students and colleagues and trekking party members. Their thanks are also due to the medical staff at the James Cochrane Practice in Kendal who have kept them going for the last 20 years and for the many kindnesses that they have been offered by so many folk met along trekking routes. Their generosity was often humbling; their friendship hugely valued.